THE SPIRITUAL MAN

Volume II

THE SPIRITUAL MAN

Watchman Nee

IN THREE VOLUMES

Christian Fellowship Publishers, Inc.
New York

PRINTED IN U.S.A.

Distributed by Premium Literature Co.

Box 55102

Indianapolis, Indiana 46205

Contents

VOLUME II

EXPLANATORY NOTES

Volume II of *The Spiritual Man* is a continuation in this series of studies. While many other books have been compiled from his spoken messages, this book translated from the Chinese is the only one of any substantial size which brother Watchman Nee himself ever wrote. At the time of writing it he felt this work might be his last contribution to the church, although since then God has graciously overruled. Long after the book's initial publication in Chinese our brother once was heard to express the thought that it should not be reprinted because, it being such a "perfect" treatment of its subject, he was fearful lest the book become to its readers merely a manual of principles and not a guide to experience as well. But in view of the urgent need among the children of God today for help on spiritual life and warfare, and knowing our brother as one who is always open to God's way and most desirous to serve His people with all that God has given him, we conclude that he would doubtless permit it to be circulated in English. Hence this translation.

Translations used. The Revised Standard Version (RSV) of the Bible has been used throughout the text unless otherwise indicated. Additional translations where employed are denoted by the following abbreviations:

Amplified—*Amplified Old Testament*
ASV—American Standard Version (1901)
AV—Authorized Version (King James)
Darby—J. N. Darby, *The Holy Scriptures, a New Translation*
Young's—Young's *Literal Translation*

Soulical and Soulish. The adjectives "soulical" and "soulish" have been used to convey distinctly different meanings. "Soulical" as herein employed pertains to those proper, appropriate, legitimate, or natural qualities, functions, or expressions of man's soul which the Creator intended from the very beginning for the soul uniquely to possess and manifest. "Soulish" appears in these pages to describe that man *in toto* who is so governed by the soulical part of his being that his whole life takes on the character and expression of the soul.

PART FOUR

THE SPIRIT

CHAPTER 1

THE HOLY SPIRIT AND THE BELIEVER'S SPIRIT

BELIEVERS TODAY very much lack knowledge as to the existence and operation of the human spirit. Many are unaware that in addition to their mind, emotion and will they also have a spirit. Even when they have heard of the spirit, many Christians either consider their mind, emotion or will as the spirit or else plainly confess they know not where their spirit is. Such ignorance enormously affects cooperation with God, control over self, and war against Satan, the performance of which in all cases requires the operation of the spirit.

It is imperative that believers recognize a spirit exists within them, something extra to thought, knowledge and imagination of the mind, something beyond affection, sensation and pleasure of the emotion, something additional to desire, decision and action of the will. This component is far more profound than these faculties. God's people not only must know they possess a spirit; they also must understand how this organ operates—its sensitivity, its work, its power, its laws. Only in this way can they walk according to their spirit and not the soul or body of their flesh.

The spirit and soul of the unregenerate have become fused into one; therefore they do not know at all the presence of the deadened spirit; on the other hand, they are very well aware of strong soulical sensation. This foolishness continues even after being saved. That is why believers sometimes walk after the spirit and sometimes after the flesh even though they have received spiritual life and have experienced to some degree victory over the things of the flesh. To be unaware of the demand, movement, supply, sense, and direction of the spirit naturally curtails the life of the spirit and allows the natural life of the soul to go unchallenged as the living principle of one's walk. The magnitude of this ignorance far exceeds common admission of it among believers. Because of their ignorance concerning the spirit's operation, those who honestly desire deeper experience upon having overcome sin may all too easily be led astray into seeking so-called "spiritual" Bible knowledge with their minds, or a burning sensation of the Lord's presence in their physical members, or a life and labor emanating from their will power. They are deceived into overly esteeming their soul experiences and thus fall into conceiving themselves as ever so spiritual. Their soul life is inordinately nourished. They become so subjective as to assess their experience as unquestionably spiritual. Accordingly, they are hindered from making any genuine spiritual progress. For this reason God's children must be very humble before Him and seek to know the teaching of the Bible and the functioning of the spirit through the Holy Spirit in order that they may walk by the spirit.

THE REGENERATION OF MAN*

Why must a sinner be born anew? Why must he be born from above? Why must there be a regeneration of the spirit?

*Compare Part One, Chapter 4.

Because man is a fallen spirit. A fallen spirit needs to be reborn that it may become a new one. Just as Satan is a fallen spirit, so is man; only he has a body. Satan's fall came before man's; we therefore can learn about our fallen state from Satan's plunge. Satan was created as a spirit that he might have direct communion with God. But he fell away and became the head of the powers of darkness. He now is separated from God and from every godly virtue. This, however, does not signify that Satan is non-existent. His fall only took away his right relationship with God. Similarly, man in his fall also sank into darkness and separation from God. Man's spirit still exists but is separated from God, powerless to commune with Him and incapable of ruling. Spiritually speaking, man's spirit is dead. Nonetheless, as the spirit of the sinful archangel exists forever so the spirit of sinful man continues too. Because he has a body his fall rendered him a man of the flesh (Gen. 6.3). No religion of this world, no ethics, culture or law can improve this fallen human spirit. Man has degenerated into a fleshly position; nothing from himself can return him to a spiritual state. Wherefore regeneration or regeneration of the spirit is absolutely necessary. The Son of God alone can restore us to God, for He shed His blood to cleanse our sins and give us a new life.

Immediately the sinner believes in the Lord Jesus he is born anew. God grants him His uncreated life that the sinner's spirit may be made alive. The regeneration of a sinner occurs *in his spirit*. God's work begins without exception within the man, from the center to the circumference. How unlike Satan's pattern of work! He operates from the outer to the inner. God aims first to renew man's darkened spirit by imparting life to it, because it is this spirit which God originally designed to receive His life and to commune with Him. God's intent after that is to work out from the spirit to permeate man's soul and body.

This regeneration gives man a new spirit as well as quickens his old one. "A *new spirit* I will put within you"—"That which is born of the Spirit is spirit" (Ezek. 36.26; John 3.6).

The "spirit" in these passages has God's life in view, for it is not what we originally possessed; it is accorded us by God at our regeneration. This new life or spirit belongs to God (2 Peter 1.4) and "cannot sin" (1 John 3.9); but our spirit, though quickened, may yet be defiled (2 Cor. 7.1) and in need of being sanctified (1 Thess. 5.23).

When God's life (which can equally be called His Spirit) enters our human spirit, the latter is quickened out of its coma. What was "alienated from the life of God" (Eph. 4.18) is now made alive again. Hence "although your bodies are dead because of sin, your spirits are alive because of righteousness" (Rom. 8.10). What we are given in Adam is a spirit made dead; what we receive in Christ at regeneration is both the dead spirit quickened and the new spirit of God's life: the latter, something Adam never had.

In the Bible God's life is often labeled "eternal life." "Life" here is *zoe* in Greek, denoting the higher life or spirit life. This is what every Christian receives at his regeneration. What is the function of that life? "This is eternal life," prayed Jesus to His Father, "that they know thee the only true God, and Jesus Christ whom thou hast sent" (John 17.3). Eternal life means *more* than mere future blessing to be enjoyed by believers; it is equally a kind of spiritual ability. Without it no one can know God nor the Lord Jesus. Such intuitive knowledge of the Lord comes solely upon receiving God's life. With the germ of God's nature within him, an individual can ultimately grow into a spiritual man.

God's aim in a regenerated man is for that man by his spirit to rid himself of everything belonging to the old creation, because within his regenerated spirit lie all the works of God towards him.

THE HOLY SPIRIT AND REGENERATION

When regenerated, man's spirit is made alive through the incoming of God's life. The Holy Spirit is the prime mover in this task. He convinces the world of sin and of righteousness and of judgment (John 16.8). He prepares human hearts to believe in the Lord Jesus as Savior. The work of the cross has been fulfilled by the Lord Jesus, but it is left to the Holy Spirit to apply this finished work to the sinner's heart. We ought to know the relationship between the cross of Christ and its application by the Spirit. The cross accomplishes all, but the Holy Spirit administers to man what it has accomplished. The cross grants us position; the Holy Spirit gives us experience. The cross brings in the fact of God; the Holy Spirit brings about the demonstration of that fact. The work of the cross creates a position and achieves a salvation by which sinners can be saved; the task of the Holy Spirit is to reveal to sinners what the cross has created and achieved so that they may in fact receive it and be saved. The Holy Spirit never functions independently of the cross: without the cross the Holy Spirit has no proper ground from which to operate: without the Holy Spirit the work of the cross is dead, that is, it produces no effect upon men even though it is already effective before God.

While it is the cross which achieves the whole work of salvation it is the Holy Spirit Who operates directly upon men for their salvation. Hence the Bible characterizes our regeneration as a work of the Holy Spirit: "that which is born of the Spirit is spirit" (John 3.6). The Lord Jesus explains further on that regenerated man is "every one who is born of the Spirit" (v.8). Believers are born anew because the Holy Spirit brings to bear the work of the cross upon them and communicates God's life to their spirit. He is none other than the Executor of God's life. "We live by the Spirit" (Gal. 5.25). If whatever men know comes through their brain without the Holy Spirit regenerating their spirit, then their knowledge will help them not one whit. If their belief rests in man's wisdom and not in God's power, they are merely excited in their soul. They will not last long, for they are not yet newly born. Regeneration comes just to those who believe in their heart (Rom. 10.10).

Besides bestowing life to believers at new birth, the Holy Spirit executes a further work of *abiding* in them. How regrettable for us if we forget this! "A new heart I will give you and a new spirit I will put within you . . . and I will put my Spirit within you" (Ezek. 36.26-27). Note that immediately after the clause "a *new spirit* I will put within you" there follows this one of "I will put *my Spirit* within you." The first statement signifies that believers shall receive a new spirit through the renewal of their deadened spirit by the incoming of life. The second has reference to the indwelling or the abiding of the Holy Spirit in that renewed spirit of theirs. Believers at new birth obtain not only a new spirit but also the Holy Spirit dwelling within. Is it not sad that many fail to understand the newness of their spirit *and* the abiding of the Holy Spirit in their new spirit? Christians need not delay many years following regeneration and then suddenly wake up and seek the Holy Spirit; they have His entire personality *abiding* in them—not just visiting them—at the moment they are saved. The Apostle exhorts us on this wise: "Do not grieve the Holy Spirit of God, in whom you were sealed for the day of redemption" (Eph. 4.30). The use of the word "grieve" here and not "anger" reveals the Holy Spirit's love. "Grieve" it says and not "cause to depart," for "he dwells with you and will be in you" (John 14.17). While every born-again believer does have the Holy Spirit permanently residing in him, nevertheless the plight of the indwelling Spirit may not be the same in all saints—He may be either grieved or gladdened.

We should understand the relationship between regeneration and the indwelling Holy Spirit. Unless a new spirit is available to Him the Holy Spirit cannot find a place to abide. The holy dove found no place whereon to set her foot in the judged world; she could take up her abode only in the new creation (see Gen. 8). How positively essential regeneration is! Without it the Holy Spirit cannot at all dwell in man. God's children receive within them the permanent abiding of God's Spirit. Just as this new spirit emerges through a life-producing relationship with God and is therefore inseparable from Him, so the abiding of the Holy Spirit is eternally unchangeable. Few are those who know they have been born anew and thus possess new life; but fewer still are those who know that from the moment they believed in the Lord Jesus they have the Holy Spirit indwelling them to be their energy, their guide, their Lord. It is for this very reason that many young Christians are slow in spiritual progress and never seem to grow. This sad state reflects either the foolishness of their leaders or their personal faithlessness. Until God's servants dissolve their prejudice which holds that "the indwelling Holy Spirit is but for the spiritual," they can hardly lead people on to any degree of spirituality.

The regenerative work of the Spirit of God embraces far more than convincing us of sin and leading us to repentance and faith in the Savior. It verily confers upon us a new nature. The promise of the Holy Spirit indwelling us follows closely the promise of having a new spirit. Actually they form two parts of one promise. In convincing men of sin and leading them to believe in the Lord, the Spirit is just preparing the groundwork for His Own indwelling. The singular glory of this dispensation of grace is that God's Spirit indwells believers in order to manifest the Father and the Son. God already has imparted to His children His Spirit; they now should faithfully acknowledge the Holy Spirit and loyally submit themselves to Him. Both the Day of Resurrection and that of Pentecost have passed; the Spirit has long since come. But many simply experience new birth without knowing in addition His abiding in them. They are living on the wrong side of Resurrection and Pentecost!

Regardless the dullness of Christians in recognizing the dwelling of the Person of God's Spirit in them, God nonetheless has given Him to them. This is an immutable fact which no condition of the Christian can gainsay. Because they have been regenerated they automatically have become a holy temple fit for habitation of the Holy Spirit. If only these would claim by faith this part of God's promise as they did the other part, they would gloriously experience both. But if they should stress new birth and be content merely with possessing a new spirit, they shall forfeit the possibility of experiencing a vigorous and joyful life and miss many blessings which God has provided them in the Lord Jesus. If on the other hand they accept God's promise in its totality, trusting in the divine fact that at regeneration God has given a new life *plus* the indwelling of the very Person of the Holy Spirit, then their spiritual life shall advance tremendously.

By faith and obedience believers may experience the abiding presence of the Spirit on the same day they receive their new spirit. The Person Who dwells within shall reveal Christ in them, sanctify them, and lead them on to true spiritual heights. Even so, Christians often do not appreciate the exalted position which this Person occupies, and thus descend to despising His indwelling and to following instead the dictates of their mind. These individuals ought to humble themselves before such light, learn to respect such a Holy Presence, and be willing to allow Him to work. They should tremble before Him for love's sake, not daring to impose their will in the slightest but always remembering how God has highly exalted them by virtue of His abiding presence. Any who desire to abide in Christ and live a holy life like His must accept by faith and obedience God's provision for them. The Holy Spirit already is in our spirit. Therefore the question before us now is, are we willing to let Him work from within?

THE HOLY SPIRIT AND MAN'S SPIRIT

Having realized how the Holy Spirit comes and dwells in believers at new birth, we must next observe exactly where He does dwell. By so doing, it is our hope that we shall know better His operation within us.

"Do you not know that you are God's temple and that God's Spirit dwells in you?" (1 Cor. 3.16) The Apostle Paul implies here that the Holy Spirit dwells in us as God so did in the temple of old. Though the entire temple symbolizes the place of God's presence and serves as a general picture of God's habitation, it is nevertheless in the Holy of Holies where God actually dwells, with the Holy Place and the outer court standing for those spheres of divine activity which are in accordance with God's presence in the Holiest. Answering truly to this typology, God's Spirit dwells now in our spirit, the antitype in our time of the Holy of Holies.

The dweller and his dwelling must share the same character. Only man's regenerated spirit—and not the mind, emotion or volition of his soul and not his body either—is fit to be God's dwelling place. The Spirit is both a builder and a dweller. He cannot dwell where He has not built: He builds to dwell and dwells only in what He has built.

The holy anointing oil may not be poured on the flesh; accordingly, it is obvious that the Holy Spirit cannot make His home in man's flesh for it includes everything man had or was before regeneration. He cannot dwell even in the spirit of an unregenerated person, not to mention in the mind, emotion or will of his soul or in his body. Inasmuch as the holy anointing oil is not poured on the flesh, just so the Holy Spirit does not abide in any part of the flesh. He has no connection with the flesh other than striving against it (Gal. 5.17). Unless there is an element within man unlike the flesh, the Holy Spirit finds Himself unable to dwell in man. It is therefore indispensable for the spirit of man to be regenerated so that He may abide in the new spirit.

Why is it so important to understand that the Holy Spirit dwells in man's innermost depth, deeper within than his organs of thought, feeling and decision? Because unless the child of God perceives this, invariably he shall seek His guidance in his soul. With understanding he shall be delivered from the deception and error of looking to what is outward. The Holy Spirit lives in the remotest recess of our being; there and only there may we expect His working and obtain His guidance. Our prayers are directed to "our Father who art in *heaven,*" but the heavenly Father guides from *within* us. If our Counsellor, our Paraclete, resides in our spirit then His guidance must come from within. How tragically deceived we will be if we seek dreams, visions, voices, and sensations in our outer man rather than seeking Him in our inner man!

Frequently many children of God turn within themselves, that is, they look into their soul to determine whether they have peace, grace or spiritual progress. This is most harmful and is not of faith. It diverts them from gazing upon Christ to a looking at themselves. There is a peering within, however, which is completely different from the above. It is faith's greatest act. It is a search for guidance by looking to the Holy Spirit Who indwells their spirit. Although a believer's mind, emotion and will cannot discern the things within, yet he ought to believe, even when in darkness, that God has given him a new spirit in which His Spirit dwells. Just as God dwelling in the darkness behind the curtain of the Holy of Holies was feared though not seen by those in the Holy Place and outer court, even so is the Holy Spirit Who dwells in man's spirit incomprehensible by the soul and the body.

Thus are we able to recognize what is authentic spiritual life. It is not to be discovered or experienced in the many thoughts and visions of the mind, nor in the many burning and exhilarating feelings of the emotion, nor in the sudden shaking, penetrating and touching of the body by outside force. It is to be found in that life which emanates from the spirit, from the *innermost* part of man. To walk truly after the Spirit is to understand the movement of this most hidden area and to follow it accordingly. However wonderful may be those experiences which occur through the components of the soul, they are not to be accepted as spiritually valid as long as they remain in the outward and run no deeper than sensations. Only what results from the operation of the Holy Spirit within man's spirit can be accounted spiritual experience. Hence to live a spiritual life requires faith.

"It is the Spirit himself bearing witness with our spirit that we are children of God" (Rom. 8.16). Man's spirit is the place where man works together with God. How do we know we have been born anew and are therefore children of God? We know because our inner man has been quickened and the Holy Spirit dwells therein. Our spirit is a regenerated, renewed one, and He Who dwells in, yet is distinct from, this new spirit is the Holy Spirit. And the two of them bear witness together.

CHAPTER 2

A SPIRITUAL MAN

A PERSON WHOSE SPIRIT is regenerated and within whom the Holy Spirit abides can still be fleshly for his spirit may yet be under the oppression of his soul or body. Some very definite actions are required if he is to become spiritual.

Generally speaking we will encounter at least two great perils in our life but are enabled to overcome not only the first but the second of them as well. These two perils with their corresponding triumphs are: that of remaining a perishing sinner or becoming a saved believer and that of continuing as a fleshly believer or developing into a spiritual one. As sinner-turned-believer is demonstrably realizable, so carnal-turned-spiritual is likewise attainable. The God Who can change a sinner into a Christian by giving him His life can equally transform the fleshly Christian into a spiritual one by giving him His life more abundantly. Faith in Christ makes one a regenerated believer; obedience to the Holy Spirit makes him a spiritual believer. Just as the right relationship with Christ generates a Christian, so the proper relationship with the Holy Spirit breeds a spiritual man.

The Spirit alone can render believers spiritual. It is His work to bring men into spirituality. In the arrangement of God's redemptive design the cross performs the negative work of destroying all which comes from Adam while the Holy Spirit executes the positive work of building all which comes from Christ. The cross makes spirituality possible to believers; but it is the Holy Spirit Who renders them spiritual. The meaning of being spiritual is to belong to the Holy

Spirit. He strengthens with might the human spirit so as to govern the entire man. In our pursuit of spirituality, therefore, we must never forget the Holy Spirit. Yet we must not set aside the cross either, because the cross and the Spirit work hand in hand. The cross always guides men to the Holy Spirit, while the Latter without fail conducts men to the cross. These two never operate independently of each other. A spiritual Christian must experimentally know the Holy Spirit in his spirit. He must pass through several spiritual experiences. For the sake of clarity we shall discuss them in a somewhat sequential fashion, although in actual practice they frequently occur simultaneously.

Quite a few remarks will bc made concerning how to be spiritual, but let us not forget what we have learned heretofore.* We should realize by now that what hinders one from being spiritual is the flesh. So if a person maintains a proper attitude towards it he shall encounter no difficulty in making progress. It is surprisingly true that the more spiritual one becomes the more he knows the flesh, because he increasingly discovers it. Had he not known it, how could he be spiritual? Hence we cannot neglect what has been discussed earlier concerning the flesh, since it serves as the basis for seeking spirituality. Unless there is this fundamental dealing with the flesh, whatever progress one may make shall inevitably be superficial, shallow, and unreal. But if one knows how to resist his flesh in all things—denying its activity, power, and opinion—he may be regarded as already spiritual. Nevertheless we would still like to cite some positive measures which are related directly to the spirit.

THE DIVIDING OF SPIRIT AND SOUL**

The salient implication of Hebrews 4.12 is whether we are living by intuitive guidance in the spirit or by the naturally good or bad influence of the soul. The Word of God must

*See Part Two, Chapters 4 and 5, the latter Chapter particularly.

**Compare Part Three, Chapter 5.

judge in this particular respect, for only God's sharp Sword can differentiate the source of our living. As a man's knife cuts and divides joints and marrow, so God's Sword too pierces and separates the most intimately linked spirit and soul. Initially such dividing may be simply a matter of knowledge, but it is essential that it enter the realm of experience; otherwise it shall in fact never be understood. Believers should allow the Lord to introduce this cleaving of spirit and soul into their practical walk. Not only must they seek it positively with consecration, prayer, and yieldedness to the operation of the Holy Spirit and the cross, but also they must actually possess such experience. Their spirit needs to be liberated from the soul's binding enclosure. These two must be parted cleanly even as the spirit and soul of the Lord Jesus were not one bit mixed. The intuitive spirit needs to be freed wholly from any influence which may come from soulical mind and emotion. The spirit must be the sole residence and office of the Holy Spirit. It must be released from every disturbance of the soul.

The various experiences of having his outer and inner man divided will make a believer spiritual. A spiritual believer differs from others for the simple reason that his entire being is governed by his spirit. Such spirit-control connotes more than the Holy Spirit's authority over the soul and body of man; it also signifies that man's *own* spirit, upon being elevated as head over the whole man through the working of the Holy Spirit and the cross, is no longer ruled by the soul and body but is powerful enough to subject them to its rule.

The division of these two organs is necessary for entering spiritual life. It is that preparation without which believers shall continue to be affected by the soul and hence shall always pursue a mixed course: sometimes walking according to the spirit life but at other times walking according to the natural life. Their pathway fails to be marked by purity, for both spirit *and* soul are their life principles. This mixture holds believers fast within a soulish framework which damages their walk as well as hinders the important work of the Spirit.

Were a believer's outer and inner life definitely separated so that he walks not according to the former but according to the latter, he would sense instantaneously any movement in his soul and immediately shake off its power and influence as though being defiled. Indeed, everything belonging to the soulish is defiled and can defile the spirit. But upon experiencing the partition of soul and spirit, the latter's intuitive power becomes most keen. As soon as the soul stirs, the spirit suffers and will resist right away. The spirit may even be grieved at the inordinate stirring of the soul in others. It will in fact repulse a person's soulish love or natural affection as something unbearable. Only after experiencing such separation do Christians come into possession of a genuine sense of cleanliness. They then know that not sin alone, but all which belongs to the soulish, is defiled and defiling and ought to be resisted. Nay, it is far more than simply knowing, for any contact with what is soulish—whether in themselves or in others—causes their intuitive spirit to feel defiled and to demand instant cleansing.

UNITED TO THE LORD IN ONE SPIRIT

In his first Corinthian letter, Paul informed his readers that whoever "is united to the Lord becomes one spirit with him" (6.17). And note that he did not say, "one soul with him." The risen Lord is the life-giving Spirit (15.45). His union with the believer is therefore a union with the believer's spirit. The soul, the seat of man's personality, belongs to the natural. All it can and is to be is a vessel for expressing the fruit of the union between the Lord and the believer's inner man. Nothing in his soul partakes of the Lord's life; it is solely in the spirit that such a union is effected. The union is one of spirits with no place for the natural. Should it be mixed in with the spirit it will cause impurity to the union of spirits. Any action taken according to our thought, opinion or feeling can weaken the experimental side of this union.

Things of the same nature unite perfectly. Inasmuch as the spirit of the Lord is pure, ours likewise needs to be as pure in order to be united truly with Him. If a believer clings to his own wonderful ideas and is unwilling to lay aside his preference and opinion, his union with the Lord will not be expressed in experience. The union of spirits permits no adulteration from anything soulish.

Wherein lies this union? It is in identification with Christ in His death and resurrection. "If we have been united with him in a death like his, we shall certainly be united with him in a resurrection like his" (Rom. 6.5). This verse explains our union with the Lord as one of being united with His death and resurrection. This simply indicates we are completely one with Him. By accepting His death as our death we enter into this union with the Lord. By additionally accepting His resurrection we who have died with Him shall be resurrected as well. Through faith's acceptance of His resurrection we shall stand experientially in the place of resurrection. Because the Lord Jesus was raised from the dead according to the Spirit of holiness (Rom. 1.4) and was made alive in the spirit (1 Peter 3.18), we too, when united with Him in resurrection, actually are united with Him in His resurrected Spirit. Henceforth we are dead to everything pertaining to ourselves and alive to His Spirit alone. This requires our exercising faith.* Once identified with His death, we lose the sinful and the natural in us; once identified with His resurrection, we are united with His resurrection life. Thus our inner being which is now united with the Lord becomes one spirit with Him. "You have died . . . through the body of Christ, so that you may belong to another, to him who has been raised from the dead . . ., so that we serve . . . in the new life of the Spirit" (Rom. 7.4,6). Through Christ's death we are joined to Christ, even in His resurrected life. Such union enables us to serve in the new life of the Spirit, free from any adulteration.

*See Part Three, Chapter 1, on the two essentials for deliverance from sin.

How marvelous is the cross! It is the foundation for everything spiritual. The purpose and end of its working is to unite the believer's spirit with the resurrected Lord into one spirit. The cross must go deeply to rid him of the sinful and the natural within him that he may be joined to the positive resurrection life of the Lord and thus become one spirit with Him. A believer's spirit, together with all which is natural and transient in him, needs to pass through death so that it may be purified and then united to become one spirit with the Lord in the freshness and purity of resurrection. Spirit is joined with Spirit to become one spirit. And the outcome will be: to serve the Lord in "newness of spirit" (Rom. 7.6 Darby). What is of the natural, of self, and of animal activities has no more place in the believer's walk and labor. Both the soul and the body may then but exhibit the purpose, work, and life of the Lord. The Spirit life leaves its imprint on everything, and everything speaks of the outflowing of the Spirit of the Lord.

This is ascension life. The believer is joined to the Lord Who sits at the right hand of God. The Spirit of the enthroned Lord flows into the spirit of the believer, who is on the earth yet not of the world; the enthroned life is accordingly lived out upon the earth. The Head and the body share the same life. With such a union He is able to pour forth the power of His life through the believer's spirit. As a tube which is connected to a fountain is able to convey living water, so too the believer's spirit which is united with the Spirit of the Lord is capable of transmitting life. The Lord is not just the Spirit; He is the *life-giving* Spirit as well. When our spirit is joined intimately with the life-giving Spirit, it is filled with life; and nothing can limit that life. How we need to have this in our spirit that we may triumph continually in our daily walk. Such a union clothes us with the victory of the Lord Jesus. It gives us the knowledge of His will and mind. It builds and expands the new creation within us by the rich inflow of the Lord's vitality and nature. Through death and resurrection our spirit ascends—even as the Lord has ascended on high—and experiences "the heavenly places," having trodden all that is earthly underfoot. Our inner being is in ascendancy, far above any obstacle or disturbance. Yes, it is continually free and fresh and discerns everything with the transparent sight of heaven. How radically different this life of heaven on earth is from one that is swayed by emotion. The former kind displays heavenly nature and is persistently spiritual.

KNOWING THE INDWELLING OF THE HOLY SPIRIT

God's children already have the Holy Spirit abiding in them, but they may not recognize Him or obey Him. They need to do so completely. They must realize that this indwelling presence is a Person, One Who teaches, guides, and communicates the reality of Christ to them. Until they are willing to acknowledge the foolishness and dullness of their soul and are ready to be taught, they block the way of this Person. It is necessary for them to let Him regulate everything so as to reveal the truth. Except they know in the depth of their being that God's Holy Spirit is indwelling them and unless with their spirit they wait for His teaching, they will not welcome His operation upon their soul life. Only as they cease to seek anything by themselves and only as they take the position of the teachable shall they be taught by the Spirit truth which they are able to digest. We know He verily abides in us when we understand that our spirit, which is deeper than thought and emotion, is God's Holy of Holies by which we commune with the Holy Spirit and in which we wait for His communication. As we acknowledge Him and respect Him, He manifests His power out from the hidden part of our being by extending His life to our soulical and conscious life.

The Christians at Corinth were of the flesh. In exhorting them to depart from their carnal state, Paul repeatedly reminded them of the fact that they were God's temple and that the Holy Spirit lived in them. Knowing He indwells them helps Christians to overcome their carnal condition.

They must know and understand perfectly by faith that He abides in them. Christians should not be content merely with knowing mentally the doctrine of the Holy Spirit as given in the Bible; they also need to know Him experimentally. They will then commit themselves without reservation to Him for renewal and submit every part of their soul and body to His correction.

The Apostle put to those at Corinth this question: "Do you not know that God's Spirit dwells in you?" (1 Cor. 3.16) Paul seemed to be surprised at their ignorance of such a sure fact. He viewed the indwelling of the Holy Spirit as the foremost consequence of salvation, so how could they miss it? However low a Christian's spiritual measure may be, even as low as that of those Christians at Corinth (alas, many probably do not rise higher than that), he nevertheless ought to be clear on this fact without which he shall long remain carnal and never become spiritual. Even if you have not yet *experienced* His indwelling, could you not at least believe he *does* abide in you?

Can we refrain from worship, respect, and praise when we consider how the Holy Spirit—Who is God Himself, One of the three Persons in the Triune God, the very life of the Father and the Son—comes to live in us who belong to the flesh? What grace for the Holy Spirit to dwell in the likeness of sinful flesh just as the Lord Jesus once took upon Himself the same likeness!

THE STRENGTHENING OF THE HOLY SPIRIT

In order for man's innermost organ to gain dominion over the soul and the body and thus serve as channel for the life of the Spirit to be transmitted to others, there must be His strengthening. Paul prays for believers "that according to the riches of his glory he may grant you to be strengthened with might through his Spirit in the inner man" (Eph. 3.16). He so prays because he considers it infinitely important. He asks God to strengthen by His Spirit their "inner man," which is the new man in them after they have trusted in the Lord.

Therefore the prayer is that the believer's spirit may be strengthened by God's Spirit.

From this we may deduce that the spirits of some saints are weak while those of others are strong. Whether they are potent or impotent depends upon whether or not they have received His strengthening. Since those at Ephesus had been sealed already with the Holy Spirit (1.13-14), the Apostle's prayer for them must be concerned with a gift other than His indwelling. His prayer indicates they must have not only the Holy Spirit indwelling them but also have His special power inundating their spirit so as to render their inner man strong. It is possible for us to possess a weak spirit although having God indwelling us.

To be filled with might in the inner man is the urgent need of Christians. However, unless they appreciate how feeble theirs is they will not ask for the invigoration of the Holy Spirit. Often the children of God cannot rise up to answer the Lord's call to service simply because, though their physical condition is good, their feelings are low, cold, and reluctant. Or even when their emotions are quite high, passionate, and willing, they find themselves unable to serve the Lord because now the body reacts lazily. Such phenomena betray the weakness of the spirit in its dominion over feeling and the physical body. The disciples found themselves in precisely that situation in the Garden of Gethsemane: "the spirit indeed is willing, but the flesh is weak" (Matt. 26.41). Willingness by itself is not sufficient; the spirit also must be strong. If it is sturdy it can overcome the infirmity of the flesh. Why do believers sometimes find themselves dragging and failing while laboring for souls? Lack of power in their spirit is the explanation. The same holds true in the case of environment. How easily we are affected by the confusion of the outside world. Were our spirits hardy we would be able to meet the most disturbing situation with peace and rest. Prayer is the acid test of the inner man's strength. A strong spirit is capable of praying much and praying with all perseverance until the answer comes. A weak one grows weary and fainthearted in the maintenance of praying. A vigorous spirit can move forward in the midst of adverse environment or feeling, but a frail one is impotent to stand against opposition. Great is the need of power in the spirit for spiritual warfare with Satan. Only those who have might in the inner man understand how to exercise their spiritual strength in resisting and attacking the enemy. Otherwise the battle will be make-believe, fought in the imagination of the mind or the excitement of the emotion, and perhaps fought with the weapons of flesh and blood.

In order for the inner man to be strengthened with power through the Holy Spirit, the children of God must discharge their responsibility. They need to yield specifically to the Lord, forsake every doubtful aspect in their life, be willing to obey fully God's will, and believe through prayer that He will flood their spirit with His power. Without delay God will answer the expectation of their heart, once all obstacles on their part are removed. Believers do not need to wait for the Holy Spirit's filling, because He has descended already. What they need only wait for is for themselves to fulfill the condition for His filling, which is, they must let the cross perform a deeper incision upon them. Should they be faithful in believing and obeying, then within a very short time the power of the Holy Spirit will saturate their spirit and strengthen their inner man for living and for laboring. Some may receive His filling immediately upon once surrendering themselves to the Lord, for they already have met the conditions for such filling.

This invasion of God's power in us, this infilling of His Spirit, happens in the human spirit. It is the inner and not the outer man which is activated by His power and thence becomes strong. This is most important to recognize, for it helps us to exercise simple faith in our desire for the filling of the Holy Spirit (Gal. 3.14), rather than to anticipate some bodily sensations such as a shaking, a jerking, or a hurling to the ground. Yet Christians need to be watchful lest they use faith as an excuse for not experiencing the empowering of the Holy Spirit. The conditions for filling must be accomplished and the attitude of believers must be firm. God will fulfill His promise.

By reading what the Apostle affirms in the succeeding verses in Ephesians 3 about apprehending, knowing, and filling, we are certain this strengthening with might in the inner man renders it highly sensitive. Like the body, the spirit has its functions and consciousness. Prior to the mighty inflow of the Holy Spirit's power into their spirit, believers scarcely can detect its intuitive power; but afterwards its intuitive force becomes most distinctive and hence readily discovered. As the inner man is energized, its intuitive power is increased. Believers are able to sense its slightest movement.

The effect of having the spirit filled with God's power is to afford it full sway over the soul and the body. Every thought, desire, sensation and intent is now governed by the spirit. The soul can no longer act independently: it becomes instead the spirit's steward. Furthermore, through the believer's spirit the Holy Spirit is able to impart God's life to thirsty and dying men. However, this filling of the Holy Spirit differs from the baptism with the Holy Spirit, because the latter is for the purpose of service while the former solves the problem of life (naturally it will affect service too).

WALKING ACCORDING TO THE SPIRIT

Transformation from soulish to spiritual does not guarantee that believers never again will walk according to the flesh. On the contrary, an ever present danger exists of falling back into it. Satan is constantly alert to seize every opportunity to cause them to plunge from their lofty position to a life below par. It is therefore highly necessary for God's children to be watchful at all times and to follow the Spirit so that they may remain spiritual.

"In order that the just requirement of the law might be fulfilled in us, who walk not according to the flesh but according to the Spirit . . . (Now) those who live according to the Spirit set their minds on the things of the Spirit. To set . . . the mind on the Spirit is life and peace" (Rom. 8.4-6). To follow the spirit is to walk contrary to the flesh. Not following the spirit is walking by the flesh. Many Christians oscillate between these two: now following the one, now following the other. They ought to walk according to the inner man *alone,* which is, to walk according to the spirit's intuition and not for a moment according to the soul or body. In thus following the spirit they invariably shall "set their minds on the things of the spirit." And the result shall be "life and peace."

To live by the spirit means to walk according to intuition.* It is to have all one's life, service, and action in the spirit, ever being governed and empowered by it. This preserves the saint in life and peace. Since he cannot remain in a spiritual state unless he walks according to the spirit, then at the very least the saint must understand its various functions and laws if he is to walk well.

To live after the spirit is the Christian's daily task. He ought to perceive that we can live neither by the noblest of feelings nor by the loftiest of thoughts. We must walk according to the guidance accorded us through our intuition. The Holy Spirit expresses His feeling through our spirit's delicate sense. He does not operate directly on our minds, suddenly inducing us to think of something. All His works are done in our innermost depths. If we desire to know His mind we should conduct ourselves in accordance with the intuition of our spirit. At times, however, we may sense something there without comprehending what it means, what it demands, or what it is communicating. Whenever this happens, we must commit ourselves to prayer, asking that our mind may be given understanding. Once we apprehend the meaning of what we have sensed intuitively, we thereafter should behave accordingly. The mind can instantly be enlightened and made to understand the meaning of intuition;

---

*See Part Five, Chapter 1.

but abrupt thoughts which originate with the mind void of intuition ought not to be followed. Solely intuitive teaching represents the Spirit's thought. Only this should we follow.

Such a walk by the spirit requires *reliance* and *faith.* We have seen before how all good actions of the flesh exhibit an attitude of independence towards God. The very nature of the soul is independency. Should believers act in accordance with their thought, feeling and desire, they have no need to spend time before God, to wait for His guidance. Those who follow "the desires of body and mind" (Eph. 2.3) need not rely upon God. Except Christians realize how useless, how undependable, and how utterly weak they are in seeking to know the will of God, they shall never cultivate a heart of reliance upon Him. To receive God's guidance in their spirit they must wait upon Him therewith; they must refrain from taking their feeling or thought as a guide. Let us remember that whatever we do or can do without trusting, seeking, and waiting upon God is or will be done in the flesh. With fear and trembling we must rely upon God for guidance in the inner depths. This is the sole way to walk according to the spirit.

To walk in this fashion requires faith of the believer. The opposite of sight and feeling is faith. Now it is the soulish person who gains assurance by grasping the things which can be seen and felt; but the person who follows the spirit lives by faith, not by sight. He will not be troubled by the lack of human assistance, nor will he be moved by human opposition. He can trust God even in utter darkness for he has faith in God. Because he does not depend upon himself, he can trust the unseen power more than his own visible power.

Walking after the spirit involves both the initiation of a work by revelation and execution of it through the Lord's strength. Frequently believers beseech God for spiritual power to do a work which has not been revealed at all in their intuition. This is simply impossible, for what is of the flesh is flesh. On the other hand believers frequently know the will of God through revelation in their intuition but bring their own strength to the work to perform it.* This likewise is impossible, for how can they begin with the Holy Spirit and end up with the flesh? Those who follow the Lord must be brought to the place of no confidence in the flesh. They must confess they can originate no good idea and must admit they possess no power to fulfill the Holy Spirit's work. All thought, cleverness, knowledge, talent and gift—which the world superstitiously worships—must be set aside in order to enable one to trust the Lord wholly. The Lord's people should persistently acknowledge their own unworthiness and incompetency. They dare not initiate anything before receiving God's order nor attempt to execute God's command in self-reliance.

To live by the spirit we must move in accordance with the delicate sense of its intuition and depend on its enabling to accomplish the revealed task. Well do we begin if we follow intuition instead of thought, opinion, feeling or tendency; well do we end if we rely on the Spirit's power and not on our talent, strength or ability. Simply keep in mind that the moment we cease to follow our intuitive sense at that very moment we begin to walk after the flesh and end up minding the things of the flesh. This in turn injects death into the spirit. Only if we "walk not according to the flesh" can we walk "according to the spirit."

Our aim is to be a spiritual man but not a spirit. If we recognize this distinction our lives shall never be cut and dried. We today are human beings and shall be so eternally, yet the highest achievement of a human being is to develop into a spiritual man. The angels are spirits; they have neither body nor soul. But we humans possess both. We are to be spiritual *men* and not spirits. The spiritual man shall continue to retain his soul and body; otherwise, he would be reduced to being a spirit instead of a man. No, what is meant by being a spiritual man is that he is under the control of his spirit

---

*See Part Two, Chapter 4.

which has become the highest organ of his whole person. Let us not be mistaken on this point. A spiritual man retains his soul and body; being spiritual does not annihilate these organs nor their respective functions, because these make man what he is. So although the spiritual man does not live by them, he certainly has not annihilated them either. They instead have been renewed through death and resurrection so that they are perfectly united to the spirit and have become instruments for its expression. Hence the emotion, mind and will remain in a spiritual man but are subject entirely to the guidance of the intuition.

The emotion of a spiritual man is completely under his spirit's regulation, no longer asserting an independent course as it once did. It does not block the spirit nor resist its move because it does not insist upon its own affection and feeling. The emotion now rejoices solely in what the spirit likes, loves only what the spirit directs, feels merely what the spirit permits. It has become its life: when the spirit stirs, emotion responds.

The mind of the spiritual man likewise cooperates with the spirit, wandering no more as in the past. It does not object to the spirit's revelation by raising its reason and argument, neither does it disturb the peace of the spirit with many confused thoughts, nor does it rebel against the spirit by boasting in its own wisdom. Quite the reverse, the mind cooperates fully with the intuition in advancing on the spiritual journey. If the spirit unfolds any revelation the mind discerns its meaning. It will assist the spirit to fight should the latter plunge into warfare. If the Holy Spirit desires to teach any truth, the mind will help the spirit to understand. The latter, though, has the authority to stop the mind's thinking as well as to initiate it.

The spiritual man also retains his will, yet it too is no longer independent of God but now decides according to the dictate of the spirit, having abandoned self as its center. The will does not insist upon its desire as before. It consequently is fit to obey God. No more is it hard and stiff but is completely broken; hence it cannot resist God or strive against Him. It has been tamed of its wild nature. Today when the spirit receives revelation and apprehends God's wish, the will decides to follow. It stands at the spirit's door like a courier, awaiting its every command.

The body of a spiritual man is subjected to the spirit as well. Because it has been cleansed by the precious blood and has had its passions and lusts dealt with by the cross, it can serve today as an obedient servant to the spirit's order as that order is communicated to the body from the spirit through the soul. By no means does it entice the soul into many sins by its passions and lusts as it formerly did. Instead the body now answers swiftly all the spirit's directions. The latter through the renewed will has complete authority over the body. Gone are the days when the body pressed a weak inner man. The spirit of a spiritual man has grown strong and the body is under its power.

The Apostle Paul has described the authentic condition of a spiritual man in I Thessalonians: "May the God of peace himself sanctify you wholly; and may your spirit and soul and body be kept sound and blameless at the coming of our Lord Jesus Christ" (5.23). Hence the portrait of the spiritual man which can be drawn from everything which has been said is as follows:

(1) He has God dwelling in his spirit, sanctifying him totally. Its life inundates his entire person so that his every component lives by the spirit life and functions in the spirit's strength.

(2) He does not live by soul life. His every thought, imagination, feeling, idea, affection, desire and opinion is renewed and purified by the Spirit and has been brought into subjection to his spirit. These no longer operate independently.

(3) He still possesses a body, for he is not a disembodied spirit; yet physical weariness, pain, and demand do not impel the spirit to topple from its ascended position. Every

member of the body has become an instrument of righteousness.

To conclude, then, a spiritual man is one who belongs to the spirit: the whole man is governed by the inner man: all the organs of his being are subject completely to it. His spirit is what stamps his life as unique—everything proceeds from his spirit, while he himself renders absolute allegiance to it. No word does he speak nor act does he perform according to himself; rather does he deny his natural power each time in order to draw power from the spirit. In a word, a spiritual man lives by the spirit.

CHAPTER 3
SPIRITUAL WORK

As a believer goes on his spiritual way he gradually begins to realize that to live for himself is a sin, yea, the greatest sin of his life. To live for himself is as it were a grain of wheat which having fallen into the earth refuses to die and hence remains alone. To seek the filling of the Holy Spirit in order to be a powerful spiritual person is solely to please himself, to make himself happy. For were he to live purely for God and His work this believer would not consider his personal happiness or feeling. He certainly would understand the meaning of spirituality. But in the depth of his heart lodges instead a soul's self-love.

All God's children are God's servants. Each of them receives some gift from the Lord: none is excepted (Matt. 25.15). God places them in His church and apportions to each a ministry to fulfill. God's objective is not to make the believer's spirit a reservoir of spiritual life which withers after a little while: if God's life becomes stagnant in him he begins to feel parched. No, spiritual life is for spiritual work; spiritual work expresses spiritual life. The secret of that kind of living lies in the incessant flowing of that life to others.

Spiritual food of a believer is nothing more nor less than accomplishing God's work (John 4.34). The kingdom of God suffers greatly at the hands of "spiritual believers" who busy themselves with prayer and Bible study and attend only to *their* spiritual need. The Lord's people should simply trust God for the sustenance of both their physical and spiritual needs. If they are willing to endure hunger in order to accomplish what God wants them to do, they shall be satisfied. Spiritual food is simply to do His will. Preoccupation with one's own supply causes lack, whereas concern with God's kingdom brings satisfaction. He who is occupied with the Father's business and not with his own shall find himself perpetually full.

The child of God should not be overanxious to make new gains; what he essentially requires is to keep what he already has, for not losing is itself a gain. The way to retain what he possesses is to engage it. Burying it beneath the earth is a sure way to lose it. When a believer allows the life in his spirit to flow freely, he not only shall gain others but shall gain himself as well. One gains by losing self for others and not by hoarding for oneself. The life within a spiritual man must be released by performing spiritual labor. If one's inner being is always open and free (it must of course be closed to the enemy), the life of God shall flow out from him to the salvation and edification of many. The moment spiritual exertion ceases, at that precise moment spiritual life is blocked. These two are inseparable.

No matter what earthly occupation the believer may have, he is apportioned a measure of work by God as well. One who is spiritual knows his place in the body of Christ; as a consequence he also knows the limits of his work. Each member has his usefulness; his work lies in discharging that usefulness. Some gifts are dispensed to benefit particular members; while others, the whole body. A Christian ought to recognize the limits of his gift and to labor within those bounds. But many fail. They either withdraw from their work and thus stifle the development of their spiritual life, or they overextend themselves to their harm. Misusing hands and feet damages a person just as much as not using his hands and feet at all. One sure means of losing life, as we have seen, is to try to keep spiritual life to oneself; yet to work indiscriminately can equally impede life.

SPIRITUAL POWER

We must desire to be filled with the Holy Spirit experientially if we desire to have power in witnessing for Christ and in combating Satan. More and more people are in hot pursuit of such experiences today. But the question should be raised as to what lies behind such a quest. How many covet that they may boast? How many desire more glory for their flesh? How many hope people will fall effortlessly under their power? We must discern clearly why we solicit the power of the Holy Spirit. If our motive is neither of God nor one with God, we certainly will not be able to obtain the power. God's Holy Spirit does not fall on man's "flesh"; He descends only on God's newly created spirit within the man. We cannot allow the outward man, that is, the flesh, to persist while petitioning God to immerse our inner man, the spirit, in His Spirit. So long as the flesh continues unscathed the Holy Spirit of God shall never descend upon man's spirit, for man would only grow more fleshly and boastful if power were granted him.

It is often observed that Calvary precedes Pentecost. The Holy Spirit is not willing to dispense power to men and women who have not been dealt with by the cross. The path which leads to the upper room in Jerusalem winds by way of Calvary. Only those who are conformed to the death of the Lord can receive the power of the Lord. The Word of God affirms that "upon man's flesh shall it (holy anointing oil) not be poured" (Ex. 30.32 Darby). God's Holy Oil will not be poured upon the flesh, whether it be exceedingly defiled or highly refined. Where the mark of the cross is lacking, there the oil of the Spirit is absent. Through the death of the Lord Jesus God pronounces His verdict upon all who are in Adam: "all must die." Just as the Heavenly Power did not descend until the Lord Jesus died, even so should the believer not expect that Power if he has yet to know the death of the Lord Jesus in experience. Historically, Pentecost followed Calvary; experientially, being filled with the power of the Holy Spirit follows the bearing of the cross.

The flesh is condemned forever before God and by God is sentenced to death. Are we not attempting the impossible if we desire not its death but rather seek to adorn the flesh with the Holy Spirit that it may be more powerful in service? What is our intention after all? Personal attraction? Fame? Popularity? The admiration of spiritual believers? Success? Being pleasing to man? Self-edification? People with mixed motives, those of double mind, shall not be able to receive the baptism in the Holy Spirit. We perhaps may judge our motive pure, but our High Priest, through different circumstances, will enable us to know our true heart. Not until the work in hand has failed and we are despised and rejected shall we begin to discern the intent of our heart. Any who are genuinely used by the Lord always have gone this way. The time when we receive the power is after the cross has performed its task.

But are there not many of God's children who, never having had the deeper experience of the cross, are yet powerful in witnessing and appear to be greatly used by the Lord? The Bible indicates that there is an oil very much like the holy anointing oil (Ex. 30.33). It is compounded *like* the holy anointing oil, but it is not the *holy* anointing oil. Do not be taken in or flattered by your own success or fame. Take note only as to whether or not the old creation, including everything which comes by birth, has gone through the cross. Any power we possess before the flesh is put to death is certainly *not* the power of the Holy Spirit. Those with spiritual insight who live on the other side of the curtain well appreciate that such success has not a shred of spiritual value.

Only after a person has actually condemned his flesh and begins to walk according to the spirit will he receive the real power from God. Otherwise it would be his flesh that would be endued with spiritual power. How can one's spirit receive special power if the flesh has not experienced death, since the flesh rules by its own energy and invariably suppresses the spirit? The power of God only descends upon that spirit which is full of His Holy Spirit. This is the sole possibility. No other way can there be for the dynamism of the Spirit to flow out. Is it not true that when a vessel is already full, any added power will naturally overflow? To receive power, therefore, it is necessary for us to die to the old creation and learn how to walk in the Spirit.

Every Christian ought to seek the power of the Holy Spirit. To understand it mentally is not enough. His spirit must be engulfed by the Heavenly Power. The effectiveness of one's work depends upon whether he has the experience of being so immersed in the Holy Spirit. God's Spirit requires an outlet, but alas, in how many can He actually find that outlet? There are hindrances of sin, of pride, of coldness, of self-will, or of reliance on the soul life. God's Power has no exit! We have too many other sources of energy besides His!

In seeking the might of the Holy Spirit we must keep our mind clear and our will alive, thereby guarding ourselves from the enemy's counterfeit. We also must let God purge from our life anything sinful, unrighteous or doubtful, that our total being may be presented to the Lord. We then should "receive the promise of the Spirit through faith" (Gal. 3.14). Rest in God trusting that He will fulfill His Word in due course. Do not, however, forget His promise. Should there be delay, use the opportunity for closer scrutiny of your life beneath His light. Gladly accept any feeling which does come with the power; but if God deems it suitable not to accompany power with feeling, simply believe He has indeed fulfilled His Word.

How does one judge whether he has received the promise or not? By looking into his experience. He who has received power has his spiritual senses sharpened and also possesses an utterance—not of this world—to witness for the Lord. His work is effective and bears lasting fruit. Power is the basic ingredient for spiritual service.

Upon receiving the enablement of the Holy Spirit a believer grows very sensitive to his spirit's senses. He should keep his inner man continually free, allowing the Holy Spirit to flow out His life in and through his being. To keep the inner man free is to maintain it in an operative condition for the Holy Spirit. Suppose God, for instance, sends a believer to lead a meeting. This one's spirit must be open. He should not come to the meeting with a spirit loaded down with many cares or weights, else this shall afflict the whole meeting with heaviness, creating a difficult and unbearable situation. The one who leads should not carry his burden to the meeting and expect the congregation to set him free. Anyone who relies on the response of the congregation to relieve him of his burden is doomed to failure. When he enters the meeting place the leader's spirit must be light and unbound. Many who attend are teeming with burdens. Hence the leader first must release them through prayer, hymn, or truth before he can deliver God's message. He cannot expect to unshackle others while he is himself bound with unbroken fetters.

It should be clearly borne in mind that a spiritual gathering is the communion of spirit with spirit. The messenger delivers his message out of his spirit, and the hearer receives God's Word with his. Were the spirit of the messenger or the hearer to be weighed down and under bondage, it would be powerless to open to God and respond to His Word. Accordingly, the leader's spirit should be free in order that initially he may unloose the spirit of the congregation and then may deliver God's message to them.

We must have the Heavenly Power to achieve powerful work; but we must keep our spirit constantly open to let that Power freely flow from our spirit. The manifestation of power varies in its measure. The experience a Christian has of Calvary measures that of Pentecost. If man's spirit is unbound, God's Spirit can work.

Occasionally in working one may experience his inner man being shut in, especially in performing personal work. This may be due to the condition of the other party. The latter may not have an open spirit or mind to receive the truth, or he may harbor improper thoughts which block the spirit's outflow. Such a state will hem in the spirit of the worker. We know quite often whether we are able to perform any spiritual service by merely observing the attitude of the other party. If we find our inner being is closed in by him, we are not able to deliver the truth to that one.

Now were we to force ourselves to labor upon encountering the shutting in of our spirit, we would probably work not with it but with our mind. Yet only work done with the spirit accomplishes lasting results. Whatever is produced by the mind lacks spiritual power. Our efforts shall lose their effectiveness if initially we do not prepare ourselves through prayer and by setting our spirit free for the delivery of God's Word. We must learn how to walk after the spirit so that eventually we may know how to work by it.

THE INAUGURATION OF SPIRITUAL WORK

To inaugurate a work is no small matter. Christians should never initiate anything presumptuously on the basis of need, profit, or merit. These may not indicate God's will in the slightest. Perhaps He will raise up others to undertake this task or He may suspend it till some other time. Men may feel regretful, but God knows what is best. Hence need, profit and merit cannot serve as indicators for our work.

The book of Acts is the best aid in approaching our work. We do not find there anyone consecrating himself as a preacher nor anyone deciding to do the Lord's work by making himself a missionary or a pastor. What we do see is the Holy Spirit Himself appointing and sending men out to do the work. God never enlists men to His service: He simply sends whom *He* wants. We do not see anyone choosing himself: it is God who chooses His worker. There is positively no ground for man's flesh. When God selects, not even a Saul of Tarsus can withstand; when God does not select, even a Simon cannot buy it. God is the sole master of His work, for He will not permit any human mixture in it. Never does man come to work, but it is always God Who *sends* out to do his work. Spiritual service consequently must be inaugurated by the Lord Himself calling us. It should not be initiated through the persuasion of preachers, the encouragement of friends, or the bent of our natural temperament. None who are shod with fleshly shoes can stand on the holy ground of God's service. Many failures and much waste and confusion which have resulted are due to men's *coming* to work, instead of being *sent out* to work.

The chosen worker is not free to move, even after he is chosen. From the fleshly viewpoint no labor is as restrained as spiritual labor. We read in the book of Acts such phrases as: "the Spirit said to him" (10.19); "being sent out by the Holy Spirit" (13.4); "having been forbidden by the Holy Spirit" (16.6). Other than obeying orders, one has no authority to decide anything. In those days the works of the Apostles were performed by heeding the mind of the Holy Spirit apprehended in their intuition. How simple it is! If spiritual work must be contrived and controlled by believers themselves, who then is competent save those who are naturally capable, clever, and learned? *But,* God has discarded all which belongs to the flesh. Believers *can* be used by the Lord to do the most effective work, but only if their spirits are holy, alive, and full of power before the Lord. God has never delegated to believers authority over the control of His work, because He desires them to listen to what He tells them in their spirit.

Despite a great revival in Samaria, Philip was not responsible for the follow-up labor of strengthening. He must leave immediately for the desert in order that a "heathen" eunuch might be saved. Ananias had not heard of Saul's conversion, but he could not refuse to go to pray for Saul when sent, though by standards of human judgment he was casting his life away by walking directly into the persecutor's hand. Peter could not resist what the Holy Spirit had set forth, even though Jewish tradition forbade Jews from visiting anyone of another nation and associating with him. Paul and Barnabas were sent by the Holy Spirit; yet He retained the authority to forbid them from entering Asia; subsequently, though, He did lead Paul to Asia and established the church at Ephesus. All acts are in the hands of the Spirit; believers simply obey. Had it been left to human thoughts and wishes, many places which ought to be visited would not have been, and many others would have been visited which ought not to be. These experiences from Acts inescapably tell us that we too must follow the guidance of God's Spirit in our intuition and not follow our thoughts, reasons or wishes. They also indicate that He does not guide us by our counsels, desires or judgments because these often contradict the guidance of the Holy Spirit in our spirits. How then dare we follow our mind, emotion or will if even the Apostles did not move on that basis?

All works which God calls us to accomplish are revealed in the intuition of the spirit.* We shall deviate from God's will if we follow the thought of our mind, the feeling of our emotion or the desire of our will. Only what is born of the Spirit is spirit; nothing else is. In all their labors Christians must wait on God until they receive revelation in their intuition; otherwise the flesh will assert itself. God will undeniably grant us the spiritual strength for the task He calls us to execute. Here, then, is an excellent principle to remember: never extend beyond the strength of our spirit. If we undertake more than what we there have, we will draw invariably upon our natural strength for help. This shall be the beginning of vexation. Overstretching in work hinders us from walking according to the spirit and disables us from achieving true spiritual accomplishment.

How people today have seized upon reason, thought, idea, feeling, wish and desire as the governing factors in work! These emanate from the soul and contain not an ounce of spiritual value. These can be good stewards but they most assuredly are not good masters. We shall be defeated if we follow them. Spiritual service must emerge from the spirit: nowhere else but here shall God reveal His will.

Workers must never permit soulical sensations to transcend spiritual relations while helping others. They should minister spiritual help in all purity; any soulical feeling can be harmful. This often is a danger and a snare to workers. Even our love, affection, concern, burden, interest and zeal must be

*See Part Five, Chapter 1.

entirely under the spirit's guidance. Negligence in keeping this law causes untold moral and spiritual defeats. If we allow natural attraction and human admiration or the lack of these to govern our efforts we will surely fail in our work and our lives shall be ruined. To obtain genuine fruitfulness we frequently need to disregard fleshly relationships or, in the case of those dearest to us, at least relegate them to a subordinate place. Our thoughts and desires must be offered completely to the Lord.

We will undertake whatever we know intuitively through the guidance of the Holy Spirit; the flesh has no possibility of participating in God's service. The measure of our spiritual usefulness depends upon how penetratingly the cross has cut into our flesh. Do not look at apparent success; rather, look at how much is done by God's crucified ones. Nothing can cover the flesh, not even good intention, zeal, or labor and though they be in the name of the Lord Jesus and for the sake of the kingdom of heaven. God Himself will work; He brooks no interference from the flesh. We should realize that in the matter of serving God there is even the possibility of offering "unholy fire," that which is unspiritual. This arouses God's wrath. Any fire which is not kindled by the Holy Spirit in our spirit is but unholy fire and is deemed sinful in God's sight. Not all deeds done for God are His deeds. Doing for Him is not enough; the question is, who is doing the doing? God will not recognize any labor as His if it simply reflects the believer's activity and is carried out in his strength. God's recognized work must be done by God Himself through the spirit of the believer. Whatever comes from the flesh shall perish with the flesh; only what comes from God remains forever. Doing what is ordered by Him can never fail.

THE AIM OF SPIRITUAL WORK

Spiritual work aims to give life to man's spirit or to build up the life in the spirit. Our labor will be nil in worth or effectiveness if it is not directed towards the spirit lying in the very depths of man. What a sinner needs is life, not some sublime thought. A believer needs whatever can nourish his spiritual life, not mere Bible knowledge. If all we communicate are excellent sermonic divisions, wonderful parables, transcendent abstractions, clever words, or logical arguments, we are but supplying additional thoughts to people's minds, arousing their emotions once again, or activating their will to make one more decision. With a moribund spirit do they come and with just as moribund a spirit do they depart despite our heavy labors on their behalf. A sinner needs to have his spirit resurrected, not to be able to argue better, shed profuse tears, or make a firmer resolve. Likewise a believer does not require outward edification, since his real lack is inward life more abundant – how he can grow spiritually. Should we focus our attention on the outward man and neglect the inward man, our work will be utterly vain and superficial. Such work equals no work at all, and perhaps it is even worse than no work, for a lot of precious time is undeniably wasted!

Man can be moved to tears, can confess his sins, can consider redemption reasonable, can profess his interest in religion, can sign a decision card, can read the Bible and pray, can even testify with joy; but still his spirit has not received God's life and therefore remains as dead as before. Why? Because man's soul is capable of performing all these things. To be sure, we do not despise these motions; nevertheless we recognize that except the spirit is quickened these pious acts are but rootless blades which will be totally withered beneath the scorching sun. When a spirit is born anew it may display these same manifestations in the outward soul: in the depth of its being, however, it receives a new life which enables the person to *know God* and to know Jesus Christ Whom God has sent. No work possesses any spiritual effectiveness save that which quickens the spirit into an intuitive knowledge of God.

We ought to perceive that it is quite possible to exercise "false faith" and experience "false regeneration." Many confuse understanding with believing. The former simply means the mind understands the reason of the truth and reckons it believable. The latter, according to the spiritual sense, involves being united; that is, by believing that the Lord Jesus died for us we unite ourselves with His death. People can understand doctrine without necessarily believing in the Lord Jesus. What we stress is that men are not saved by their good deed, rather do they obtain eternal life through believing the Son of God. Men must *believe* in God's Son. Many believe the doctrine of atonement but fail to believe in the Savior Who atones. Their regeneration is false should they only fill the basin with the blood of the lamb without applying it on the doors of their heart. Countless are the professing Christians who lack the intuitive knowledge of God, although they live like true regenerated Christians—clean, pious, helpful, frequently praying and reading the Bible, even attending services. They can hear and converse about God, yet they do not *know God,* they have no personal knowledge of Him. "My own know me . . . and they will heed my voice" (John 10.14, 16). Those who neither know the Lord nor heed His voice are not His sheep.

Since man's relationship with God begins at regeneration and is carried on completely in the spirit, it is evident that all our work must have its center here. To court apparent success by merely whipping up people's enthusiasm results in a work without God. Once having learned the central place of the spirit, our efforts should undergo a drastic change. We do not labor without objective, simply following what we think is good; we have a distinctive aim, that of building up man's inner depths. In the past we laid stress on the natural; now must we emphasize the spiritual. Spiritual service means nothing other than our working by our spirit for the quickening of the spirits of others. Nothing else can be so termed.

When in fact we recognize that nothing *we* have can impart life to man, then we shall discover how utterly useless we in ourselves are. When we cease depending upon ourselves and using what we have we will see indeed how very weak we are. Not until then will we learn how much power our inner man has. Since we usually rely so heavily on the soul by which to live, we naturally do not appreciate how weak our spirit actually is. Now that we trust solely in the spirit's power we come to perceive the real dynamic of our spiritual life. If we are determined to give life to man's spirit and not just assist the mind to understand, the emotion to be stirred, or the will to decide, we will realize instantly that unless the Holy Spirit verily uses us we are absolutely undone. "Who were born not of blood nor of the will of the flesh nor of the will of man, but of God" (John 1.13). How can we beget them if God does not beget them? We now know all works must be done by God; we are but *empty* vessels. Nothing in us is able to beget them: nothing in them is capable of self-begetting. It is God Who pours out His life through our spirit. Spiritual work is therefore God doing His work. Whatever is not done by Him is not accounted as such.

We should beseech God to reveal the nature and greatness of His work to us. If we understand how much His work requires His great power, we shall be ashamed of our ideas and abashed by our self-reliance. We shall see that all our efforts are but "dead works." Though at times God in special mercy blesses our labors far beyond their due, we should nonetheless refrain from interpreting this as a green light to proceed on that course. Whatever is achieved by ourselves is worthless as well as dangerous. We ought to recognize that God's work is accomplished neither by charged atmosphere, attractive environment, romantic thought, poetic imagination, idealistic view, rational suggestion, burning passion, nor excited will. These might well be suitable were spiritual work merely a dream and not a reality. But such an endeavor is to regenerate the spirit of man and to give resurrection life to him. It can accordingly be accomplished only by God Himself in that Power which raised the Lord Jesus from death.

Thus we see that unless we communicate *God's life* to men our labor merits no praise in heaven. Whatever does not originate in the inward man where God's Spirit dwells is powerless to impart life, no matter how compatible or how incompatible that work may be with reason and feeling. False spiritual enablement may produce results seemingly alike but it can never grant authentic life to man's dead spirit. It may achieve anything and everything except the one real objective of spiritual work.

If we truly aim to bring life to others the power we use must obviously be God's. But in case we employ soul power, failure is inevitable because the soul, though itself alive (Gen. 2.7 Darby), cannot quicken others; for "it is the spirit that gives life" (John 6.63). Note also that "the last Adam (the Lord Jesus) became a life-giving spirit" (1 Cor. 15.45). As the Lord Jesus "poured out his soul to death" (Is. 53.12), so everyone who would serve as a channel for His life must likewise deliver his natural life to death in order that he may work with spirit life for the regeneration of others. However attractive the soul life may be, it possesses no reproductive force. It is impossible to draw on natural power as the energizing force for performing spiritual labor. Old creation can never be the source for new creation, nor can the old serve as the helper to the new. If we labor by the revelation of the Holy Spirit and in His strength, our audience shall be convinced and have their spirits enlivened by God. Else what we give them simply becomes a masterful idea which may stimulate temporarily but leaves no lasting result. The same work may be employed in both cases, but what originates with spirit power becomes spiritual life while that which draws upon self-power turns into natural reasoning. Furthermore, whatever is done in the energy of our natural life will whet people's appetite for more of such feeling and reasoning, automatically and unavoidably drawing them to the one who supplies such needs. The ignorant regard this as spiritual success since many are being gathered; but the discerning can perceive that no life exists in their spirit. The effect of such endeavor in the realm of religion is similar to that of opium or alcohol on the body. Man needs life, not ideas or excitement.

The responsibility of Christians is consequently just this: to present their spirits to God as vessels and to consign to death everything pertaining to themselves. Should they neither block their spirit nor attempt to give to others what they have in and of themselves, God can use His children greatly as channels of life for the salvation of sinners and the upbuilding of the saints. Without that, then whatever the listener receives is but the thought, reason and feeling of the worker; he never accepts the Lord as Savior nor is his dead spirit quickened. Realizing that our aim is to furnish life to man's spirit, we ourselves obviously must be duly prepared. By genuinely relinquishing our soul life and relying entirely on the inner man, we shall see that the words the Lord speaks through *our* mouths continue to be "spirit and life" (John 6.63).

THE CESSATION OF SPIRITUAL WORK

Spiritual work invariably flows with the current of the Holy Spirit—never reluctantly, never under compulsion, hence without need of fleshly strength. This does not imply of course that there is no opposition from the world or attack from the enemy. It simply means the work is done in the Lord with the consciousness of having His anointing. If God still requires the work, the believer will continue to sense himself flowing in the current, no matter how difficult his situation may be. The Holy Spirit aims at expressing spiritual life. Labor accomplished in Him correspondingly develops life in the spirit. Unfortunately many of God's servants frequently are pressed by environment or other factors into working mechanically. As soon as the individual is aware of it, he ought to inquire whether such "mechanical work" is desired by the Spirit or whether God would call him away to other service. God's servants should know that a task begun spiritually—that is, in the Spirit—may not necessarily continue that way. Many works are initiated by Him, but after He has no more need of them men often desire to keep them going. To regard as forever spiritual whatever is begun by the Holy Spirit is inevitably to change the spiritual into the fleshly.

A spiritual Christian can no longer enjoy the anointing of the Spirit in a work that has become mechanical. When a task is already given up by God as unnecessary and yet is maintained by the Christian because of the outside organization (with or without form) which surrounds it, then it must be carried on by drawing upon his own resources rather than upon the power of God. Should a saint persist in laboring after the spiritual work is terminated, he must employ his soul power as well as physical power to continue on with it. In true spiritual service one must completely deny his natural talent and gift; only in this way can he produce fruit for God. If not, each effort not led by the Holy Spirit does collapse if not supported by one's brain, talent, or gift.

A worker must observe carefully which part of his labor the Holy Spirit anoints. Then he will be able to cooperate with Him and operate within the current of His power. The worker's duty is to discern the current of the Spirit and to follow it. A task should be discontinued if it no longer enjoys God's anointing, is out of His current, and creates a sluggish, languid feeling. Another undertaking should be found which flows with the current. The spiritual man discerns more quickly than others. The matter for him to determine is, where is the Holy Spirit's current? Where is it flowing? Any labor that oppresses spiritual life, that fails to express the life of the spirit, or that hinders God's Spirit from overflowing has become a definite obstacle, however well it began. That work should be either cancelled or corrected so that the believer can obey life in the spirit. The worker may have to alter his relationship to the work.

Many cases can be cited to illustrate how the Lord's people are entangled in "organization," to the detriment of their life. At first these servants of God received tremendous spiritual power and were mightily used by God to save and build up man. Later arose the need for some kind of "organization" or "method" to preserve the grace that was given. Due to needs, requests, and sometimes orders, these servants were required to undertake so-called "edifying" work. Thus they were bound by environment and no longer had the freedom to follow the Holy Spirit. Gradually their spiritual life ebbed, though the outside organized work still continued in prosperity. Such has been the story of numberless defeats.

What tragedy lurks within spiritual work today! Many consider their labor a burden. Are there not many who say: "I am so busy with work that I have little time to commune with the Lord. I hope I can find the opportunity to suspend the work temporarily so that I may repair my spirit for the next task." How fraught with danger this is! Our work ought to be the fruit of our spirit's fellowship with the Lord. Every task should be undertaken joyfully as the overflow of the life of the spirit. If it becomes a weight and separates the life of the spirit from the Lord Jesus, then it ought to be terminated. Since the current of the Spirit has changed its course, one must seek to discover its re-location and follow accordingly.

Wide is the disparity between the Holy Spirit terminating our work and Satan hindering it. Yet people frequently are confused by these two. If God should say "Stop" and the believer continue, he will descend from working with his spirit into maintaining the work with his brain, talent, and strength. He may attempt to resist the enemy; without the anointing of the Holy Spirit, however, he cannot succeed. The whole warfare becomes fake. Whenever a child of God encounters resistance in the spirit he should distinguish immediately whether this opposition emanates from God or from the enemy. Should it be the latter his resistance by the *spirit* through prayer will release his inner man and thus he can advance with God. But if it is not from the enemy, the believer shall find as he advances that his own spirit becomes more oppressed, heavily burdened, and void of liberty.

In sum, then, the servants of God today must set aside every work which is not appointed by Him, that should long have been forsaken, which monopolizes everything, that does not come from the spirit, which oppresses the spirit and deflects spiritual work, and that is even good but nonetheless deprives them of other and nobler tasks.

CHAPTER 4
PRAYER AND WARFARE

ALL PRAYER OUGHT TO BE SPIRITUAL. Unspiritual prayers are not genuine and can produce no positive result. What abundant spiritual success there would be were every prayer offered by believers on earth in fact spiritual! But sad to say, fleshly prayers are far too numerous. Self-will found therein deprives them of spiritual fruitfulness. Nowadays Christians appear to treat prayer as a means to accomplish *their* aims and ideas. If they possessed just a little deeper understanding, they would recognize that prayer is but man uttering to God what is *God's* will. The flesh, no matter where displayed, must be crucified; it is not permitted even in prayer. No mixing of man's will in God's work is possible, for He rejects the best of human intentions and man's most profitable prospects. God does not will He should follow what man has initiated. Other than following God's direction, we have no right to direct Him. We have no ability to offer save to obey God's guidance. God will do no work which originates with man, no matter how much man may pray. He condemns such praying as fleshly.

As believers enter the true realm of the spirit, immediately they shall see how empty they themselves are, for absolutely nothing in them can impart life to others or work havoc upon the enemy. Instinctively they will therefore reckon on God. Prayer then becomes imperative. True prayer uncovers the emptiness in the petitioner but the fullness in the Petitioned. Unless the flesh has been reduced to a "vacuum" by the cross, what use is prayer and what can it possibly signify?

Spiritual prayer does not proceed from the flesh nor the

thought, desire, or decision of the believer; rather does it follow purely from that which is offered according to the will of God. It is prayed in the spirit, that is to say, spiritual prayer is made after one has discerned the will of God in his intuition. The command insisted upon in the Bible is to "pray at all times in the spirit" (Eph. 6.18). If that is not the way we are praying we must be praying in the flesh. We should not open our mouths too hastily upon approaching God. On the contrary, we first must ask God to show us what and how to pray before we make our request known to Him. Have we not consumed a great deal of time in the past asking for what *we* wanted? Why not now ask for what *God* wants? Not what we want but what He wants. If such be the case, then the flesh is provided no footing here. It takes a spiritual man to offer true prayer.

All spiritual prayers have their source in God. God makes known to us what we ought to pray by unfolding to us the need and by giving that need as a burden in our intuitive spirit. Only an intuitive burden can constitute our call to pray. Yet how we have overlooked many delicate registrations in the intuition through carelessness. Our prayer should never exceed the burden in our intuition. Prayers which are not initiated or responded to in the spirit originate instead with the believer himself. They are therefore of the flesh. So that his prayer may not be fleshly but may be effectual in the spiritual domain, the child of God ought to confess his weakness that he does not know how to pray (Rom. 8.26), and petition the Holy Spirit to teach him. He next should pray according to His instruction. God gives us utterance to pray just as he gives us utterance to preach. The need for the former equals that of the latter. In acknowledging our total weakness, we then are able to depend on the movement of the Holy Spirit within our spirit for uttering His prayer. How empty that work is which is done by the flesh; how likewise fruitless is that prayer which is offered in the flesh.

Not only should we pray with the spirit; we should "pray with the mind also" (1 Cor. 14.15). In praying, these two must work together. A believer receives in his spirit what he needs to pray and understands in his mind what he has received. The spirit accepts the burden of prayer while the mind formulates that burden in prayerful words. Only in this way is the prayer of a believer perfected. How often the Christian prays according to the thought in his mind without possessing any revelation in his spirit. He becomes the origin of the prayer himself. But true prayer must originate from the throne of God. It initially is sensed in the person's spirit, next is understood by his mind, and finally is uttered through the power of the Spirit. Man's spirit and prayer are inseparable.

To be able to pray with the spirit a Christian must learn first to walk according to the spirit. No one can pray with his spirit if during the whole day he walks after the flesh. The state of one's prayer life cannot be too greatly disconnected from the condition of his daily walk. The spiritual condition of many too often disqualifies them from praying in the spirit. The quality of a man's prayer is determined by the state of his living. How could a fleshly person offer spiritual prayer? A spiritual person, on the other hand, does not necessarily pray spiritually either, for unless he is watchful he also shall fall into the flesh. Nonetheless, should the spiritual man pray often with his spirit, his very praying shall keep his spirit and mind continually in tune with God. Praying exercises the spirit which in turn is strengthened through such exercising. Negligence in prayer withers the inner man. Nothing can be a substitute for it, not even Christian work. Many are so preoccupied with work that they allow little time for prayer. Hence they cannot cast out demons. Prayer enables us first inwardly to overcome the enemy and then outwardly to deal with him. All who have fought against the enemy on their knees shall see him routed upon their rising up.

Now the spiritual man grows stronger through such exercises. For if a believer prays often with his spirit, his spiritual efficiency shall be increased greatly. He will develop sharp sensitivity in spiritual affairs and will be delivered from all spiritual dullness.

The current need of the spiritual Christian is to learn by God's revelation in his spirit how to detect the enemy's attack and subsequently through prayer to disclose it. He should quickly understand any movement in his spirit so that he may achieve immediately through prayer what God desires him to accomplish. Prayer is work. The experiences of many children of God demonstrate that it accomplishes far more than does any other form of work. It is also warfare, for it is one of the weapons in fighting the enemy (Eph. 6. 18). However, only prayer in the spirit is genuinely effectual.

Praying in the spirit is most productive in attacking the enemy or resisting his wiles. It can destroy as well as build up. Whatever issues from sin and Satan it destroys, but whatevery belongs to God it edifies. Prayer is thus one of the most significant instruments in spiritual work and warfare. Yes, spiritual work and warfare turn on the matter of prayer. If a believer fails in prayer, he in fact fails in everything.

SPIRITUAL WARFARE

Broadly speaking, a Christian who has not yet experienced the baptism in the Holy Spirit is rather vague about the reality of the spiritual realm. He is like the servant of Elisha whose eyes were closed to that sphere. He may receive instructions from the Bible, yet his understanding is confined to the mind because he still lacks revelation in his spirit. But upon experiencing the baptism his intuition becomes acutely sensitive and he discovers in his spirit a spiritual world opening before him. By the experience of the baptism in the Holy Spirit he not only touches the supernatural power of God but contacts God's Person as well.

Now it is just there that spiritual warfare begins. This is the period when the power of darkness disguises himself as an angel of light and even attempts to counterfeit the Person and the work of the Holy Spirit. It is also the moment when the intuition is made aware of the existence of a spiritual domain and of the reality of Satan and his evil spirits. The Apostles were taught in the Scriptures by the Lord after Calvary; but they were made conscious of the real existence of a spiritual realm following Pentecost. Spirit-baptism marks the starting point of spiritual warfare.

Once a believer has contacted the Person of God via the baptism in the Holy Spirit, he then has his own spirit released. He now senses the reality of the things and beings in the spiritual domain. With such knowledge (and let us call to mind that the knowledge of a spiritual man does not accrue to him all at once; some of it may, and usually does, come through many trials), he encounters Satan. Only those who are spiritual perceive the reality of the spiritual foe and hence engage in battle (Eph. 6.12). Such warfare is not fought with arms of the flesh (2 Cor. 10.4). Because the conflict is spiritual so must the weapons. It is a struggle between the spirit of man and that of the enemy—an engagement of spirit with spirit.

Before he arrives at such a juncture in his spiritual walk, the child of God neither understands, nor can he engage in, the battle of the spirits. Only after his inner man has been strengthened by the Holy Spirit does he know how to wrestle with the adversary in his spirit. As he spiritually advances he begins to discover the reality of Satan and his kingdom and then it is that he is given to understand how to resist and attack the foe with his spirit.

The reasons for such conflict are many, with the enemy's tactic of attack and blocking constituting the greatest. Satan frequently either unsettles the emotions of the physical bodies of spiritual believers, or he blocks the works of the spiritual ones, or he may disturb their environments. The need to fight for God forms still another reason for this warfare. As Satan plots in the air and works on earth against God, so His people fight back with spiritual power, destroying the enemy's plots and plans through their prayers. Though at times saints do not know for sure what Satan's scheme is nor what he is doing at the moment, they nevertheless continue to press the fight with no let up, for they understand who their antagonist is.

Beyond the above two explanations, spiritual combat has for its existence yet another cause: the need to be delivered from Satan's deception and to deliver deceived souls.* In

---

*Consult Part Eight, Chapter 3 and Part Nine, Chapter 4.

spite of the fact that their spirit's intuition becomes sharp and sensitive after they are baptized in the Holy Spirit, believers may nonetheless fall into deception. To preclude their plunging into the wiles of the adversary, they need not only spiritual sensitivity but also spiritual knowledge. Should they be ignorant of the manner in which the Holy Spirit leads, they may assume a passive position and thereby become captives of the enemy. The easiest error Christians can commit at this moment is to follow some irrational feeling or experience rather than the leading in their inner man. Once baptised in the Holy Spirit, they have entered the supernatural realm. Unless believers appreciate their own weakness, that is, know how incompetent they are in themselves to encounter the supernatural, they shall be deceived.

The Christian's spirit can be influenced by either of two forces: the Holy Spirit or the evil spirit. He commits a fatal blunder who thinks his spirit can be controlled solely by the Holy Spirit and not be so by the evil spirit too. Let it be forever known that aside from the Spirit that is from God, there is additionally "the spirit of the world" (1 Cor. 2.12), which is in fact the spiritual foe of Ephesians 6.12. Except the Christian shuts up his spirit to resist, he may find the evil one usurping his spirit through deceit and counterfeit.

When a child of God becomes spiritual he is subject to the influence of the supernatural world. At this point it is vital for him to know the difference between "spiritual" and "supernatural," the confusion of which forms the cause of many deceptions. Spiritual experiences are those which originate with the believer's spirit, while those of the supernatural may not necessarily come from there. They may arise from physical senses or from the soulical sphere. A Christian ought never interpret a supernatural experience as always being a spiritual one. He should examine his experiences and determine whether they enter through the outer sensual organs or come via the inner spirit. Whatever emanates from outside, however supernatural it may be, is never spiritual.

The Lord's saints should not receive everything supernatural unquestioningly, for Satan too can perform supernatural deeds. No matter how the feeling is during the moment of experience nor how the phenomenon appears or declares itself to be, believers should investigate its source. The charge of 1 John 4.1 must be strictly observed: "Beloved, do not believe every spirit, but test the spirits to see whether they are of God; for many false prophets have gone out into the world." The counterfeits of the adversary often exceed the believer's expectation. If the Lord's people will humble themselves by admitting that deception is quite possible to them, they will be the less deceived. Because of the counterfeits of the enemy, spiritual warfare looms inevitable. Unless *with their spirits* soldiers of Christ take to the field to meet the foe, they shall find him coming in to suppress their spiritual strength. In spiritual conflict the spirit of the Christian wars against the enemy evil spirit. Now should the Christian be deceived already, then he fights to regain his freedom. If not, then he strives to rescue others and to prevent the foe from attacking. He takes the positive stance of subjugating the enemy by opposing every one of Satan's plans and works.

Such battles are fought in the strength of the spirit. It requires power there to wage war. A Christian must understand how to wrestle against the assailant with his spirit. Otherwise he cannot detect how the enemy will attack or discern how God will direct him to fight. But if he walks by the spirit he learns how to pray incessantly therein against the wicked powers. And with each battle his inner man waxes that much stronger. He comes to realize that by applying the law of the spirit he not only can overcome sin but also Satan.

From that part of the Scriptures in which the Apostle touches on spiritual warfare we can readily estimate how important strength is in such conflict. Before he mentions the problem of spiritual warfare (Eph. 6.11-18), Paul first exhorts his readers to "be strong in the Lord and in the strength of his might" (v.10). Where should there be this strength of which he speaks? Paul tells us in Chapter 3: "strengthened with might through his Spirit in the inner man" (v.16). The inner man is man's center, the spirit of man. And right there is where the powers of darkness attack the man. Now if the inner man is weak everything else becomes weak. A frail spirit produces fear in the heart which automatically weakens the believer's stand in the day of evil. What he needs pre-eminently is a firm spirit. Except he understands the nature of the conflict a believer is not capable of resisting *in his spirit* against the principalities and the powers.

Many Christians find their spirit feathery and free when all is sweetness and light; but just let there be eruptive war, and their spirit becomes disturbed, fearful, and worried, until finally it is submerged. They do not know why they are defeated. Satan's aim is victory, and to this end he attempts to remove believers from their ascension position by causing their spirit to sink so that *he* can ascend. Position is a primary factor in battle. When the saint's spirit tumbles, he loses his heavenly position. Christians must consequently maintain a strong spirit and yield no ground to the enemy.

Upon realizing how his inner man is strengthened with might through God's Holy Spirit, a spiritual child of God learns the absolute necessity of overcoming the enemy. His inner man grows sturdier as he attacks the foe with prayer and wrestling. In the same manner that the muscles of the wrestler develop in physical combat, just so the strength of the believer's spirit increases as he battles the adversary. The latter mounts an assault in order to depress the believer's inner man and thus to afflict his soul. If the child of God has come to appreciate the wiles of his assailant, he will not surrender at any point but will instead resist; and his emotional soul is thereby protected. Resistance in the inner man forces the enemy to go on the defensive.

Resistance is one of the indispensable elements in spiritual combat. The best defense is a continuous offense. Oppose with the will as well as with the strength in the spirit. Giving opposition means struggling free from the power of suppression. The opponent will be routed if one fights his way out by the spirit. But should one allow the enemy to attack and not resist in return, then that one's spirit will surely be depressed, sink very low, and may require many days before it regains its ascendancy. The spirit that does not withstand the enemy is often a suppressed one.

How shall we resist? With the Word of God which is the Sword of the Holy Spirit. As a believer receives God's Word it becomes "spirit and life" to him. Hence he can employ this as his weapon of resistance. A heavenly believer knows how to use the Word of God advantageously to break down the enemy's lie. Even now a battle is raging in the world of the spirit. Though unobserved by the eyes of the flesh, it is sensed and proven by those who are seeking heavenly progress. Many who are deceived and bound by the enemy need to be released. Not only is there need for release from sin and self-righteousness; many who are bound as well by supernatural experience need release also. Due to curiosity and the prospect of pleasant sensations, Christians gladly welcome these supernatural phenomena, not recognizing that these merely puff up their pride without producing any real or lasting result in terms of a holy and righteous life or spiritual work. When the evil spirits succeed in their deceptions they gain a footing in the believer. From this ground the enemy gradually enlarges his frontiers until finally he renders the believer as one who walks in the flesh.

Now obviously he who himself is bound cannot possibly set others free. Only when wholly freed experientially from the powers of darkness can the believer himself overcome the foe and rescue others. The incidence of the danger of deception increases in proportion to the number of those who experience the baptism in the Holy Spirit. The need today is for a company of overcoming saints who know how to wage war for the release of those under the enemy's deception. The church of God shall be defeated if she lacks members who know how to walk by the spirit and how to fight therewith against the enemy. May God raise up such!

SOMETHING TO GUARD AGAINST IN SPIRITUAL WARFARE

Each stage of the believer's walk possesses its particular hazard. The new life within us wages a constant war against all which opposes its growth. During the physical stage, it is a war against sins; in the soulish phase, it is a battle against the natural life; and lastly, on the spiritual level, it is an onslaught against the supernatural enemy. It is solely when a Christian turns spiritual that the evil spirit in that realm launches its assault against his spirit. Accordingly, this is called spiritual warfare. It is fought between spirits and with spirit. Such a phenomenon rarely if ever occurs with unspiritual believers. Do not imagine for a moment, therefore, that when one actually reaches the spiritual plateau he is beyond conflict. A Christian life is an unending engagement on the battlefield. The Christian has no possibility of laying down his arms until he stands before the Lord. While soulish, he faces conflict with the flesh and its danger; when spiritual, he encounters spiritual warfare and its peculiar hazards. Initially there is the war against Amalek in the wilderness. Upon entering Canaan there is next the struggle against the seven tribes of Canaan, wherein the attack of Satan and his evil hosts against the believer's spirit is mounted only after the believer has become spiritual.

Since the enemy focuses particular attention on the spirit, how necessary for spiritual believers to keep their own spirit in its normal state and frequently to exercise it as well. They must control with utmost caution all bodily sensations and carefully distinguish all natural and supernatural phenomena. Their mind must be kept perfectly calm without any disturbance; their physical senses too must be maintained in quiet balance without agitation. Spiritual Christians should exercise their will to deny and oppose any falsehood and seek to follow the inner man with their whole heart. Should they at any time follow the soul instead of the inner man they have lost precious ground already in spiritual warfare. Furthermore, they must be very careful to guard their spirit from being passive in this warfare.

Now we have mentioned before that all our guidance must proceed from the inner man: we must wait with our spirit for the guidance of the Holy Spirit. All this is fundamentally true; however, we need to exercise extreme prudence here lest we fall into grievous error. For while we are waiting in our spirit for the Holy Spirit to move and guide us, a danger readily arises wherein our spirit and our entire being may slide into a state of passivity. Nothing can provide more ground for Satan to work from than this state of inaction. On the one side we ought not to do anything in our own strength save to obey the Holy Spirit; yet on the other side we need to be watchful lest our spirit or any part of our being turns mechanical and plunges into inertia. Our inner man must vitally govern our total being and must cooperate actively with God's Spirit.

When our spirit tumbles into passivity the Holy Spirit is left with no way to use it. This is because His operation in a human life is absolutely diametrical to that of Satan. The Holy Spirit *requires man to cooperate livingly with Him.* He desires man to work actively with Him because He never violates the believer's personality. By contrast, Satan demands a full stop in man so that he may *take over* and do everything in man's stead. He wishes man to accept his work passively. Satan wants to turn man into an automaton. Oh, how we should guard against whatever is extreme and guard against misunderstanding in spiritual doctrine. We need not fear being radical in obeying the Lord, that is for sure; nor do we need to guard against being extreme in denying the works of the flesh. But most vigilant must we be that we not be led to any extremes through misconception.

We said most emphatically earlier that we ought to seek God's work, for vain are those things which belong to man and spring from him. We have said that no spiritual value is possible except from what is done by the Holy Spirit through our inner man and that we should therefore wait with our spirit for revelation from God. Yes, this that we have affirmed is quite true. And blessed is he who is willing to follow this truth. Nonetheless, herein lies one of the gravest perils of all—that of going to the extreme through misunderstanding. Countless believers mistake this truth that we have enunciated as the call to inertia. They conceive the idea that their mind should be emptied for the Holy Spirit to think for them, that their emotion should be suppressed in order for Him to put His affection in them, and that their will should make no decision so that He can decide for them. They mistakenly assume they should accept without question whatever comes to them. Their spirit should not cooperate actively with the Holy Spirit but should wait passively for His moving. And then if there be any movement, it automatically is assumed to be from Him.

This constitutes a very serious misjudgment. It *is* a fact that

God wants to destroy every work of our flesh, but He never desires to destroy our *personality.* He takes no pleasure in transforming us into automata; rather does He delight in having us cooperate with Him. God does not wish us to be a people void of thoughts, feelings, and decisions: He yearns for us to think what He thinks, feel what He feels, desire what He desires. The Holy Spirit never supplants us in thinking, feeling, and desiring; we ourselves must think, feel and desire, but all according to God's will. If our mind, emotion and will plunge into a state of quiescence—in which we are no longer active but idly waiting for an outside force to activate us, then our spirit too cannot escape being passive at the same time. And thus Satan benefits immeasurably when we are unable to exercise our spirit but expect instead to be prodded by some external force.

A fundamental difference obtains between the work of the Holy Spirit and that of the evil spirit. *The Holy Spirit moves people themselves to work, never setting aside man's personality; the evil spirit demands men to be entirely inactive so that he may work in their place, reducing man's spirit to a robot.* Hence a passive spirit not only provides the evil one an opportunity to function but binds the hand of the Holy Spirit as well, because He will not operate without the cooperation of the believer. Under these circumstances the evil power inevitably will attempt to exploit the situation. Before a Christian becomes spiritual he is not confronted by this danger of contacting the satanic power; but once he becomes spiritual the wicked one naturally will assault his inner man. The fleshly Christian never experiences this passivity of spirit; the spiritual alone encounters the hazard of developing an errant spirit.

Due to his misconception of the destruction of the flesh, a child of God may allow his inner man to sink into an inert state. This affords the evil one a chance to simulate the Holy Spirit. If the believer forgets that the enemy may influence his spirit as much as the Holy Spirit can, he unwittingly may accept every moving in his spirit to be from the Holy Spirit and thereby cede ground to Satan for pursuing his aim of destroying the moral, mental, and physical well-being of the saint and making him suffer unspeakable pains.

This is exactly what has happened to many who have experienced "the baptism in the Holy Spirit." They do not understand that such an experience necessarily initiates them into a closer relationship with the spirit world and exposes them to the influence of both the Holy Spirit *and* the evil spirit. While they are experiencing a baptism in the spirit they consider all supernatural experiences to be baptism in the Holy Spirit. Truly they have been baptised in the spirit, but the searching question is, in what spirit have they been baptised—in the Holy one or in the evil one? Both of these may be viewed as "baptised in the spirit." Not recognizing that the Holy Spirit requires *their* spirit's cooperation and that He never does violence to their personality, many saints allow their inner man to descend into passivity and to permit some outside force to burn, twist, or overthrow them. They, in a word, have been baptised in the evil spirit.

Some Christians genuinely have been baptised in the Holy Spirit, yet being unable to distinguish between spirit and soul they are deceived afterwards. Because of their special experience, they maintain that now that the Holy Spirit is in full control they should not take any active step but remain completely passive. And so their inner man is submerged in total inertia. Satan begins to feed them many excessive pleasant sensations and numerous visions, dreams, and supernatural experiences too. They receive them all as from the Holy Spirit, not realizing that their inert spirit like a magnet draws in these counterfeit experiences. Had they known how to distinguish the sensational and the supernatural from the spiritual, these believers would have examined those experiences. Now, however, because of a lack of discernment combined with a passive spirit, they settle deeper and deeper into the enemy's deception.

As the believer's spirit grows increasingly quiescent, his conscience of course follows suit. Once his conscience is rendered passive, he next expects to be led *directly* by the Holy Spirit, either by voice or by Scripture verse. He concludes that He no longer will lead him by his conscience or by decisions emanating from his intuition; instead he will be led in the highest way. The Holy Spirit, he now assumes, will speak either directly to him or indirectly through some Bible verses. By ceasing to employ his conscience and by letting it drop into inaction, the saint is deceived into minding Satan in his daily walk. The Holy Spirit, however, true to His Own working principle, will always refrain from taking over man's conscience and using it for him. Satan alone will seize the occasion to replace the guidance of the believer's conscience and intuition with supernatural voices and other devices.

As conscience grows more passive and the evil spirit supplies his guidance, some Christians begin to lower their moral standard—thinking they henceforth live according to a higher life principle, and therefore treat immoral matters as not quite so immoral any more. They also cease to make any progress in life or work. Instead of *exercising* their intuitive power to detect the thought of the Holy Spirit or of engaging their conscience to discern right and wrong, they simply follow the supernatural voice which comes from outside and reduce themselves to robots. These Christians mistake the supernatural voice for the voice of God. They disregard their reasoning, their conscience, and other people's advice. They turn out to be the most stubborn individuals in the world: they refuse to listen to anyone. They picture themselves as obeying a higher law of life than the rest of their spiritual confreres. How they fit perfectly the description of the Apostle: "whose consciences are seared"! (1 Tim. 4.2) Their consciences are void of conviction!

Hence to sum up: in our spiritual warfare we must ever and anon preserve our inner man in an active state—wholly yielded to the Holy Spirit, yet not in passive submission; otherwise we shall be deceived by the enemy. Even should the adversary not assault us, we still shall retreat into a shut-in position if our spirit is not operative and outstretched. For the enemy would have the chance anyway to seal off all outlets for our spirit to work, to serve, and to war. It would suffer as though suppressed. Our inner man must accordingly be active and outgoing. It must resist Satan constantly or else it will be attacked from all sides.

Another very important principle to learn in spiritual warfare is that we must attack Satan incessantly. This is to prevent ourselves from being attacked. When a believer has crossed into the domain of the spiritual he daily ought to maintain a combat attitude in his spirit, praying therewith for the overthrow of all the works of Satan done through the evil powers. If not, he shall discover his spirit shall fall from heaven, grow very weak and feeble, gradually lose its senses, and finally become scarcely detectable. This is all because the believer's inner man has collapsed into such a passive condition that it has ceased to launch out in attack. Hence ground is surrendered to the enemy from which to assail, surround and shut in his spirit. But if the Christian daily "lets out" his spirit and continually resists the foe, he will keep his spirit mobilized. And with each passing day it shall wax stronger and stronger.

A Christian must be delivered from every misconception with respect to spiritual life. He often surmises, before he enters the spiritual sphere, that if only he could be as spiritual as his brother how happy he would be! He visualizes the spiritual odyssey as a most happy affair; and so he contemplates spending his days in perfect joy. Little does he know that the opposite is the truth. The spiritual path does not yield any enjoyment to the person himself; it is instead a life of daily fighting. To remove warfare from a spiritual life is to render it unspiritual. Life in the spirit is a suffering way, filled with watching and laboring, burdened by weariness and trial, punctuated by heartbreak and conflict. It is a life utterly outpoured entirely for the kingdom of God and lived in complete disregard for one's personal happiness. When a Christian is carnal he lives towards himself and for his own "spiritual" enjoyment. Of little real value is he in God's hand. Only as he dies to sin and to his personal life shall he be able to be used by God.

A spiritual life is one of spiritual usefulness because it is lived to mount assault upon assault against God's spiritual enemy. We ought to be zealous for God, relentlessly attacking that enemy and never allowing this most useful spirit of ours to sink into passivity.

PART FIVE

AN ANALYSIS OF THE SPIRIT

CHAPTER 1
INTUITION

To UNDERSTAND more clearly what spiritual life is we must analyze the spirit explicitly and assimilate all its laws. Only after we are really acquainted with its different functions are we able to know the laws which govern them; only after we become familiar with those laws can we walk according to the spirit; that is, according to the laws of the spirit. This is indispensable for experiencing the spiritual life. We should never fear appropriating too much knowledge concerning the spirit; but we should be extremely apprehensive if we use our mind excessively in such pursuit.

God's glad tidings to men is that the fallen can be regenerated and the fleshly can receive a new spirit. This new spirit serves as the basis for new life. What we commonly term spiritual living is but to walk by this spirit which we obtain at regeneration. It is something to be deplored that believers are so ignorant of the functions of the spirit as well as of other matters pertaining to it. Although they may know the relationship of the spirit to man in name, they are unable to identify their spirit in experience. Either they do not realize where their spirit is or else they interpret their own feelings or thoughts to be functions of the spirit. An analysis of its functions hence becomes absolutely essential, for without them no believer can move according to the spirit.

THE FUNCTIONS OF THE SPIRIT

Mention was made previously that the functions of the spirit could be classified as intuition, communion, and conscience. While these three *can* be distinguished, still, they are closely entwined. It is therefore difficult to treat of one without touching upon the others. When we talk for example about intuition, we naturally must include communion and conscience in our discussion. Thus in dissecting the spirit we necessarily must look into its triple functions. Since we have seen already how the spirit comprises these three abilities, we shall proceed next to uncover what these exactly are in order that we may be helped to walk according to the spirit. We may say that such a walk is a walk by intuition, communion and conscience.

These three are merely the *functions* of the spirit. (Furthermore, they are not the *only* ones; according to the Bible, they are but the *main* functions of the spirit). None of them *is* the spirit, for the spirit itself is substantial, personal, invisible. It is beyond our present comprehension to apprehend the substance of the spirit. What we today know of its substance comes via its various manifestations in us. We will not attempt here to solve future mysteries but only attempt to discover spiritual life; sufficient for us is the knowledge of these abilities or functions and of the way to follow the spirit. Our spirit is not material and yet it exists independently in our body. It must therefore possess its own spiritual substance, out of which arise various abilities for the performance of God's demands on man. Hence what we desire to learn is not the substance but the functions of the spirit.

Previously we have compared man to the temple and man's spirit to the Holy of Holies. We shall proceed further with this metaphor by comparing the intuition, communion and conscience of the spirit to the ark in the Holy of Holies. First, within the ark lies the law of God which instructs the Israelites what they should do; God thereby reveals Himself and his will through the law. In like manner God makes Himself and His will known to the believer's intuition that he may walk accordingly. Second, upon the ark and sprinkled with the blood is the mercy seat whereon God manifests His glory and receives man's worship. Similarly, every person redeemed by the blood has the spirit quickened; through this quickened spirit he worships and communes with God. As God formerly communed with Israel on the mercy seat, so He today communes with the believer in his blood-cleansed spirit. Third, the ark is called "the Ark of Testimony" because therein are kept the Ten Commandments as God's testimony to Israel. Just as the two tablets of law silently accused or excused the doings of Israel, so the believer's conscience, on which God's Spirit has written the law of God, bears witness for or against the conduct of the believer. "My conscience bears me witness in the Holy Spirit" (Rom. 9.1).

Observe with what respect the Israelites paid the ark! In crossing the Jordan River they had no other guidance save the ark, but they followed it without hesitation. In fighting against Jericho, they did nothing except march behind it. Later, they could not stand before the Philistines when they tried to use the ark according to their way. Was not Uzzah smitten to death as he put out his fleshly hand to hold the ark? How joyful Israel was when they had prepared a habitation for it (Ps. 132). These incidents ought to teach us to be exceptionally careful with our ark, which is our spirit with its threefold functions. If we walk in this fashion, we shall have life and peace; if we allow the flesh to interfere, we can encounter nothing but total defeat. Victory depended not on what or how Israel thought but on where the ark led. Spiritual usefulness lies in the teaching of our intuition, communion and conscience and not in the thought of man.

INTUITION

As the soul has its senses, so too has the spirit. The spirit is intimately related to the soul and yet is wholly unlike it. The soul possesses various senses; but a spiritual man is able to detect another set of senses—lodged in the innermost part of his being—which is radically dissimilar from his set of soulical senses. There in that innermost recess he can rejoice, grieve, anticipate, love, fear, approve, condemn, decide, discern. These motions are sensed in the spirit and are quite distinct from those expressed by the soul through the body.

We can learn about the sensing of the spirit and its many-sided character from the following verses:

"The spirit indeed is *willing*" Matt. 26.41
"*Perceiving* in his spirit" Mark 2.8
"He *sighed* deeply in his spirit" Mark 8.12
"My spirit *rejoices* in God my Savior" Luke 1.47
"The true worshipers will *worship* the Father in spirit and truth" John 4.23
"He was deeply *moved* in spirit and *troubled*" John 11.33
"When Jesus had thus spoken, he was *troubled* in spirit" John 13.21
"His spirit was *provoked* within him as he saw that the city was full of idols" Acts 17.16
"He had been instructed in the way of the Lord; and being *fervent* in spirit" Acts 18.25
"Paul *purposed* in the spirit" Acts 19.21 ASV
"I go *bound* in the spirit unto Jerusalem" Acts 20.22 ASV
"(Be) *fervent* in spirit" Rom. 12.11 ASV
"For what person *knows* a man's thoughts except the spirit of the man which is in him" 1 Cor. 2.11
"I will *sing* with the spirit" 1 Cor. 14.15
"If you *bless* with the spirit" 1 Cor. 14.16
"I had no *rest* in my spirit" 2 Cor. 2.13 Darby
"We have the same spirit of *faith*" 2 Cor. 4.13
"A spirit of *wisdom* and of *revelation*" Eph. 1.17
"Your *love* in spirit" Col. 1.8 literal

From these many passages we can see readily that the spirit clearly senses and that such sensing is manifold. The Bible is not telling us here how our heart senses but rather how our *spirit* does. And it would appear that the sensing of the spirit is as inclusive as that of the soul. The spirit like the soul has its thoughts, feelings, and desires. But how we must learn to distinguish the spiritual from the soulical! We shall come to appreciate this difference if we are matured through the deeper work of the cross and the Spirit.

It is while a Christian lives spiritually that his spiritual sense develops fully. Before he experiences the dividing of soul and spirit and union with the Lord in one spirit, his spiritual sense is rather dull. But once he has had the power of the Holy Spirit poured into his spirit, his inner man is strengthened and it possesses the sense of the matured. Only then can he fathom the various senses of his spirit.

This spiritual sensing is called "intuition," for it impinges *directly* without reason or cause. Without passing through any procedure, it comes forth in a *straight* manner. Man's ordinary sensing is caused or brought out by people or things or events. We rejoice when there is reason to rejoice, grieve if there is justification to grieve and so forth. Each of these senses has its respective antecedent; hence we cannot conclude them to be expressions of intuition or direct sense. Spiritual sense, on the other hand, does not require any outside cause but emerges directly from within man.

Great similarities do exist between the soul and the spirit. But believers should not walk according to the soul, that is, they should not follow its thoughts, feelings and desires. The way God ordains for His children is a walk after the spirit; all other paths belong to the old creation and hence possess no spiritual value. But how to walk after the spirit? It is living by its intuition because the latter expresses the thought of the spirit which in turn expresses the mind of God.

Oftentimes we think of a certain thing we have good reason to do and our heart delights in it and finally our will decides to execute it; yet somehow, in the inner sanctuary of our being there seems to arise *an unuttered and soundless voice* strongly opposing what our mind, emotion or volition has entertained, felt, or decided. This strange complex seems to infer that this thing ought not to be done. Now such an experience as this may change according to altered conditions. For at other times we may sense in the inner depths that same wordless and noiseless monitor greatly urging, moving and constraining us to perform a certain thing which we view as highly unreasonable, as contrary to what we usually do or desire, and as something which we do not like to do.

What is this complex which is so unlike our mind, emotion and will? It is the intuition of the spirit: the spirit is expressing itself through our intuition. How distinctive the intuition is from our emotional feeling. Frequently we feel inclined to execute a certain act, but this inward, unarticulated intuition sharply warns against it. It is totally counter to our mind. The latter is located in the brain and is of a reasoning nature, while intuition is lodged elsewhere and is often opposed to reasoning. The Holy Spirit expresses His thought through this intuition. What we commonly refer to as being moved by the Spirit is but the Holy Spirit making us know His will intuitively by working upon our spirit. Just here can we differentiate between what comes from God's Spirit and what from ourselves and Satan. Because the Holy Spirit dwells in our spirit which is at the center of our being, His thought, expressed through our intuition, must arise from that innermost region. How contrary this is to thought which originates at the periphery of our being. If a notion should come from our outward man—that is, from the mind or emotion—then we realize it is but our own and not that of the Holy Spirit; for whatever is His must flow from the depths. The same distinction applies to what comes forth from Satan (those of demon possession excepted). He dwells not in our spirit but in the world: "he who is in you (the Holy Spirit) is greater than he who is in the world (Satan)" (1 John 4.4). Satan can only attack us from the outside in. He may work through the lust and sensations of the body or through the mind and emotion of the soul, for those two belong to the outward man. It therefore behooves us to learn to distinguish our feelings as to whether they originate with the inner, or come from the outer, man.

THE ANOINTING OF GOD

The intuition of which we have been speaking is exactly the locus where occurs the anointing that teaches: "you have been anointed by the Holy One, and you all *know*. . . . But the anointing which you received from him *abides in you*, and you have *no need that any one should teach you;* as his anointing teaches you about everything, and is true, and is no lie, just as it has taught you, abide in him" (1 John 2.20, 27). This portion of Scripture informs us quite lucidly where and how the anointing of the Holy Spirit teaches us.

But before we delve into this passage may we first explain the meaning of "knowing" and "understanding." We usually do not make a distinction between these two words; in spiritual matters, however, the difference between them is incalculable: the spirit "knows" while the mind "understands." A believer "knows" the things of God by the intuition of his spirit. Strictly speaking, the mind can merely "understand"; it can never "know." Knowing is the work of intuition; understanding, the task of the mind. The Holy Spirit enables our spirit to know; our spirit instructs the mind to understand. It may appear difficult to distinguish these two in the abstract, but they are as disparate as wheat from weed in experience. So ignorant are modern believers in their quest to know the thought of the Holy Spirit that they do not even realize how to distinguish "knowing" from "understanding."

Is it not true that we frequently experience this indescribable sense within us which makes us *know* whether or not to do a certain thing? We may say we know the mind of the Holy Spirit in our spirit. Nevertheless our mind may still fail to *understand* what the meaning of it all is. In spiritual matters it is possible for us to know without understanding it. Are there not times when, reaching our wit's end, we receive the teaching of the Holy Spirit in our spirit and jubilantly shout "I know it!"? And are there not times when our mind receives light and understands what the Holy Spirit has meant *long after* we have obeyed and acted on what He has expressed in our intuition? Do we not at that moment exclaim "*Now* I understand it"? These experiences show us that we "know" God's thought in our spirit's intuition but "understand" His guidance in the mind of our soul.

The Apostle John speaks of the operation of intuition when he asserts that the anointing of the Lord, Who dwells in the believer, shall instruct him in all things and enable him to know all so that he has no need for anyone to teach him. The Lord gives the Holy Spirit to every saint in order that He may dwell in him and lead him into all truth. How does He lead? Through the intuition. He unfolds His mind in the believer's spirit. Intuition possesses the inherent ability to discern His movement and its meaning. Just as the mind instructs us in mundane affairs, so intuition teaches us in spiritual affairs. Anointing in the original signifies "applying ointment." This suggests how the Holy Spirit teaches and speaks in man's spirit. He does not speak thunderously from heaven nor does He cast the believer to the ground by an irresistible force. Rather does He work very quietly in one's spirit to impress something upon our intuition. In the same way that a man's body feels soothed when ointment is applied, so our spirit gently senses the anointing of the Holy Spirit. When intuition is aware of something, the spirit is apprehending what He is saying.

To perform God's will a Christian need simply heed the direction of his intuition. There is no necessity to ask others, nor even to ask himself. The Anointing teaches him concerning everything. Not once will the Anointing leave him nor permit him to choose independently. Any who wish to walk after the spirit ought to recognize this. Our responsibility is none other than to accept instruction from the Anointing. We need not decide our own way; indeed, He will not allow us so to do. Whatever is not of the leading of the Anointing is but our doing. The Anointing functions independently; He does not require our help. He expresses His mind independently of our mind's searching or our emotion's agitating. The Anointing operates in man's spirit to enable intuition to know His thought.

DISCERNMENT

Reading the context of this same portion of Scripture reveals how the Apostle is concerned with many false teachings and antichrists. He assures his readers that the same Holy One Who anoints them also teaches them to differentiate truth from lies and what is of Christ from what is of the antichrists. Christians do not require other men to instruct them since the indwelling Anointing teaches them everything. This is spiritual discernment, something greatly needed today. If we must pore over many theological references and reason, compare, research, observe and think with our mind until we ultimately reach an understanding of what is lie or what is truth, then only Christians with good minds and education would escape deception. But God has no respect for the old creation; He concludes that all except the newly created spirit must die and be destroyed. Can the wisdom which God demands to be destroyed assist people to know good and evil? No, most emphatically no! God puts His Spirit in every believer's spirit, regardless how sinful or dull he is. The indwelling Spirit shall teach him what is of God and what is not. This is why sometimes we can conjure up no logical reason for opposing a certain teaching, yet in the very depth of our being arises a resistance. We cannot explain it, but our inner sense tells us this is an error. Or contrarily we may hear some teaching which is entirely different from what we generally hold and which we will not like to follow, but is there not occasionally a still small voice that speaks persistently within us and contends that this is the way, walk you in it? Though we may muster many arguments against it, even overwhelming it with reason, nevertheless this inner small voice still insists that we are wrong.

Such experiences inform us that our intuition, the organ for the working of the Holy Spirit, is capable itself of distinguishing good from evil without any assistance from the mind's observation and investigation. No matter what his natural intellect may be, any individual who honestly and faithfully follows the Lord will be taught by the Anointing. The most learned doctor shares in the same foolishness with the dullest country folk when it comes to spiritual affairs; nay, the learned may make more mistakes than the dullard. False teachings are currently rampant. Many there are who with deceiving words disguise lies as truths. How necessary is this power of discernment in the spirit! The most appealing teaching, the cleverest brain, and the most enlightened advisors are undependable; only those who adhere intuitively to the teaching of the Anointing are preserved from being deceived in this time of theological confusion and supernatural manifestations. We should ask the Lord to make our spirit more active and pure. We should follow the still small voice that comes from our intuition instead of being overawed by people's knowledge and drawn away from the warning sounded within us. Otherwise we shall fall into heresy or become fanatical. If we quietly follow the teaching of the Anointing we shall be delivered from the compulsion of a noisy emotion and a confused mind.

DEALING WITH PEOPLE

Never should we judge other people; yet we surely need to know them so that we may comprehend both how to live with them and how to assist them. The ordinary way for man to know others is to inquire, observe and investigate—all of which, unfortunately, often lead us to blunder. Now we are not suggesting that these are categorically useless, but we do affirm that they occupy merely a secondary place in the knowledge of people. A pure spirit frequently discloses unmistakable discernment. Well do we remember when as children how we made certain remarks concerning various individuals we saw. As time went on how accurate these remarks proved to be. Many years have now passed; our knowledge, experience and observation have altogether been increased; yet somehow our ability to know people seems to be diminishing. When we made those remarks as children we had no suitable reason to advance for doing so other than that we felt that way in our hearts. Many years later our "sense" of that time was shown to have been correct. As a child we never spoke out after once having carefully investigated or inquired, nor could we have ever given any good reason for so speaking. What was it then? It was the operation of a pure intuition. Obviously the example we have just set forth pertains to the natural. Nonetheless, in the things of God our spiritual condition must be converted and become as a little child if we desire to discern spiritually.

Let us observe our Lord Jesus. "And immediately Jesus, perceiving in his spirit that they thus questioned within themselves, said to them" (Mark 2.8). Do we not see there the working of intuition? The Scripture does not state that the Lord Jesus thought or felt in his heart nor does it say the Holy Spirit told Him. It was His spirit that displayed this perfect ability. The spiritual sense in the man Jesus Christ was exceedingly pure, sensitive and noble; hence His spirit detected immediately how the surrounding people questioned in their heart. He spoke to them according to what He intuitively knew. This ought to be the normal condition of every spiritual person. Our spirit indwelt by the Holy Spirit is free to work and, filled with the power of knowledge, it can exercise control over our whole being. Just as the human spirit of the Lord Jesus operated during His earthly pilgrimage, even so shall our spirit be activated by the indwelling Spirit.

REVELATION

To know things in our intuition is what the Bible calls revelation. Revelation has no other meaning than that the Holy Spirit enables a believer to apprehend a particular matter by indicating the reality of it to his spirit. There is but one kind of knowledge concerning either the Bible or God which is valuable, and that is the truth revealed to our spirit by God's Spirit. God does not explain Himself via man's reasoning; never does man come to know God through rationalization. No matter how clever man's mind is nor how much it understands about God, his knowledge of God remains veiled. All he can do is rationalize what is behind the veil, because he has not penetrated the reality hidden from view. Since he has not yet "seen," man can "understand" but never can he "know." If there is no revelation, personal revelation, Christianity is worth nothing. Everyone who believes in God must have His revelation in his spirit, or else what he believes is not God but mere human wisdom, ideals or words. Such a faith cannot endure the test.

This kind of revelation is not a vision, a heavenly voice, a dream, or an external force which shakes the man. One may encounter these phenomena and still not have revelation. Revelation happens in the intuition—quietly, neither hastily nor slowly, soundless and yet with a message. How many denominate themselves Christians, though the Christianity they embrace is simply a kind of philosophy of life or of ethics, a few articles of truth, or some supernatural manifestations. Such an attitude will issue neither in a new birth nor in a new spirit. Numerous are these "Christians" whose spiritual usefulness measures up to zero. Not so are those who have received Christ, for by the grace of God they have perceived in their spirit the reality of the spiritual realm, which opens to them like the lifting of a veil. What they today *know* is far more profound than what their mind has comprehended; yea, it seems as though a new meaning has been imparted to all which they had only understood or comprehended in the past. Now everything is thoroughly and genuinely known, because the spirit has seen it. "We speak of what we *know*, and bear witness to what we *have seen*" (John 3.11). This is Christianity. Searching with intellect never delivers men; revelation in the spirit alone gives true knowledge of God.

ETERNAL LIFE

Many say, "If we believe, we have eternal life." What is this life we secure? It does point, to be sure, to future blessing. But what does eternal life mean for *today*? "And *this* is eternal life, that they *know* thee the only true God, and Jesus Christ whom thou has sent" (John 17.3). This life constitutes for the here and now a new ability to know God and the Lord Jesus. This is indeed true. Whoever believes in the Lord and enjoys eternal life has obtained an intuitive knowledge of God which he never possessed before. Having eternal life is not a slogan; it is a reality which can be demonstrated and exhibited in this present hour. Those without this life can rationalize about God but they enjoy no personal knowledge of Him. Only after one has received new life in regeneration does he intuitively and *actually know* God. People may understand the Bible, yet their spirit abides in death. They may be familiar with theology, still their spirit remains unquickened. They may even zealously serve in the name of the Lord, but no new life is engendered within their spirit. The Bible perceptively asks, "Canst thou by searching find out God? Canst thou find out the Almighty unto perfection?" (Job 11.7 ASV) No amount of mental laboring can equip us to know God. Apart from the quickened spirit within man no one is able to apprehend Him, not even with his brain. The Bible recognizes just one kind of knowledge, and that is the knowledge in the spirit's intuition.

GOD'S WAY OF GUIDING

As at the beginning a believer acquires his first knowledge of God in his spirit, even so must he continue to know God in his spirit. In a Christian life nothing is of any spiritual benefit unless it flows from revelation in the intuition. Whatever does not issue from the spirit is not of God's will. Whatever we think or feel or decide, if not preceded by revelation in the spirit, is reckoned as dead in the eyes of God. Should a believer follow his sudden thought, the "burning fire" in his heart, his natural inclination, his perfect reason, or his rationalization, he is but activating his old man again. God's will is not to be so known; He reveals Himself solely to man's spirit. What is not revealed there is purely human activity.

The head is where God's will is understood, but it is never the source of His will. The will of God originates in Himself, Who by His Holy Spirit reveals it to the spirit of man. In turn the latter causes the outward man to understand through the mind what the inner man has known. Thus the Christian is able to practice God's will. Now if instead of seeking His purpose in the spirit a Christian should daily search his mind, he will be confused, since thoughts often change. He who follows his mind is not capable of saying at any moment, "I *truly* know this is the will of God." Such deep faith and assurance emerges only when one has received revelation in his spirit.

The revelation of God in our spirit is of two kinds: the direct and the sought. By direct revelation we mean that God, having a particular wish for the believer to do, draws nigh and reveals it to the latter's spirit. Upon receiving such a revelation in his intuition the believer acts accordingly. By sought revelation we mean that a believer, having a special need, approaches God with that need and seeks and waits for an answer through God's movement in his spirit. The revelation young believers receive is mostly the sought type; that of the more matured ones is chiefly the direct kind. We should quickly add, however, that these are not exclusively so, only predominantly so. There lies the difficulty with the young believer. While he ought to wait before the Lord, denying his thought, feeling and desire, he often becomes impatient waiting for His revelation and substitutes his own disguised will for that of God. As a consequence he falls under the accusation of his conscience. Granted that he genuinely has a heart to follow God's intent, he nonetheless unwittingly follows the thought of his mind because he lacks spiritual knowledge. Who can avoid mistakes if he walks without revelation?

Now we find true spiritual knowledge in this: only what is appropriated in the spirit is spiritual knowledge; the rest is wholly the mental kind. Let us inquire a moment, how does God know things? How does He make His judgment? By what knowledge does He control the universe? Does He ascertain with His mind like man? Does He need to think carefully before He understands? Does God depend upon philosophy, logic and comparison to know a matter? Must He search and investigate before He hits upon the solution?

Is the Almighty compelled to rely upon His brain? Decidedly not. God has no necessity to indulge in such sweating exercises. His knowledge and judgment is intuitive. As a matter of fact intuition is the common faculty of all spiritual beings. The angels obey what they know as God's will intuitively; they do not arrive at a conclusion by way of argument, reason or contemplation. The difference between knowing intuitively and knowing mentally is immeasurable. Upon this very distinction hangs the outcome of spiritual success or defeat. If it had been intended that a believer's action or service was to be governed by rationalization and common sense, no one would ever have attempted to carry out those many glorious spiritual works of the past and the present, because all of them supersede human reasoning. Who would have dared do them if he had not first known God's will intuitively?

Everyone who walks intimately with God, enjoying secret communion and spiritual union, will receive God's revelation in his intuition and know unmistakably what he should do. His actions obviously will attract no sympathy from men, for they know not what he has seen. According to worldly wisdom, his actions are utterly meaningless. Do not spiritual believers suffer many oppositions of this kind? Have not the worldly-wise labeled them as mad? Even their fleshly brethren pass similar judgment on them. And the reason? Because the old created life in worldly people or in believers cannot understand the way of the Holy Spirit. How the more rational believers do in fact criticize their less rational brethren as "blindly zealous," not realizing that these "blindly zealous" are the truly spiritual ones, walking by the revelation they intuitively have received.

We should be careful not to confuse intuition with emotion. In their zeal emotional Christians may display many phenomena similar to those of spiritual Christians, but the origin of these phenomena cannot be traced to intuition. Likewise in discernment rational Christians may act in many ways like those who are spiritual, yet once again no revelation in intuition is involved. As emotional believers are soulical, so are the rational. The spirit possesses a zeal which surpasses the emotional kind. The spiritual are "justified in the spirit" (1 Tim. 3.16 ASV), not approved by the affections or reasons of the flesh. Should we drop from the exalted position of the spirit into following the feeling and reasoning of the flesh, we shall lose ground instantly and shall retreat, like Abraham of old, into the visible and tangible Egypt for help. The spirit and the soul move independently. As long as the spirit has not yet ascended to hold sway over the total man, the soul shall never cease to strive against it.

When a person's spirit has been quickened and subsequently strengthened by the power and discipline of the Holy Spirit, his soul cedes its usurped place and returns to submission. Increasingly the soul becomes the spirit's servant; similarly, the body, once subdued, becomes the soul's servant. The spirit receives revelation of God in its faculty of intuition, while the soul and the body unitedly execute the will of the spirit. There is no end to such progress. Some of the Lord's people may have more to deny than others, for their spirit is not as pure because they have been far too long saturated with mental knowledge and affections. Many are so full of prejudice that they do not enjoy an open spirit to accept God's truth. What they need are those requisite dealings which can free their intuition to receive everything from God.

We need to appreciate how fundamental is the difference between spiritual and soulical experiences: spiritual experience is so designated because it begins with *God* and is known in our *spirit*: soulical experience arises from the *man himself* and does *not* emerge through the spirit. It is therefore quite possible for an unregenerated man to know fully the Bible, to grasp accurately and expertly the essential doctrines of Christianity, to apply zealously all his talents to service, and to sway his audience with wonderful eloquence, and yet remain within the realm of the soul without so much as having crossed over one step, his spirit as dead as ever. People shall never enter the kingdom of God through our encouragement, persuasion, argument, inducement, excitement, or attraction; entrance can be gained only by new birth, by nothing less than the resurrection of the spirit. The new life which invades us at regeneration brings with it many inherent abilities, not the least of which is the intuitive power of knowing God.

Does it hence mean that man's mind or brain is totally useless? Of course not. It obviously has its part to play. But we need to remember that intellect is of secondary, not of primary, importance. We do not sense God and the realities of God by our intellect; else eternal life would be meaningless. This eternal life or new life is the spirit mentioned in John 3. We apprehend God through this newly obtained eternal life or spirit. The mind's role is to explain to our outward man what we know in our spirit and additionally to form it into words for others to understand. Paul stresses most emphatically in his letters that the gospel he preaches does not originate with man: it is not acquired wholesale from one man's mind and retailed to the mind of others but is discovered through revelation. Although a believing man may have the best of minds, his teaching is nevertheless not to be derived from his thinking, whether sudden or progressive. His mind merely cooperates with his spirit in communicating to others the revelation his intuition has received. The brain is but the transmitting, not the receiving, mechanism of spiritual knowledge.

God communes with us entirely in the spirit. Save by its intuition there is no way of knowing God. In his spirit man soars into the eternal unseen realm of God. Intuition may be characterized as the brain of the inner sanctuary. When we say man's spirit is dead, we are indicating his intuition is insensitive to God and His realities. When we say the spirit controls the whole man, we mean the various parts of the soul and all the members of the body adhere closely to God's intuitively known will. We wish to underscore our point that regeneration is totally indispensable. Man's soulical faculties cannot perceive God: nothing else can be a substitute for intuition. Except a man receives a new life from God and has his intuition resurrected, he is eternally separated from God.

How fundamental new birth is. It is not just a term, nor is it purely a moral alteration, but the life of God actually enters our spirit and quickens its intuition. How utterly impossible for man to please God with his good deeds: they are simply the operations of the soul: his intuition is dead to God. Equally impossible is it for man to beget himself anew, because there is nothing in him which can produce new life. Unless God generates him he is not able to beget himself. Also worthless in the work of God is man's understanding of teachings, for the work must be done by *God.* What then can man do other than deliver himself into the hands of God for Him to work? His spirit shall remain forever dead unless he confesses that everything pertaining to man is useless and unless he stands in the place of death with the Lord Jesus and accepts His life.

Man's way cannot envisage acceptance of the Lord Jesus as Savior and a quickening of his spirit's intuition, but insists on substituting his mind for intuition. He thinks and cogitates until he creates many philosophies, ethics, or religions. But what is God's pronouncement? "As the heavens are higher than the earth, so are my ways higher than your ways and my thoughts than your thoughts" (Is. 55.9). However intensively man may contemplate, his thoughts are earthly and not heavenly. After regeneration, God enables our intuition to know His thought and to apprehend His way so that we may follow Him. Yet how forgetful believers are! We forget what we learned at regeneration. Countless are those saints who daily walk by their head and heart. In service we still attempt to move people's mind, emotion and will by our intellect, zeal and effort. God desires to teach us the fact that in service the soul, ours and everyone else's, is void of any spiritual value or worth. He actually allows us to be defeated in spiritual work and to become despondent, cold and fruitless in order that He may destroy our natural life with its wisdom, fervor, and ability. Such a lesson as this cannot be learned in one or two days. God must instruct us throughout our lifetime in order to make us realize that apart from following the spirit's intuition everything else is vain.

Now comes the crisis. Which will we follow when intuition and soul clash in their opinions? This will determine who is to rule over our life and which way we shall go. Our outer man and our inner man—the man of the flesh and the man of the spirit—are struggling for supremacy. In the early days of our Christian walk our spirit fought with the lusts of our flesh; today it is a battle between our spirit and our soul. Formerly the engagement was over the issue of sin; presently it is not a matter of good and evil but of natural good versus God's goodness. We contended for the quality of things before, but now we are concerned with the source of things. It is a conflict of the inward against the outward man, a war between God's will and man's good intention. To learn how to walk after the spirit is a lifetime's occupation for the new man. If one wholly follows the spirit, he shall overcome the man of the flesh completely. Through the strengthening by the Holy Spirit of the spirit in the new man, the believer shall be able to destroy totally his minding of the flesh so as to mind the things of the spirit. This is life and peace.

CHAPTER 2
COMMUNION

WE COMMUNICATE with the material world through the body. We communicate with the spiritual world through the spirit. This communication with the spiritual is not carried on by means of the mind or emotion but through the spirit or its intuitive faculty. It is easy for us to understand the nature of the communion between God and man if we have seen the operation of our intuition. In order to worship and fellowship with God man must possess a nature similar to His. "God is *spirit,* and those who worship him must worship in *spirit* and truth" (John 4.24). There can be no communication between different natures; hence both the unregenerate whose spirit obviously has not been quickened and the regenerate who does not use his spirit to worship are equally unqualified to have genuine fellowship with God. Lofty sentiments and noble feelings do not bring people into spiritual reality nor do they forge personal communion with God. Our fellowship with Him is experienced in the deepest place of our entire being, deeper than our thought, feeling and will, even in the intuition of our spirit.

A close scrutiny of 1 Corinthians 2.9-3.2 can provide a very clear view of how man communes with God and how man knows the realities of God through the spirit's intuition.

THE HEART OF MAN

"What no eye has seen, nor ear heard, nor the heart of man conceived, what God has prepared for those who love him" (v.9). The larger context of this one verse speaks of

God and the things of God. What He has prepared can neither be seen or heard by man's outward body nor conceived by his inward heart. The "heart of man" includes among other facets man's understanding, mind and intellect. Man's thought cannot envisage God's work, for the latter transcends the former. It is therefore evident that he who desires to know and commune with God cannot depend solely upon his thought.

THE HOLY SPIRIT

"God has revealed to us through the Spirit. For the Spirit searches everything; even the depths of God" (v.10). This verse sets forth the fact that the *Holy Spirit searches* everything and not that our mind conceives all. Only the Holy Spirit knows the depths of God. He knows what man does not know. By His intuition the Spirit searches everything. God is thus able to reveal through Him what our heart has never conceived. This "revealing" is not acquired after much thinking, for our heart cannot even conceive it. It is a revelation; it does not require the help of our thought.

The next two verses tell us how God reveals Himself.

THE SPIRIT OF MAN

"For what person knows a man's thoughts except the spirit of the man which is in him? So also no one comprehends the thoughts of God except the Spirit of God. Now we have received not the spirit of the world, but the Spirit which is from God, that we might understand the gifts bestowed on us by God" (vv.11 and 12). No one knows man's thoughts except the spirit of man; likewise, no one knows the things of God but the Holy Spirit. Man's spirit as well as God's Spirit apprehend things directly, not by deducing or searching. They perceive through the faculty of intuition. Since the Holy Spirit alone knows the things of God, we must receive the Holy Spirit if we also would know those things. The spirit of the world is cut off from communication with God. It is a dead spirit: it cannot effect communion with Him. The Holy Spirit, on the other hand, comprehends the things of God; therefore, by receiving in our intuition what the Holy Spirit knows, we too shall understand the realities of God. "We have received . . . the Spirit which is from God, that we might understand the gifts bestowed on us by God."

How then do *we know?* Verse 11 tells us man knows by his spirit. The Holy Spirit unfolds to our spirit what He knows intuitively so that we too may know intuitively. When the Holy Spirit discloses the matters pertaining to God He does so not to our mind nor to any other organ but to our spirit. God knows this is the sole place in man which can apprehend man's things as well as His things. The mind is not the place for knowing these things. While it is true that the mind can think and conceive many matters, it nonetheless cannot *know* them.

From this we can appreciate how highly God esteems the regenerated spirit of man. Before new birth man's spirit was dead. God had no way of unfolding His mind to such a man. The cleverest brain fails to know the mind of God. Both God's fellowship with man and man's worship of God are contingent upon the regenerated spirit of man. Without this revitalized component God and man are hopelessly separated—neither can come or go to the other. The first step towards communion between God and man must be this quickening of man's spirit.

Because man enjoys a free will he has authority to decide his own matters. That explains why he continues to encounter many temptations following new birth. Due to his foolishness or perhaps his prejudice he may not yield the rightful position to his spirit and its intuition. God accepts this spirit as the one place where He will commune with man and man with Him. But the believer still walks by his mind or emotion. How many times he completely ignores the voice of intuition. His principle of living is to adhere to what he himself considers reasonable, beautiful, delightful, or interesting. Even should he have a heart to do God's will, he usually will take either his impulsive idea or his more logical thought as the mind of God, not realizing that what he ought to follow is the thought expressed by the Holy

Spirit in his intuition. He sometimes may be willing to hear the voice of intuition, but failing to keep his feelings quiet he finds that voice blurred and confused. Walking after the spirit consequently becomes an occasional affair instead of forming a daily continuous experience in the Christian's life.

If the *initial* knowing of God's will is so difficult, who can wonder at the lack of further and more profound revelation? How then can we ever truly know in our spirit God's plan for the end of this age, the reality of spiritual warfare, and the deeper truths of the Bible? For our worship merely corresponds to what we think is best or what we feel on the spur of the moment. And to commune with the Lord in our intuition naturally becomes an unheard of phenomenon.

A believer must recognize that the Holy Spirit alone comprehends the things of God—and that intuitively. He is the one Person Who can convey this knowledge to man. But for anyone to obtain such knowledge he must appropriate it through the proper means; namely, he must receive with his intuition what the Holy Spirit intuitively knows. The conjunction of these two intuitions enables man to apprehend the mind of God.

"And we impart this in words not taught by human wisdom but taught by the Spirit, interpreting spiritual truths to those who possess the Spirit" (v.13). How are we going to impart to others the things of God which we have discerned in our spirit's intuition? Having come to know the realities of God, our responsibility now is to proclaim them. The Apostle Paul declares he does not transmit them in terms taught by human wisdom. That wisdom belongs to a man's mind and is the product of man's brain. Paul categorically asserts that he does not employ the words which come from the mind to communicate what his spirit knows concerning the things of God. Paul in himself possesses great wisdom. He is perfectly able to formulate many new and wonderful phrases and to deliver his message eloquently with good organization and illustrative parables. He knows how to make his audience understand what he means to say. He nevertheless refuses to use the terminology taught by human wisdom. This declaration and attitude of the Apostle Paul indicate that man's mind is not only useless in *knowing* the things of God but is also secondary in *imparting* spiritual knowledge.

The Apostle articulates God's realities in phraseology taught by the Spirit. In his intuition he receives His instruction. Nothing in the life of a Christian is of any value save that which is in his spirit. Even in relating spiritual knowledge he needs to employ spiritual words. Intuition appropriates not only the thing which the Holy Spirit unfolds but also the words taught by the same Spirit, in order to explain to others what has been revealed. How often a believer tries to impart to others what has been revealed so clearly to him by God; yet try as he may, he finds no words to convey the fundamental meaning of what has been disclosed. Why? Because he has not received words in his spirit. At other times, as he waits before the Lord, the believer senses something rising in the center of his being—perhaps but a few words. With those few words, however, he is able to communicate adequately at a meeting what has been revealed to him. He comes to realize how God actually uses him to testify for the Lord.

Such experiences attest the importance of the "utterance" given by the Holy Spirit. There are two kinds of utterance, the natural and the Spirit-given. The type of utterance recorded in Acts 2.4 is indispensable in spiritual service. However eloquent our natural utterance, it remains powerless to truly communicate the things of God. We may view ourselves as having spoken quite well; yet we have not succeeded in expressing the thought of the Spirit. Spiritual words, that is, terminology received in the spirit, can alone articulate spiritual knowledge. If we are burdened with the message of the Lord in our spirit, as though a fire were burning within, and yet have not the means to discharge that burden, we should wait for the "utterance" to be given by the Spirit so that we may proclaim the message of our spirit and discharge that burden. Should we inadvertently employ language taught by human wisdom instead of waiting for the words bestowed intuitively by the Holy Spirit, we shall find our spiritual effectiveness comes to nought. Speech merely grounded in earthly wisdom can only move people to say that the theory advanced is indeed good. Sometimes we enjoy many spiritual experiences, but we are at a loss how to articulate them until other believers unlock them with a word. This is because until the moment we heard others uttering our experience in simple terms, we still had not received in our spirit explicit words from the Lord.

Spiritual truths must be explained with spiritual phrases. We must employ spiritual means to reach spiritual ends. This is what the Lord especially wishes to teach us today. Spiritual goals need to be perfected through corresponding spiritual processes. The fleshly as fleshly will never become spiritual. If we hope to arrive at our spiritual objectives with our minds and emotions, we as it were are expecting sweet water to pour forth from fountains of bitter water. All matters pertaining to God—such as seeking His will, obeying His commandments, proclaiming His message—are effective only if they arise out of fellowship with God in the spirit. Whatever is performed through our thoughts, talents or methods is accounted by God as dead.

THE SOULICAL AND THE SPIRITUAL

"The unspiritual (original, *soulical*) man does not *receive* the gifts of the Spirit of God, for they are folly to him, and he is not able to *understand* them because they are spiritually discerned" (v.14). The soulical are those who have not yet been born anew and who hence do not possess a new spirit. Since their intuitive faculty is dead to God, all which they have are the faculties of the soul. They are well able to decide what they like through reason and affection but, not having a regenerated spirit, they are powerless to receive the things of the Spirit of God. Although these individuals can think and observe, they still lack basic intuitive power; they cannot take in what God reveals exclusively to man's spirit. How utterly inadequate are the natural endowments of man. He truly has much, but nothing can substitute for the operation of intuition. Because man is dead to God, no organ exists in him by which he can take in the things of God. Nothing in a soulical man is capable of communing with Him. Man's most respectable mind, intellect and reasoning are as corrupt as his lusts and passions; both equally are incompetent to apprehend God. Even a regenerated man, if he attempts to communicate with God by using his mind and observation (just as the unregenerate does) instead of exercising his renewed spirit, is absolutely impotent to perceive the realities of God. Those elements which belong to us naturally do not change their operations following regeneration. A mind is still a mind and a will, a will: these can never be turned into organs capable of communion with God.

Not only can the soulical person not receive the things of God, he even regards them as folly. According to the valuation of his mind, matters known by intuition are downright foolishness because they are all unreasonable, against human nature, contrary to worldly wisdom, or in conflict with common sense. The mind delights in whatever is logical, open to analysis, and psychologically appealing. God, however, is not governed by man's law and hence His actions are folly to the soulical. The folly mentioned in this particular chapter unquestionably refers to the crucifixion of the Lord Jesus. The word of the cross speaks not only of the Savior Who died in our stead but also of the believers who have died with the Savior. Everything naturally belonging to believers must go through the death of the cross. The mind may accept this as a theory, but it surely will oppose it as a practice.

Since the soulical person does not welcome this word of the cross, he obviously cannot comprehend what it is all about. Reception precedes knowledge. The ability or inability to receive tests the presence or absence of a quickened spirit. The capacity or incapacity to know manifests the vital or the moribund character of the intuitive faculty. The spirit first must be quickened before one is able to take in the things of God. With an enlivened spirit one is also given the intuitive ability to appropriate the things of God. Who knows a man's thoughts except the spirit of the man? A soulical person cannot discern God's realities because he does not enjoy that new spirit which carries within it the intuitive power of discernment.

The Apostle Paul proceeds to explain why the soulical man is incompetent to receive and to know matters pertaining to God: "Because they are spiritually discerned." Do we not notice how the Holy Spirit repeatedly stresses the fact that man's spirit is the place of communion with God? The focal point of this particular portion of Scripture is to prove and demonstrate that man's spirit is basic to, and exclusive in, any fellowship with God and the knowledge of divine matters.

Each element has its own particular use. The spirit is employed to know the heavenly realities. Now we are not trying to disparage the use of the soul's faculties. They *are* useful, but here they must play a *secondary* role. They should be under control and not be the controller. The mind should submit to the spirit's rule and should follow what intuition fathoms of the will of God. It ought not conceive its own ideas and then demand that the whole man comply. Emotion too should obey the dictates of the spirit. Its love or hate must follow the affection of the spirit and not its own. The will also should bend to what God has revealed intuitively in the spirit. It must not prefer those choices which are other than the will of God. Were these soulical faculties kept in secondary position the believer would make tremendous strides in his spiritual walk. Unfortunately most Christians give them first place, thus eliminating the spirit's position. Is it any wonder that they do not live a spiritual life nor are of any spiritual worth? The spirit needs to be restored to its ordained position. A believer must learn to wait *in the spirit* for the revelation of God. Unless it ascends to its rightful place a man is barred from knowing what the spirit alone can know. That is why verse 13 adds, "interpreting spiritual truths to those who possess the Spirit," for only the spiritually sensitive can know things in the spirit.

"The spiritual man judges all things, but is himself to be judged by no one" (v.15). The spiritual man is one whose spirit dominates and who has a highly sensitive intuition. It is qualified to perform its functions because its quietness is undisturbed by the mind, emotion and will of the soul.

Why can the spiritual man judge all matters? Because his intuition leans on the Holy Spirit for its knowledge. Why is he not judged by anyone? Simply because no one knows how and what the Holy Spirit imparts to his intuition. If a believer's knowledge depends on his intellect, then besides those who are naturally talented no one can judge in all respects. Learning and worldly education would be indispensable. And such a learned one would also be judged by those who are as wise or even wiser than he, for they certainly could understand the train of his thought. Spiritual knowledge, however, is based on the spirit's intuition. There is no limit to a Christian's knowledge if he is spiritual and possesses a sensitive intuition. His mind may be dull but the Holy Spirit is able to lead him into spiritual reality and his spirit is able to enlighten his mind. The way the Spirit reveals Himself does indeed surpass the expectation of man.

"For who has known the mind of the Lord so as to instruct him? But we have the mind of Christ" (v.16). Here is posed a problem. No one in the world has known the mind of the Lord so as to instruct Him because all men are soulical. The only way to apprehend God is by intuition. How can a person whose spirit is dead ever know the mind of God? This explains why no such persons as this can judge the spiritual man, for none of these have known the mind of the Lord. These are naturally the soulical people. On the other hand, the spiritual ones know the mind of the Lord for they have a responsive intuition. But the soulical cannot know because their intuition is not operative; hence they enjoy no fellowship with God. The meaning here is that the soulical can neither know the mind of the Lord nor that of those spiritual ones who are fully committed to Him.

"But we . . ." indicates that the "we" is different from those soulical people. "We" includes all the saved believers, many of whom perhaps continue to be fleshly. "But we have the mind of Christ." We who have been regenerated, whether babes or grownups, possess the mind of Christ and discern His thoughts. Because we have a resurrected intuition we are able to know and have known already what Christ has prepared for us in the future (v.9). The soulical do not know, but we, the regenerate, do know. The difference is in having or not having the spirit.

THE SPIRITUAL AND THE FLESHLY

"But I, brethren, could not address you as spiritual men, but as men of the flesh, as babes in Christ. I fed you with milk, not solid food; for you were not ready for it; and even yet you are not ready" (3.1-2). These words are closely related to the preceding verses and their teaching follows the line laid down above which speaks of the spirit of man. Now we all recognize that the dividing of the Scriptures into chapters and verses was contrived for the convenience of the readers and was not something at all revealed by the Holy Spirit. These words of verses 1 and 2 of 1 Corinthians 3 should be read in connection with those of the preceding chapter.

How incisive is Paul's spiritual sense. He is acquainted with all his readers, whether they are spiritual or fleshly, whether wholly controlled by the spirit or frequently governed by the flesh. He does not therefore disregard the condition of his readers' receptivity and pour out his thoughts at random simply because he is speaking of spiritual affairs. He will only communicate "spiritual things with spiritual" (v.13 RSV marginal). Paul's communication depends not on how much *he* knows, but on how much his *readers* can assimilate. There is no boasting here of his own knowledge. The Apostle has spiritual phraseology as well as spiritual knowledge; he accordingly knows how to deal with believers of all kinds. Not all terms which articulate the deep mystery of God are spiritual terms; only those which are taught in the spirit by the Holy Spirit are. And they are not necessarily profound words: they may in fact be very common and ordinary: yet *these* words are taught by the Holy Spirit and apprehended in the spirit. When these are uttered they then produce considerable spiritual results.

What the Apostle writes in these two verses and in verse 15 of the previous chapter resolves one interesting paradox; namely, if the spirit of man knows the things which belong to man and the spiritual man judges all things, why then are there so many spirit-renewed Christians who nonetheless do not sense that they have a spirit or who are not able to know the deep things of God through their spirit? The answer is: "the *spiritual* man judges all things" (v.15). Though all Christians *possess* a regenerated spirit, not all Christians are *spiritual*. Many are still fleshly. Man's intuition has in truth been quickened, but man must give intuition its rightful place, providing it opportunity to operate. Or else it will be suppressed, unable to commune with God, or to know what it could know. Spiritual Christians do not walk by their soul life; they have delivered all its faculties to the cross and relegated them to a position of submission so that their intuition can receive God's revelation freely. Afterwards their mind, emotion and will voluntarily comply with this revelation. Such is not the case with fleshly Christians. Regenerated and alive to God intuitively, they have every opportunity to be spiritual; but they remain bound to the flesh instead. The lusts of the flesh remain so exceedingly powerful as to drive these Christians to sin. Their carnal mind is still full of wandering thoughts, reasons and plans; their emotion runs wild with many carnal interests, desires and tendencies; and their will formulates many worldly judgments, arguments and opinions. They are so occupied in following the flesh that they have neither time nor inclination to listen to the voice of intuition. Since the voice of the spirit is usually very soft, it cannot be heard unless it is listened to attentively with everything else quieted. How then can it be heard if the various parts of the flesh are inordinately active? When believers are governed by the flesh they become influenced by it to such an extent that their spirit grows dull and they are unable to take solid food.

The Bible compares a newly regenerated believer to a baby. The life in his spirit which he newly possesses is as tiny and weak as a baby naturally born. There is nothing wrong with his being a baby as long as he does not remain too great a time in that stage. Every adult must begin as a child. But should he persist as such very long, his spirit never progressing beyond what it was when he was first regenerated some years before, then something is drastically wrong. Man's spirit can grow; the spirit's intuition is able to wax stronger. A newly regenerated person is like a new-born baby who has no self-consciousness and whose nerves are wobbly in function. His spirtual life may be compared to a spark of fire. His intuitive power is extremely weak and not effective. But a baby must grow daily. His knowledge must increase continuously through exercise, training, and growth until he has become fully self-conscious and knows how to skillfully exercise all his senses. Even so must a believer. Upon regeneration he needs to gradually exercise his intuition. Each exercise means an increase in experience, knowledge and spiritual stature. Just as a man's senses are not born with matured awareness, so a believer's intuition is not born highly sensitive.

All this does not signify, however, that the soulish Christians who long remain babes have no outward dealings with their sins, experience no increase in their knowledge of the Bible, exert no effort to serve the Lord, or receive no gift of the Holy Spirit. The saints at Corinth encountered all of these. They "were enriched in (Christ) with all speech and all knowledge . . . not lacking in any spiritual gift" (1 Cor. 1.5,7). From the human point of view, are these not signs of growth? We probably would regard the Corinthian believers as most spiritual; yet the Apostle viewed them as babes, as men of the flesh. Why is it that the increase in speech, knowledge and gifts was not considered growth? This uncovers an intensely significant fact, which is, that though the saints at Corinth grew in these outward endowments they failed to grow in their *spirit*. Their intuition did not wax stronger. Increase in preaching eloquence, Bible knowledge and spiritual gift is not reckoned as increase of spiritual life! If the believer's spirit—that which is capable of communing with God—does not grow stronger and keener, God judges that he has not grown at all!

How many of the Lord's people today are developing in the wrong direction! Many assume that upon being saved they must seek higher Bible knowledge, better utterance in preaching, and more spiritual gifts. They forget it is their spirit that must advance. Speech, knowledge and gift are purely outward matters; by contrast intuition is inward. Quite sad is the sight of that Christian who allows his spirit to persist as a babe, but who concomitantly fills his soul life with speech, knowledge and gift. These articles are valuable, but how can they be compared with the value of the spirit? What God has newly created in us is this spirit (or spiritual life), and what should develop into matured manhood is likewise this spirit. Should we commit the serious mistake of seeking the enrichment of the soul life instead of the increase of this spiritual life with its intuition, we shall have made no progress at all in God's eye. God considers our spirit all-important; and so He cares for its growth. No matter how much our mind, emotion and will may gain by speech, knowledge and gift, it is all deemed by God as vain if our spirit is not developing.

We daily expect to have more power, more knowledge, more gifts, more eloquence; yet the Bible contends that even if we have more of these elements we do not necessarily progress in spiritual life. On the contrary, our spiritual walk may remain the same without advancing a mile. Paul candidly reminds the believers at Corinth: "You were not ready for it; and *even yet* you are not ready." In what were they unprepared? They were not prepared to serve God with their intuition, to know more of God intuitively, to receive His revelation in their intuition. They were obviously not ready when they first believed in the Lord; but now years later, though enriched in speech, knowledge and gifts, they still were not so. By those two words—"even yet"—the Apostle signified that though they were replete with outward enrichments their spiritual life had made no progress since they first believed. Real advancement is measured by the growth of the spirit and its intuition; the rest belongs to the flesh. This should be impressed indelibly on our hearts.

How sad that believers today seem to achieve progress in almost every sphere except in that of their spirit. After trusting the Lord for many years, they continue to lament: "I do not feel I have a spirit." The difference between our mind and God's mind is wide. We, like those at Corinth, try successfully to garner much so-called spiritual knowledge by exercising the intellect of our mind. Unfortunately the increase of our mind does not and cannot substitute the maturing in our intuition. To God we appear unchanged. We must henceforth remember that the increase God preeminently desires is not in our outward man but in the inward man and its intuition. He expects the new life which we receive at regeneration to enlarge. And all which belongs to the old creation He expects to be denied.

A believer fails to be spiritual because he is influenced too much by the flesh. Only one whose intuition is alive and who enjoys uninterrupted communion with God knows the deep truths of God. If the intuitive power is weak, what else can be absorbed except milk? Milk is pre-digested food. What this denotes is that the soulish believer cannot maintain clear fellowship with God in the spirit's intuition and hence must depend upon other more advanced Christians for the things of God. Matured Christians fellowship with God in their intuition and then transform what they have been shown into milk for the babes in Christ. The Lord permits such a thing in the life of a beginner, but He takes no pleasure in having His people remain dull and powerless in communing directly with Him. Feeding on milk indicates the person is far less capable of communing with God directly and instead relies on others to transmit God's message to himself. The matured has his intuition fully exercised to distinguish good from evil. We are of no spiritual utility if we have many ideas but do not possess the ability to commune with God and know His realities with our intuition.

The Christians at Corinth ranked high in speech, knowledge, gifts, but how was their spiritual life? Almost totally inactive. The church at Corinth was a carnal church, for all she had she had in the mind.

Many of the Lord's people currently commit the same error as did the saints at Corinth. The words of the Lord are spirit and life, but these people do not accept the words accordingly. They investigate theological problems with a very cold mind and search the hidden meaning of the Bible with the design of presenting the best interpretation. They satisfy their lust for knowledge. They communicate what they have found by writing and preaching. Excellent though their thoughts, arguments and outlines may be, seemingly most spiritual too, God nevertheless looks on these achievements as dead weights because they have not been achieved in the spirit. They have simply passed from one man's mind to another man's mind. Some readers or hearers may protest that they are helped, but the question is, *what* is helped? Beyond assisting the mind to acquire additional ideas, nothing else has happened. Such knowledge adds nothing to spiritual effectiveness. Only what comes from the spirit can enter the spirits of others; that which comes from the mind can only reach the minds of others. Finally, what comes from the Holy Spirit enters our spirit, and whatever the Holy Spirit transmits through our spirit can reach the spirits of others.

THE SPIRIT OF WISDOM AND REVELATION

In our communion with God the spirit of wisdom and revelation is imperative. "The God of our Lord Jesus Christ, the Father of glory, may give you a spirit of wisdom and of revelation in the knowledge of him" (Eph. 1.17). When a new spirit is received at regeneration its functions await development, for they presently lie dormant there. The Apostle Paul prayed for the regenerated believers at Ephesus, desiring that they receive the spirit of wisdom and revelation so that they might know God intuitively. Whether this ability is a hidden function of the believer's spirit which is activated through prayer or whether it is something added by the Holy Spirit to the believer's spirit as a result of prayer, we do not know. Yet one thing is certain: this spirit of wisdom and revelation is essential to one's communion with God. We also recognize that it can be obtained through prayer.

Although our intuition is capable of communing with God it requires wisdom and revelation. We need it to know what is of God and what is of ourselves. We must have wisdom to discern the enemy's counterfeit as well as his attack. We also require it to know how to conduct ourselves among men. In a thousand different ways we need God's wisdom, for we are foolish and prone to make mistakes. How difficult for us to execute God's will in all matters, but He will grant us the necessary equipment. He does not impart it to our brain; rather, He dispenses the spirit of wisdom to us so that we may have wisdom in our spirit. God gives it to our intuition for He will lead us through intuition into the way of wisdom. While our mind may indeed remain dull, our intuition is full of wisdom. Often when our own wisdom seems to have reached its end, there gradually rises from within us another kind to guide us. Wisdom and revelation are closely linked because all God's disclosures are those of wisdom. If we live naturally we have no way to figure out God. Nothing but darkness resides in the natural man. God and matters divine stretch far beyond the reaches of our mind. And although our spirit may even be quickened, it still dwells in darkness if there is no unfolding from the Holy Spirit. A *quickened* spirit only indicates that it is *at last capable of receiving God's revelation. It does not mean that it can now move independently.*

In our communion with God He frequently gives revelation. We ought to pray for such. The spirit of revelation implies that God reveals in the spirit. The spirit of wisdom and revelation signifies where God reveals Himself and how He imparts to us His wisdom. An impulsive thought is not to be interpreted as belonging to the spirit of revelation. Only what we intuitively know of the mind of God through the operation of the Holy Spirit in our spirit ever constitutes the spirit of revelation. God communes with us there and nowhere else.

The spirit of wisdom and revelation affords us true knowledge of God; all else is skin deep, imaginary, superficial, and therefore false. We frequently speak of God's holiness, righteousness, mercy, love, and other virtues. Man's mind *is* capable of conceiving these attributes of God, yet such mental knowledge is like looking through a stone wall. When however a believer has received revelation from God concerning His holiness, he sees himself corrupted to the core and void of any cleanliness before the light of God's dwelling in unapproachable light where no sinful, natural man can draw nigh. Oh, that many among us might be given such an experience as *that*. And thereafter let us compare the one who has received such a disclosure of God's holiness with the other who has no such experience yet easily speaks of His holiness. They may perhaps employ the same terminology, but the word articulated by the first seems to be many times weightier than that of the second person. The first one appears to speak with his whole being and not just with his lips. The spirit of revelation alone explains it. And this applies equally to all other truths in the Bible. Sometimes we understand a certain truth and recognize its importance, but only after that particular truth is gradually unfolded by God to our spirit are we able to speak with a special emphasis.

Whatever we gather outwardly which is not inwardly disclosed can neither move ourselves nor others. Revelation in the spirit alone contains spiritual potency. To commune with God is to receive His revelation in the spirit. Rare are God's disclosures for many of us because rarely do we wait on Him for them. How can we compare a preoccupied natural life with a life walked according to revelation? But if we are willing to provide God the opportunity, we shall receive revelation quite often indeed. The life of the Apostles abundantly substantiates this assertion.

SPIRITUAL UNDERSTANDING

There is a soulish as well as a spiritual wisdom. The first springs from man's mind while the second is supplied to the spirit by God. Education may remedy any lack of understanding and wisdom in a natural man, but it cannot alter his natural endowment. Spiritual wisdom, though, may be realized through believing prayer (James 1.5). One thing which we ought to keep in mind is, that in redemption "God shows no partiality" (Acts 10.34). He places all sinners, wise or foolish, on the *same* footing, and confers upon them the *same* salvation. As the entire being of the wise is totally corrupted so is that of the foolish. In God's sight the mind of the wise is as nonefficacious as that of the foolish. Both need the regeneration of the spirit; and after that it is no easier for the wise man than for the foolish to know the words of God. Now of course it is quite difficult for a very foolish person to know God; but is it less difficult for the wisest among men? Not at all, because God must be known in the spirit by everyone. Their minds may be unalike, yet both their spirits are dead and hence equally foolish and deficient in divine matters. Man's natural cleverness does not help him to know God and God's truth. No doubt the wise one is easier to reason with and is quicker in understanding, but it is altogether limited to the mental realm, utterly contrary to intuitive knowledge.

Do not assume that after regeneration the wise have advantage over the foolish in making spiritual progress. Unless they are more faithful and submissive, their better mental comprehension adds nothing to their intuitive knowledge. Man's old creation never serves as the source of the new creation. Spiritual advancement is measured by faithful obedience. Natural endowment does not affect spiritual life one way or the other, although it yields priority to the flesh. In spiritual experience everybody begins at the same starting point, passes through the same processes, and obtains the same results. All regenerated believers, including the naturally wise, must consequently seek spiritual understanding, without which no one can maintain normal fellowship with God. Nothing can take the place of spiritual understanding.

"That you may be filled with the knowledge of his will in all spiritual wisdom and understanding, to lead a life worthy of the Lord, fully pleasing to him, bearing fruit in every good work and increasing in the knowledge of God" (Col. 1.9-10). This is what Paul prayed for on behalf of the saints at Colossae. In this prayer we find that true knowledge of God's will is preceded by spiritual understanding and followed by: (1) leading a life worthy of the Lord, fully pleasing to Him; (2) bearing fruit in every good work; and (3) increasing in the knowledge of God.

No matter how good man's natural endowment is, he cannot know God's will by that means. It requires spiritual comprehension to know His will and to commune with Him. Only spiritual understanding can penetrate the spiritual realm. The natural kind may grasp some teachings but these stay in the mind and are unable to flow as life. Because spiritual understanding comes from the spirit it can transform what is understood into life. Have we now perceived that all true knowledge emerges from the spirit? The spirit of revelation moves hand in hand with spiritual understanding. God grants us the spirit of wisdom and revelation as well as spiritual comprehension. The wisdom and revelation we obtain in the spirit needs to be understood spiritually. Revelation is what we receive from God; understanding assists us to comprehend what is revealed. Spiritual understanding furnishes us the meaning of all the movements within our spirit so that we may comprehend God's will. Communion with God includes receiving His revelation in the spirit—that is, in the spirit's intuition—and then apprehending the meaning of this revelation by spiritual understanding. Our comprehension does not arise naturally but is enlightened by the spirit.

It is clear from these two verses in Colossians that if we desire to please God and to bear fruit we must know God's will in our spirit. Our spirit's relationship with God is the foundation for pleasing Him and bearing fruit. How vain for us to expect God's pleasure while walking according to the soul. God is pleased with nothing but His Own will. Nothing else can satisfy His heart. Our anguish is that we do not know God's will. We search and think, yet we seem unable to touch His mind. We should therefore remember that the way to know God's mind lies not in much searching and judging but in spiritual understanding. Nothing but man's spirit can judge God's will, for it has an intuitive power to discern His movement.

If we apprehend God in this way continuously we shall increase in the knowledge of Him. Intuition can grow and grow. It knows no bounds. Its development means the development of the believer's entire spiritual life. Each true communion we have with God trains us to commune better next time. We should seek to be perfect; accordingly, we must seize every opportunity to train our spirit to know God better. Today our need is to *truly* know Him, to appropriate Him in the depth of our being. How often we think we have discerned His will and yet later we discover we have been mistaken. Since our need is to know God and His will, we must seek to be filled with the knowledge of that will in all spiritual understanding.

CHAPTER 3
CONSCIENCE

BESIDES THE FUNCTIONS OF INTUITION and communion, our spirit performs still another important task—that of correcting and reprimanding so as to render us uneasy when we fall short of the glory of God. This ability we call conscience. As the holiness of God condemns evil and justifies good, so a believer's conscience reproves sin and approves righteousness. Conscience is where God expresses His holiness. If we desire to follow the spirit (and since we never reach a stage of infallibility), we must heed what our inward monitor tells us regarding both inclination and overt action. For its works would be decidedly incomplete if it were only *after* we have committed error that conscience should rise up to reprove us. But we realize that even before we take any step—while we are still considering our way—our conscience together with our intuition will protest immediately and make us uneasy at any thought or inclination which is displeasing to the Holy Spirit. If we were more disposed today to mind the voice of conscience we would not be as defeated as we are.

CONSCIENCE AND SALVATION

While we were sinners our spirit was thoroughly dead; our conscience was therefore dead as well and unable to function normally. This does not mean the conscience of a sinner stops working altogether. It does continue to operate, though in a state of coma. Whenever it comes out of this coma it does nothing but condemn the sinner. It has no strength to lead men to God. Dead as it is to Him, God nonetheless desires the conscience to perform some feeble work in the heart of man. Hence in man's dead spirit conscience appears to do a little more work than the other functions of the spirit. The death of intuition and of communion seems to be a greater one than that of conscience. There is of course a reason for the variation. As soon as Adam ate the fruit of the tree of the knowledge of good and evil his intuition and communion died completely towards God, but his power of distinguishing good and evil (which is the function of conscience) was increased. Even today, while the intuition and communion of a sinner are altogether dead to God, his conscience retains something of its movement. This does not imply that man's conscience is alive; for according to the Biblical meaning of aliveness only that which has the life of God is reckoned as living. Anything void of God's life is considered dead. Since the conscience of a sinner does not embrace the life of God it is accounted dead, though it may appear to be active according to man's feeling. Such activity of the conscience augments the anguish of a sinner.

In initiating His work of salvation the first step of the Holy Spirit is to awaken this comatous conscience. He uses the thunders and lightnings of Mount Sinai to shake and enlighten this darkened conscience so as to convince the sinner of his violation of God's law and of his inability to answer God's righteous demand and additionally to convict him as one who is condemned and who deserves nothing but perdition. If one's conscience is willing to confess whatever sins have been committed, including the sin of unbelief, it will be sorrowful in a godly way, earnestly desiring the mercy of God. The tax-collector in our Lord's parable who went up to the temple to pray illustrates such a work of the Holy Spirit. It is what the Lord Jesus meant in his statement: "When (the Holy Spirit) comes, he will convince the world of sin and of righteousness and of judgment" (John 16.8). Should a man's conscience be closed to the conviction, however, then he can never be saved.

The Holy Spirit illuminates a sinner's conscience with the light of God's law so as to convict him of sin; the same Spirit also enlightens man's conscience with the light of the gospel so as to save him. If a sinner, upon being convicted of his sin and hearing the gospel of God's grace, is willing to accept the gospel and by faith take it, he will see how the precious blood of the Lord Jesus answers all the accusations of his conscience. Doubtless there is sin, but the blood of the Lord Jesus has been shed. What ground is left for accusation since sin's penalty has been fully paid? The blood of the Lord has atoned for all the sins of a believer; hence there is no more condemnation in the conscience. "If the worshipers had once been cleansed, they would no longer have any consciousness of sin" (Heb. 10.2). We may stand before God without fear and trembling because the blood of Christ has been sprinkled on our conscience (Heb. 9.14). Our salvation is confirmed by the fact that the precious blood has quieted this voice of condemnation.

Since the terrifying light of the law and the merciful light of the gospel both shine upon it, dare we overlook man's conscience in the preaching of the Word? Is our aim in preaching merely to make people understand in their mind, be moved in their emotion, and decide with their will without in the slightest touching their conscience? The Holy Spirit cannot do the work of regeneration through the precious blood if one's conscience has not been convicted of sin. We must stress the precious blood and the conscience proportionally. Some strongly insist on the latter but overlook the former; consequently sinners try hard to repent and to do good, hoping in this way to propitiate God's wrath with their own merits. Others emphasize the precious blood but neglect conscience. This results in a mental acceptance of the blood and a rootless "faith" because their conscience has not been reached by the Holy Spirit. Thus these two must be presented equally. Whoever is aware of an evil conscience will accept the full meaning of the precious blood.

CONSCIENCE AND COMMUNION

"How much more shall the blood of Christ, who through the eternal Spirit offered himself without blemish to God, purify your conscience from dead works to serve the living God" (Heb. 9.14). In order to commune with God and to serve Him one first must have his conscience cleansed by the precious blood. As a believer's conscience is cleansed he is regenerated. According to the Scriptures the cleansing by the blood and the regeneration of the spirit occur simultaneously. Here we are informed that before one can serve God he must receive a new life and have his intuition quickened through the cleansing of the conscience by the blood. A conscience so cleansed makes it possible for the intuition of the spirit to serve God. Conscience and intuition are inseparable.

"Let us *draw near* with a true heart in full assurance of faith, with our hearts sprinkled clean from an evil conscience and our bodies washed with pure water" (Heb. 10.22). We do not draw near to God physically as did the people in the Old Testament period, for our sanctuary is in heaven; nor do we draw near soulically with our thoughts and feelings since these organs can never commune with God. The regenerated spirit alone can approach Him. Believers worship God in their quickened intuition. The verse above affirms that a sprinkled conscience is the basis for communion with God intuitively. A conscience tinged with offense is under constant accusation. That naturally will affect the intuition, so closely knit to the conscience, and discourage its approach to God, even paralyzing its normal function. How infinitely necessary to have "a true heart in full assurance of faith" in a believer's communion with God. When conscience is unclear one's approach to Him becomes forced and is not true because he cannot fully believe that God is for him and has nothing against him. Such fear and doubt undermine the normal function of intuition, depriving it of the liberty to fellowship freely with God. The Christian must not have the slightest accusation in his conscience; he must be assured that his every sin is entirely atoned by the blood of the Lord and that now there is no charge against Him (Rom. 8.33-34). A single offense on the conscience may suppress and suspend the normal function of intuition in communing with God, for as soon as a believer is conscious of sin his spirit gathers all its powers to eliminate that particular sin and leaves no more strength to ascend heavenward.

A BELIEVER'S CONSCIENCE

A believer's conscience is quickened when his spirit is regenerated. The precious blood of the Lord Jesus purifies his conscience and accordingly gives it an acute sense that it should obey the will of the Holy Spirit. The sanctifying work of the Holy Spirit in man and the work of conscience in man are intimately related and mutually joined. If a child of God desires to be filled with the Spirit, to be sanctified, and to lead a life wholly after God's will, he must adhere to the voice of conscience. Should he not grant it its rightful place, he shall fall inescapably into walking after the flesh. To be faithful to one's conscience is the first step toward sanctification. Following its voice is a sign of true spirituality. If a Christian fails to let it do its work he is barred from entering the spiritual realm. Even if he regards himself (and is so regarded by others) as spiritual, his "spirituality" nevertheless lacks foundation. If sin and other matters contrary to God's will and unbecoming to saints are not restrained as dictated by its voice, then whatever has been superimposed through spiritual theory shall ultimately collapse because there is no genuine foundation.

Conscience testifies as to whether we are clear towards God and towards men and as to whether our thoughts, words and deeds follow the will of God and are not in any way rebellious to Christ. As Christians advance spiritually the witness of conscience and the witness of the Holy Spirit seem to close ranks. This is because conscience, being fully under the control of the Holy Spirit, daily grows more sensitive until it is attuned perfectly to the voice of the Spirit. The Latter is thereby able to speak to believers through their consciences. The Apostle's word that "my conscience bears me witness in the Holy Spirit" (Rom. 9.1) carries within it this meaning.

If our inward monitor judges us to be wrong we must in fact be wrong. When it condemns, let us repent immediately. We must never attempt to cover our sin or bribe our conscience. "Whenever our hearts condemn us" can we be less condemned by God, since "God is greater than our hearts"

(1 John 3.20)? Whatever conscience condemns *is* condemned by God. Can the holiness of God pursue a lower standard than our conscience? If conscience insists we are wrong, we must be wrong indeed.

What should we do when we are wrong? Cease proceeding to do the incorrect thing if we have not yet done it; repent, confess, and claim the cleansing of the precious blood if we have done it already. It is to be regretted that so many Christians today do not follow these rules. Immediately after the reproof of their inner voice, they lay plans to quench its protest. They usually employ two methods. One is to argue with it, trying to marshal reasons for their action. They suppose that anything reasonable must be God's will and will be condoned by the conscience. What they do not understand is that conscience never argues or reasons. It discerns God's will through intuition and condemns everything which is not according to Him. Conscience speaks for God's will, not for reason. Christians ought not walk by reason but by God's will as disclosed in their intuition. Whenever they disobey any movement there, conscience raises its voice to condemn. Explanation may satisfy the mind but never conscience. As long as the issue condemned is not removed it shall not cease condemning. During the initial stage of a Christian's walk conscience only bears witness to right and wrong; as spiritual life grows, it bears witness as well to what is of God and what is not of God. Although many things appear good to human eyes, they are nonetheless condemned by conscience because they do not originate with God' revelation but are initiated instead by the Christians themselves.

The other method is to ease conscience with many other works. To solve the dilemma of refusing to obey their inner voice of accusation on the one hand but continuing to be afraid of its condemnation on the other, believers resort to many good works. They replace God's will with laudable deeds. They have not obeyed God, yet they insist that what they now do is just as good as what He has revealed—perhaps even better, broader in scope, more profitable, greater in influence. They highly esteem such works; God, however, deems them of no spiritual account whatsoever. He looks neither at the aggregate of fat nor at the number of burnt offerings but solely at the sum of obedience to Him. Nothing, regardless how commendable the intention, can move God's heart if the revelation in the spirit has been neglected. Doubling the consecration will not silence the accusing monitor; its voice must be followed; that and nothing else can ever please God. Conscience simply demands our obedience; it does not require us to serve God in any spectacular way.

Let us therefore not deceive ourselves. In walking according to the spirit we shall hear the directions of conscience. Do not try to escape any inward reproach; rather, be attentive to its voice. By constantly walking in the spirit we are constrained to humble ourselves and to heed the correction of conscience. Children of God should not make a general confession by acknowledging their innumerable sins in a vague manner, because such confession does not provide conscience opportunity to do its perfect work. They ought to allow the Holy Spirit through their conscience to point out their sins one by one. Humbly and quietly and obediently they should permit their conscience to reprove and condemn them of every individual sin. Christians must accept its reproach and be willing, according to the mind of the Spirit, to eliminate everything which is contrary to God. Are you reticent to let conscience probe your life? Dare you let it explore your real condition? Will you allow it to parade before you one after another all the things in your life as they are beheld by God? Will you grant conscience the right to dissect every one of your sins? In case you dare not, in case you are not willing to be so examined, then does not such drawing back prove that there remain many elements in your life which have not been judged and committed to the cross as they ought to have been: that there are still matters in which you have not wholly obeyed God nor fully followed the spirit: that some issues continue to hinder you from having perfect fellowship with God? If so, you cannot contend before God that "there is nothing between You and me."

Only an unconditional and unrestricted acceptance of the reproach of conscience with a corresponding willingness to do what is revealed can show how perfect is our consecration, how truly we hate sin, how sincerely we desire to do God's will. Often we express a wish to please God, to obey the Lord, to follow the Spirit; here is the test as to whether our wish is real or fancied, perfect or incomplete. If we are yet entangled in sin and not completely severed from it, most likely our spirituality is largely a pretense. A believer who is unable to follow his conscience wholly is unqualified to walk after the spirit. Before conscience has its demand realized, what else but an imaginary spirit will lead the person, since the true spirit within him continues to petition him to listen to the monitor within? A believer can make no genuine spiritual progress if he is reluctant to have his evil conscience judged in God's light and clearly dealt with. The truth or falsity of his consecration and service depends on his willing obedience to the Lord—both to His command and to His reproach.

After one has permitted conscience to begin operating, he should allow it to perfect its work. Sins must be treated progressively one by one until all have been eliminated. If a child of God is faithful in his dealing with sin and faithfully follows his conscience, he shall receive light increasingly from heaven and have his unnoticed sins exposed; the Holy Spirit shall enable him to read and to understand more of the law written upon his heart. Thus is he made to know what is holiness, righteousness, purity and honesty, concerning which he had had only vague ideas before. Moreover, his intuition is strengthened greatly in its ability to know the mind of the Holy Spirit. Whenever a believer is therefore reproved by his conscience his immediate response should be: "Lord, I am willing to obey." He should let Christ once again be the Lord of his life; he should be teachable and should be taught by the Holy Spirit. The Spirit shall surely come and help if a person is honestly minding his conscience.

Conscience is like a window to the believer's spirit. Through it the rays of heaven shine into the spirit, flooding the whole being with light. Heavenly light shines in through the conscience to expose fault and to condemn failure whenever we wrongfully think or speak or act in a way not becoming saints. If by submitting to its voice and eliminating the sin it condemns we allow it to do its work, then the light from heaven will shine brighter next time; but should we not confess nor extirpate the sin, our conscience will be corrupted by it (Titus 1.15), because we have not walked according to the teaching of God's light. With sin accumulating, conscience as a window becomes increasingly clouded. Light can barely penetrate the spirit. And there finally comes a day when that believer can sin without compunction and with no grief at all, since the conscience has long been paralyzed and the intuition dulled by sin. The more spiritual a believer is the more keenly alert is his inner monitor. No Christian can be so spiritual as to have no further necessity to confess his sin. He must be fallen spiritually if his conscience is dull and insensitive. Excellent knowledge, hard labor, excited feeling and strong will cannot substitute for a sensitive conscience. He who does not heed it but seeks mental and sensational progress is retrogressing spiritually.

The sensitivity of the conscience can be increased as well as decreased. Should anyone give ground to his conscience to operate, his spirit's window will let in more light next time; but should he disregard it or answer it with reason or works other than what it demands, then his conscience will speak more and more softly each time it is rejected until ultimately it ceases to speak. Every time a believer does not listen to conscience he damages his spiritual walk. If this self-inflicted wounding of his spiritual life continues unabated, he shall sink into the state of being fleshly. He will lose all his former distaste for sin and former admiration of victory. Until we learn to face squarely the reproach which arises from conscience, we do not actually appreciate how meaningful to our walk in the spirit this heeding of the voice of conscience is.

A GOOD CONSCIENCE

"I have lived before God in all good conscience up to this day" (Acts 23.1). This is the secret of Paul's life. The conscience he refers to is not that of an unregenerated person but of a Holy Spirit-filled conscience. Bold in approaching God and perfect in his communion with Him, the Apostle's regenerated conscience gives him no reproach. He does everything according to it. Never does he do anything that his conscience objects to, nor does he ever permit one item to remain in his life which it condemns. He is therefore bold before God and man. We lose our confidence when our conscience is murky. The Apostle "always (took) pains to have a clear conscience toward God and toward men" (Acts 24.16), for "if our hearts do not condemn us, we have confidence before God; and we receive from him whatever we ask, because we keep his commandments and do what pleases him" (1 John 3.21-22).

Believers simply do not realize how very significant their conscience is. Many have the idea that as long as they walk after the spirit all is well. They do not know that an unclear conscience means loss of confidence in approaching God and that this loss in turn means disruption of one's communion with Him. In fact, a muddied conscience can hinder our intuitive communion with God more than anything else. If we fail to keep His commandments and to do what pleases Him our monitor within shall naturally reprove us, rendering us fearful before God and hence keeping us from receiving what we seek. We can serve God only with a clear conscience (2 Tim. 1.3). An opaque one shall surely cause us to shrink back intuitively from God.

"Our boast is this, the testimony of our conscience that we have behaved in the world, and still more toward you, with holiness and godly sincerity, not by earthly wisdom but by the grace of God" (2 Cor. 1.12). This passage speaks of the testimony of conscience. Only a conscience without offense will testify for a believer. It is good to have the testimony of others, but how much better to have the testimony of our own conscience. The Apostle asserts that this is what he is boasting of here. In our walk after the spirit we need to have this testimony continually. What other people say is subject to error because they cannot fully know how God has guided us. Perhaps they may misunderstand and misjudge us just as the Apostles were misunderstood and misjudged by the believers in their day. At times they also may overpraise and over-admire us. Many times men criticize us when we actually are following the Lord; on other occasions they praise us for what they see in us, though it is largely the result of a temporary emotional outburst or a cleverly conceived thought on our part. Hence outside praise or criticism is inconsequential; but the testimony of our quickened conscience is momentous. We should pay extreme attention to how it bears us witness. What is its estimate of us? Does it condemn us as hypocritical? Or does it testify that we have walked among men in holiness and godly sincerity? Does conscience affirm that we already have walked according to all the light we have?

What is the testimony of Paul's conscience? It testifies that he has "behaved in the world . . . not by earthly wisdom but by the grace of God." Conscience in fact can testify to nothing else. What it contends for and insists upon in the believer is solely for that life to be lived by the grace of God and not by earthly wisdom. Earthly wisdom is totally nil in God's will and work. It equally amounts to nothing in a believer's spiritual life. Man's mind is altogether useless in his communion with God; even in his communication with the material world the mind occupies but a subordinate position. A child of God lives on earth exclusively by the grace of God, and grace implies something entirely done by Him, with men having no part in it (Rom. 11.6). Except as one lives exclusively by God—not permitting himself to take any initiative nor allowing his mind to have control over him—can conscience testify that he lives in the world in holiness and godly sincerity. In other words, it operates together with intuition. Conscience bears witness to everything done according to revelation in intuition, but it resists every action which is contrary to intuition, no matter how compatible it is with human wisdom. To sum up, conscience approves only the revelation of intuition. Intuition leads believers, while conscience constrains them to follow their intuition.

A good conscience which attests God's good pleasure in the believer (since there is nothing between him and God) is absolutely essential to a life walked after the spirit. That attestation ought to be the believer's goal: he should be satisfied with nothing less. This indicates what should be a normal Christian's life: as it was the testimony of the Apostle Paul, so must it be with us today. Enoch was a man of good conscience for he knew God was pleased with him. This attestation of God's satisfaction with us helps us to move forward. We must be very careful here, however, lest we exalt our "self" as though we have pleased God. All glory belongs to Him. We should take pains always to have a clear conscience; but should ours in fact be clear, we then must guard against the intrusion of the flesh.

If our conscience consistently attests God's satisfaction with us, we shall have boldness to look to the blood of the Lord Jesus for cleansing each time we unfortunately fail. To have a good conscience we must not depart for a moment from that blood which continually and forever cleanses us. Confessing our sin and trusting in the precious blood are unavoidable. Moreover, because our sinful nature is still within us, we will not be able to recognize many hidden works of the flesh until we have matured spiritually. What we formerly considered harmless may now become sinful to us. Without the cleansing of the precious blood we could never be at peace. But once it is sprinkled on our conscience it shall continue to do its work of cleansing.

The Apostle confides that what he seeks is to have a good conscience towards God and men. These two directions, Godward and manward, are deeply entwined. If we wish to maintain a good conscience towards men, it must first be clear with respect to God. An unclear conscience towards God automatically brings in an unclear one towards men. Consequently all who want to live spiritually must seek to have a clear conscience towards God (1 Peter 3.21). This does not in any way signify that it is unimportant to have a good conscience before men. On the contrary, there are many things which can be done towards God but not towards men. Only a clear conscience towards men effects a good testimony before them. Man's misunderstanding does not affect the testimony: "keep your conscience clear, so that, when you are abused, those who revile your good behavior in Christ may be put to shame" (1 Peter 3.16). Good conduct cannot appease an evil conscience; but neither will much reviling by man cast a shadow over a good conscience.

A good conscience also enables us to receive God's promises. Christians nowadays frequently complain that their little faith is the cause for failure to live a perfect spiritual life. Naturally there are many reasons for not possessing greater faith, but the gravest of these is probably an evil conscience. A good conscience is inseparable from a great faith. The moment it is offended, at that very moment faith is weakened. Let us observe how the Bible joins these two elements: "whereas the aim of our charge is love that issues from a pure heart and a good conscience and sincere faith" (1 Tim. 1.5). Again: "holding faith and a good conscience" (1 Tim. 1.19). Conscience is the organ of our faith. God hates sin intensely, for the apex of God's glory is His infinite holiness. His holiness will not tolerate sin, not even for a moment. If a believer does not purge—according to the dictate of conscience—everything contrary to God's mind, he shall lose his fellowship with God instantaneously. All the promises which God grants us in the Bible may be considered conditional. None are bestowed to gratify one's fleshly lust. No one shall experience the Holy Spirit, communion with God, and answered prayer if he does not deal away with his sin and flesh. How can we claim the promise of God with boldness if our voice within is accusing us? How can anyone, whose conscience does not bear him witness that he has lived on earth in holiness and godly sincerity, be a man of prayer who is able to ask God for unlimited rewards? What is the use of praying if our inward monitor reproves us when we lift up our hands to God? Sin first must be forsaken and cleansed before we can pray with faith.

We need to possess a conscience void of offense, not in the sense that it is better than before or that much evil has been done away but that it is without offense and confident before God. This ought to be the normal condition of our conscience. If we prostrate ourselves before it and allow it to reprove us: if we offer ourselves entirely to the Lord and are willing to perform all His purposes: then our confidence shall increase until it is possible for us to regard our conscience as void of offense. We dare to tell God that now we have nothing left which is concealed from Him. So far as we are concerned we know of nothing between us and Him. In walking by the spirit we should never permit the tiniest offense to stir up our conscience. Whatever it condemns must be confessed immediately, cleansed by the precious blood and forsaken, so that no trace be left behind. Each day we should seek to have a good conscience, because no matter how short a time conscience may be offended it renders great harm to the spirit. The Apostle Paul has set us a good example in always having a good conscience. Therein alone shall we maintain uninterrupted fellowship with God.

CONSCIENCE AND KNOWLEDGE

In abiding by the spirit and listening to the voice of conscience we should remember one thing, and that is, conscience is limited by knowledge. It is the organ for distinguishing good and evil, which means it gives us the knowledge of good and evil. This knowledge varies with different Christians. Some have more while others have less. The degree of knowledge may be determined by individual environment or perhaps by the instruction each has received. Thus we can neither live by the standard of others nor ask other people to live by the light we have. In a Christian's fellowship with God an unknown sin does *not* hinder communion. Whoever observes all the will of God known to him and forsakes everything known to be condemned by God is qualified to enjoy perfect fellowship with Him. A young Christian frequently concludes that due to his lack of knowledge he is powerless to please God. *Spiritual* knowledge is indeed quite important, but we also know that the lack of such knowledge does not hinder one's fellowship with God. In the matter of fellowship God looks not at how much we apprehend of His will but rather at what our *attitude* towards His will is. If we honestly seek and wholeheartedly obey His desires, our fellowship remains unbroken, even though there should be many unknown sins in us. Should fellowship be determined by the holiness of God, who among all the most holy saints in the past and the present would be qualified to hold a moment's perfect communion with Him? Everyone would be banished daily from the Lord's face and from the glory of His might. That sin which is unknown to us is under the covering of the precious blood.

On the other hand, were we to permit to remain even the tiniest little sin which we know our conscience has condemned, we instantly would lose that perfect fellowship with God. Just as a speck of dust disables us from seeing, so our known sin, no matter how infinitesimal, hides God's smiling face from us. The moment the conscience is offended immediately fellowship is affected. A sin unknown to the saint may persist long in his life without affecting his fellowship with God; but as soon as light (knowledge) breaks in, he forfeits a day's fellowship with Him for every day he allows that sin to remain. God fellowships with us according to the level of the knowledge of our conscience. We shall be very foolish if we assume that, since a certain matter has not hindered our fellowship with God for so many years, it cannot later be of any consequence.

This is because conscience can condemn only to the extent of its newest light; it cannot judge as sinful that of which it is not conscious. As the knowledge of a believer grows, his conscience too increases in its consciousness. The more his knowledge advances the more his conscience judges. One need not worry about what he does not know if he but completely follows what he already does know. "If we walk in the light"—that is, if we are walking in the light which *we have already*—"as he is in the light, we have fellowship with *one another,* and the blood of Jesus his Son cleanses us from all sin (though many are still unknown to us)" (1 John 1.7). God has unlimited light. Although our light is limited, we shall have fellowship with God and the blood of His Son shall cleanse us if we walk according to the light we have. Perhaps there are still sins today unremoved from our life, but we are not conscious of them; hence we can continue to have fellowship with God today. Let us keep in mind that, important as conscience is, it nevertheless is not our standard of holiness, because it is closely related to knowledge. *Christ Himself* is alone our single standard of holiness. But in the matter of fellowship with God, His one condition is whether or not we have maintained a conscience void of offense. Yet, having fully obeyed the dictates of conscience, we must not visualize ourselves as now "perfect." A good conscience merely assures us that so far as our knowledge goes we are perfect, that is, we have arrived at the *immediate* goal, but not the ultimate one.

Such being the case, our standard of conduct rises higher to the degree our knowledge of the Scriptures and spiritual experience increase. Only when our lives become holier as our light progresses can we preserve a conscience without offense. It shall invariably accuse us if we accompany this year's knowledge and experience with only last year's conduct. God did not cut off His fellowship with us last year because of our sins unknown to us then; but He certainly shall sever it today if we do not forsake the sins unknown last year but now known this year. Conscience is a God-given *current* standard of holiness. Whoever violates that standard is assumed to have committed sin.

The Lord has many words for us, but in view of the immaturity of our spiritual understanding He has to wait. God deals with His children according to their respective conditions. Due to varying degrees of knowledge in the conscience some are not conscious of sins regarded as very great by their fellow-believers. Hence, let us not judge one another. The Father alone knows how to handle His children. He does not expect to find the strength of "young men" in His "little children" nor the experience of "fathers" in the "young men." But He does wait for *each* of his children to *obey* Him according to what he *already knows*. Were we to know for sure (which is not easy) that God has spoken to our brother on a particular matter and that our brother has failed to listen, then we can persuade him to obey. Yet we should never force our brother to follow what our conscience says to us. If the God of perfect holiness does not reject *us* because of our past unknown sins, how can we, on the basis of our current standard, judge our brother who only knows now what we knew last year?

In fact, in helping other people we should not coerce obedience from them in small details but only advise them to follow faithfully the dictate of their own conscience. If their volition yields to God they will obey Him when the Holy Spirit sheds light on the words clearly written in the Bible. As long as his volition is yielded, a believer will follow God's desire the moment his conscience receives light. The same is applicable to ourselves. We should not overextend ourselves to the point of exciting the strength of our soul to understand truths beyond our present capacity. If we are disposed to obey today's voice of God, we are considered acceptable. On the other hand, we should not restrain ourselves from searching any truth which the Holy Spirit may lead us intuitively to search. Such restraint would mean lowering our standard of holiness. In a word, there is no problem for that one who is willing to walk by the spirit.

A WEAK CONSCIENCE

A few moments ago we remarked that the standard of our holy living is Christ, not conscience, though the latter nonetheless is of great significance. It testifies whether or not in our everyday life we have pleased God; it consequently serves as a criterion for the *current* degree of holiness. If we live by what conscience teaches we have arrived at the place we should be for the present moment. It is therefore a prime factor in our daily walk after the spirit. In whatever matter we disobey the dictate of our conscience we shall be reprimanded by it. As a result we shall lose peace and shall be cut off temporarily from having fellowship with God. There is no question that we must follow what conscience demands; but how perfect its demand is remains a question.

As we have seen, conscience is limited by knowledge. It can guide only by the knowledge it possesses. It condemns every disobedience to what it knows, but it cannot condemn what it itself does not know. Hence a vast distance obtains between the measure of conscience and the measure of God's holiness. Just here we find at least two defects. First, a conscience with limited knowledge condemns only what it knows as wrong and leaves untouched in our life numerous matters which are not according to God's will. God and those more matured saints know how imperfect we are, and yet we continue to walk in our old fashion for lack of new light. Is not this an enormous defect? This imperfection is nonetheless bearable because God does not judge what we do not know. Despite this flaw we can fellowship with Him and be accepted if we simply obey whatever our conscience dictates.

But the second defect, unlike the first, *does* interfere with our fellowship with God. Just as a limited knowledge fails to judge what ought to be judged, so it may also judge what should not be judged. Does it mean that conscience is faulty in its guidance? No, the leading of conscience is correct and must be heeded by believers. But there are different degrees of knowledge among the saints. Many things which can be done with knowledge are condemned as sins by the conscience of those who lack knowledge. This manifests the disease of believers' immaturity. The fathers can do many things with perfect liberty for they have advanced knowledge, experience and position, but for the little children to do them would be entirely wrong because they simply do not possess such knowledge, experience and position. This does not imply that there are two different standards for the Christian's conduct. It just shows, however, that the standard of good and evil is bound up with individual position. This law applies to the secular, as well as to the spiritual, realm. Many matters agree perfectly with God's will when done by matured believers, but these very items become sins if copied by immature ones.

The reason for this variance is the different degrees of knowledge in our consciences. When one believer does what his conscience deems good he is obeying the will of God; but the conscience of another person may judge the same thing as evil, and he will be sinning against God if he does it. The absolute will of God is always the same; but He reveals His mind to each person according to the limitation of their spiritual position. Those with knowledge have a stronger conscience and consequently enjoy more liberty; while those without knowledge harbor a weaker conscience and hence experience more bondage.

This is distinctly illustrated in the first letter to the Corinthians. There was much misunderstanding among the Christians at Corinth concerning the eating of food offered to idols. Some of them regarded idols as possessing no real existence since there is no God but One (1 Cor. 8.4). So for them there could be no difference between the food offered to idols and food not so offered: both with propriety could be eaten. But others, having long been accustomed to idols, could not help viewing the food as though it were truly offered to an idol. They felt uneasy when eating it. Because their conscience was weak while eating the food, they were defiled (v.7). The Apostle treated this divergence of view as a matter of knowledge (v.7). The former had light and therefore did not sin when they ate, for their conscience did not bother them; the latter, however, not enjoying such knowledge, felt uneasy while eating and so were guilty. Thus we see the great importance of knowledge. The increase of it sometimes may increase the condemnation of conscience but it may equally decrease its condemnation.

It is advisable for us to beseech the Lord to grant us more knowledge in order that we may not be bound unreasonably, but this knowledge must be kept in humility lest we, like the Corinthians, fall into the flesh. In case our knowledge is inadequate and our conscience continues its censure, we must obey its voice at all cost. We should never philosophize that since this thing is not wrong according to God's highest standard, we can do it in spite of what our conscience says. Let us not forget that conscience is our current standard of God's leading. We need to submit to it, else we sin. God judges whatever conscience judges.

What we have discussed here concerns merely outward items such as food. In those items of a more spiritual character there can be *no* such difference of liberty and bondage, however much our knowledge grows. Only in these external physical matters does God deal with us according to our age. In the young believers He pays much attention to their food, clothing and other external issues, because He desires to put to death the evil deeds of the body. If the young genuinely have a heart to follow the Lord they shall find Him frequently calling them, through their spirit's conscience, to subdue themselves in these matters. But those with deeper experience in the Lord seem to enjoy more liberty in their conscience with respect to these items because they already have learned how to obey Him.

Yet the more advanced ones are confronted by one of the most serious hazards here. Their conscience becomes so strong as to drift into cold numbness. Young Christians who follow the Lord wholeheartedly obey Him at many points, for their conscience is sensitive and easily moved by the Holy Spirit. Old believers, on the other hand, have so much knowledge that they tend to overdevelop their mind so as to numb the sensitivity of the conscience. They are tempted to do things according to the knowledge of their mind and seemingly render themselves immovable by the Holy Spirit. This is a fatal blow to spiritual life. It removes the freshness from a believer's walk and causes it to become old and dull. Regardless how much knowledge we possess, let us be careful not to follow it but the conscience of our spirit. Should we disregard what is condemned intuitively by our conscience and take our knowledge as our standard of conduct, we have already settled into walking after the flesh.

Is it not true that our conscience sometimes can be greatly disturbed when we set out to do what is absolutely legitimate according to the truth we know? That which conscience condemns is reckoned as not in accordance with God's will, even though by the knowledge of our mind it is good. This is because our knowledge is acquired through the searchings of our intellect and not by revelations in our intuition. Hence the leading of conscience and of knowledge can prove to be quite conflicting.

Paul indicates that one's spiritual life shall be impaired enormously if he disregards the reproach of conscience and follows the knowledge of his mind instead. "For if any one sees you, a man of knowledge, at table in an idol's temple, might he not be encouraged, if his conscience is weak, to eat food offered to idols? And so by your knowledge this weak man is destroyed, the brother for whom Christ died" (1 Cor. 8.10-11). Seeing a believer with knowledge eating food offered to idols, the one without knowledge tends to think he too can so eat. But if the latter eats against the voice of his conscience he falls into sin. Let us never for a moment, then, walk by the knowledge we have. However much of it we have accumulated, we ought only to heed the intuition and conscience of the spirit. Perhaps one's knowledge may influence his conscience; even so, what he must follow directly is his conscience. God is looking more for our obedience to His will than for the "correctness" of our conduct. Our listening to the voice of conscience guarantees the genuine character of our consecration and obedience. Through our conscience God examines our motive—whether we desire to obey Him or we seek something else.

Another thing one must guard against is the blocking of his conscience. It often loses its normal operation through a kind of blockage. When we are surrounded by those whose conscience is deadly numb, ours may be numbed also through their argument, conversation, teaching, persuasion or example. Beware of teachers with hardened consciences: beware of man-made consciences: reject all attempts of man to mold yours. Our consciences must be responsible directly to God in all regards. We ourselves must know His will and be responsible for executing it. We will fail if we neglect our conscience to follow that of another.

Let us recapitulate. The conscience of the believer constitutes one of the indispensable faculties of his spirit. We ought to follow its guidance fully. Though it is influenced by knowledge, its voice nonetheless represents God's highest will for His children today. It is well for us to arrive at the highest for today. Other matters we need not worry about. Let us continuously maintain our conscience in a healthy condition. Do not permit any sin to hurt its feeling. If at any time we discover that it has become cold and hard as though nothing can move us, let us recognize by this that we have fallen *deeply* into the flesh. In such a case, all the Bible knowledge we have acquired is but stored in the mind of the flesh and is lacking in living power. We ought to follow the intuition of our spirit unceasingly, being filled with the Holy Spirit, in order that our conscience may increase daily in sensitivity and our repentance may be as instantaneous as our knowledge of anything wrong between us and God. Do not be concerned purely with the mind and neglect the intuitive conscience. The extent of spirituality is measured by the sensitivity to our conscience. Countless are those Christians who have disregarded their conscience in the past and are now unlively, merely holding some dead knowledge in their brain. May we be ever watchful lest we stumble into the same trap. Do not be afraid to be easily moved. Never fear to have the conscience exercised too much; only fear for it not to be moved enough. Conscience serves as a monitor for God. It informs us where something has gone wrong or needs to be repaired. We can avoid much destructive consequences later if we but listen to conscience earlier.

PART SIX

WALKING AFTER THE SPIRIT

CHAPTER 1
THE DANGERS OF SPIRITUAL LIFE

NOTHING IS MORE VITAL to the Christian life than to walk daily after the spirit. It is this that maintains the Christian in a constant spiritual state, delivers him from the power of the flesh, assists him to obey God's will always, and shields him from the assault of Satan. Now that we understand the operations of our spirit, we must immediately walk by it. This is a moment by moment affair from which there can be no relaxing. In these days we must be keenly alert to the peril of receiving the teaching of the Holy Spirit while subsequently rejecting His leading. On this very point have many saints stumbled and fallen. To acquire teaching alone is not sufficient; we must also accept the leading. We should not be content with just spiritual knowledge but treasure as well the walk after the spirit. Often we hear people drop the words, "the way of the cross"; but what is this way after all? It is in reality nothing else but walking by the spirit, since to walk in that fashion necessitates the committing of our ideas, wishes and thoughts to death. Exclusively following the spirit's intuition and revelation demands our bearing the cross daily.

All spiritual believers know something of the operation of the spirit. Their experience of it, however, is often sporadic because they have not fully understood all the laws which govern its functioning. But with their intuition well-developed they could walk steadily after the spirit without any interference from the outside (note: all that is outside the spirit is considered the outside realm). But not having assimilated the laws of the spirit, they interpret life in the spirit as oscillatory, devoid of rule, and arduous to practice. Many are determined to heed God's will and to follow the leading of the Holy Spirit, but they lack a positive forward-propelling heart because they are not sure if the guidance of their intuition is wholly dependable. They have yet to learn to understand the indication of their intuition as to whether to advance or to stay. They are additionally igornant of what the normal state of the spirit is and are thus incapacitated from being led continually by it. Frequently their inner man loses its power to operate for the simple reason that they do not know how to keep it in a right condition. Though they sometimes do experience revelation in their intuition, they nevertheless wonder why it is, when they are earnestly seeking, that at times their intuition does receive revelation but at other times does not. This of course is due to the fact that on some occasions they unconsciously walk according to the law of the spirit and so obtain revelation whereas at other moments, though asking, they are not asking according to this law and therefore do not secure any revelation. Were they to walk by the law of the spirit continually rather than unconsciously following intermittently, they could always receive the revelation. Unfortunately they are unaware of this possibility. It is nonetheless certain that for us to consistently experience revelation we must know the laws of the spirit and the will of God and must do the things which please Him. Since all movements in the spirit are meaningful, we need to learn their import if we wish to walk faithfully. Understanding the laws of the spirit is therefore indispensable.

There are countless Christians who consider the occasional working of the Holy Spirit in their spirit to be the most sublime of their life experiences. They do not expect to have such an experience daily because they surmise that such a special event could happen but a few times in life. Were they to live by the spirit according to its law, however, they would discover that these are everyday occurrences. What they deem extraordinary—something one cannot permanently sustain—is actually the *ordinary* daily experiences of believers. "Extraordinary" indeed if believers should desert this ordinary life experience and abide in darkness.

Suppose we have received a certain thought. Are we able to discern whether this comes from our spirit or from our soul? Some thoughts burn in the spirit while others blaze in the soul. Believers ought to understand how the various parts of their being operate or they shall not be able to distinguish the spiritual from the soulical. When thinking, they should recognize the source of their thought; in feeling, they should detect the direction from which such feeling comes; and in working, they should be clear as to what strength they use. Only thus can they follow the spirit.

We know our soul provides us with self-consciousness. One aspect of self-consciousness is self-examination. This is most harmful since it causes us to focus upon ourselves and thereby enhance the growth of self life. How often self-exaltation and pride are the consequences of such self-examination. But there is a kind of analysis of incalculable help to the spiritual pilgrimage. Without it we are incompetent to know who we really are and what we are following. Harmful self-examination revolves around one's own success or defeat, stimulating attitudes of self-pride or self-pity. Profitable analysis searches only the *source* of one's thought, feeling or desire. God wishes us to be delivered from self-consciousness, but at the same time He certainly does not intend for us to live on earth as people without intelligent awareness. We must not be overly self-conscious, yet we must apprehend the true condition of all our inward parts through the knowledge accorded us by the Holy Spirit. It is postively necessary for us to search out our activities with our heart.

Many regenerated believers seem unconscious of possessing a spirit. Though they do have one, they simply are not conscious of it. Perhaps they have spiritual sense but they do not realize such sense arises from the spirit. What every truly born-again person should rely on for living is the life of the spirit. If we are willing to be taught, we shall know what is our spiritual sense. One thing is unmistakable: the soul is affected by outside influences, but not the spirit. For example, when the soul is provided with beautiful scenery, serene nature, inspiring music, or many other phenomena pertaining to the external world, it can be moved instantly and respond strongly. Not so the spirit. If the spirit of believers is flooded with the power of the Holy Spirit, it is independent of the soul. Unlike the latter the spirit does not require outside stimuli by which to be activated but is able to be active on its own initiative. It can move under any circumstances. Hence those who are genuinely spiritual can be active whether or not their soul has feeling or their body has strength. These ones live by the ever-active spirit.

Now as a matter of fact the sense of the soul and the intuition of the spirit are distinctly opposite; nevertheless, occasionally they appear to be quite similar. Their similarity can be so close as to confuse Christians. Should they be hasty to move, they will not easily escape being deceived at these times of similarity. Yet if they would wait patiently and test the source of their feelings again and again, they would be told the real source by the Holy Spirit at the right hour. In walking after the spirit we must avoid all haste.

Soulish Christians generally bend to certain directions. Most of them lean either towards emotion or towards reason. Now when these people become spiritual they tend to fall towards the *opposite* extreme from what they formerly were. Emotional persons will then be tempted to adopt their own cold reason as the leading of the spirit. Because they appreciate how soulish their former passionate life was, they now mistake their own reasoning to be spiritual. Likewise those who were rational believers may subsequently accept their passionate feeling to be the leading of the Holy Spirit. They too are conscious of the soulish cast of their hitherto cold and quiet life; consequently they now interpret their emotion to be of the spirit. These are equally ignorant of the fact that the reversal of position between emotion and reason does not render them a shade less soulish. Let us therefore remember the functions of the spirit. To be led by the spirit is to follow its intuition. All spiritual knowledge, communion and conscience come via the intuition. The Holy Spirit leads the saints by this intuition. They need not themselves figure out what possibly is spiritual; all that is required is to abide by their intuition. In order to listen to the Spirit we must apprehend His mind intuitively.

Some seek the gifts of the Holy Spirit with genuine earnestness. Yet often what they crave is but some joy, for the "I" is hidden behind their quest. They believe if they can feel the Holy Spirit descending upon them or some external force controlling their body or some warm fire burning from head to foot, that then they have been baptized in the Spirit. However true it may be that He does sometimes allow people to so feel Him, it is very damaging for men to seek Him by means of emotion. For this not only can excite their soul life but also may evoke the enemy's counterfeit. What is really valuable before God is not how we emotionally feel the presence of the Lord or how we even feel love towards Him; rather is it how we follow the Holy Spirit and live according to what He has revealed to our spirit. Frequently we meet "Holy Spirit-baptized" people of this kind who continue to live by their natural life and not by their spirit. They lack a sensitive intuition to discern matters in the spiritual world. Not emotion but communion with the Lord in the spirit is what is valuable before God.

Through our lengthy discussion of the functions of the spirit as described in the Bible, we now can realize that the spirit can be as passionate as emotion and as cool as reason.

Only those who are experienced in the Lord can distinguish what is of the spirit and what is of the soul. Those who try to reason out the movement of the Holy Spirit or, as more frequently happens, attempt to feel His movement rather than to seek to truly know God in their intuition and walk accordingly, commit themselves to a life in the flesh. They permit their spiritual life to sink into oblivion.

It may help us to see more clearly the significance of following the spirit's intuition if we examine the life of Paul. God "was pleased to *reveal* his Son *to me,* in order that I might preach him among the Gentiles, (and) I did not confer with *flesh and blood,* nor did I go up to Jerusalem to those who were apostles before me, but I went away into Arabia; and again I returned to Damascus" (Gal. 1.16-17). Revelation, as we have indicated before, is given by God and received in the spirit. When the Apostle John obtained revelation to write, he secured it in the spirit (Rev. 1.10). The Bible consistently testifies that revelation is something which occurs in the believer's spirit. Now the Apostle Paul informs us here that he was walking by the spirit when he received revelation in his spirit to know the Lord Jesus and to be sent to the Gentiles. He did not confer with flesh and blood because he had no need to listen further to man's opinion, thought or argument. He did not go to Jerusalem to see those who were spiritually senior to him so as to obtain their view. He simply followed the leading of his spirit. Since he had received *God's revelation* in his intuition and had known God's will, he no longer sought other evidence. He deemed revelation in his spirit sufficient for guidance. At that time, proclaiming the Lord Jesus to Gentiles was a new departure. Man's soul naturally would suggest amassing more information, especially the opinions of those who had more preaching experience. But Paul followed the spirit alone. He cared not what men, not even the most spiritual apostles, would say.

Thus ought we to follow the direct leading of the Lord in our spirit rather than the words of spiritual people. Does this then imply that the words of the spiritual fathers are useless? No, they are most useful. The exhortation and teaching of the fathers are most helpful, but we nonetheless ought to "weigh what is said" (1 Cor. 14.29). We must be instructed by the Lord directly in our spirit. When we are uncertain whether a movement in the spirit is actually of God or not, we can be helped greatly by those who have been taught deeply in the Lord. But if we already *have known for sure*—as Paul was—that God has so revealed His mind, then we ought not inquire of men, not even of apostles, should they still exist today.

From the context of this passage we can see the Apostle stresses that the gospel he preaches was disclosed to him by God rather than taught him by other apostles. This is a point of immense significance. The gospel we preach must not be just something we hear from men or read from books or even conceive through our meditation. Unless it is delivered to us by God, it can serve no spiritual utility. Young Christians today welcome the idea of "instructors" and the spiritually mature wish to impart an orthodox faith to the second generation. But who knows what really produces spiritual value? If what we believe and preach does not originate in revelation it counts for nothing. We can gather from the mind of others some beautiful thoughts; yet our spirit remains impoverished and empty. Obviously we are neither to expect a new gospel nor to demean what the servants of God teach, for the Bible distinctly instructs us not to despise prophesying (1 Thess. 5.20). We are simply emphasizing the utter necessity of revelation.

Without revelation, all that has been written is vain. If we desire to be spiritually effective in preaching, we initially must apprehend God's truth in our spirit. Whatever and however much is acquired wholesale from men counts for nought spiritually. Revelation in the spirit should occupy a large place in a Christian servant's life. It is actually the first qualification for a worker. This alone empowers one to perform spiritual service and to walk by the spirit. How multiplied are the workers who trust in their own intellect and mind for accomplishing spiritual work! Even among the most evangelical believers it is perhaps chiefly a mental acceptance of the truth and amounts to nothing but death. Should we not ask ourselves whether what we preach emerges from God's revelation or comes from men?

THE ATTACKS OF SATAN

In view of the significance of our spirit, which is the site of communion between the Holy Spirit and the saints, should we marvel if Satan is most unwilling to let us know the functions of the spirit for fear we may follow it? The enemy aims to confine the saint's life within the soul and to quench his spirit. He will give many strange physical sensations to believers and fill their mind with various wandering thoughts. He intends to confuse one's spiritual awareness by these sensations and thoughts. While confused, God's children are incompetent to distinguish what is of the spirit and what emanates from the soul. Satan well recognizes that victories of believers rest in their knowing how to "read" their spiritual sense (alas! how many are ignorant of this principle). He musters his whole force to attack the believer's spirit.

Let us reiterate that in such spiritual warfare Christians must never make any move according to their feelings or sudden thoughts. Never assume that such thoughts cannot be wrong because we have already prayed. It is a mistake to consider every notion which comes to us in prayer as being of God. We seem to innocently think that prayer can right the wrong and that whatever has been prayed out is bound to be all right. True, we have sought the will of God, but it does not mean necessarily that we *have already known* His will. God makes it known to our spirit, not to our mind.

Satan employs even more drastic measures against believers than that of enticing them into living by the soul instead of following the spirit. Upon succeeding in luring them—through their thoughts or feelings—to live by the outward man, Satan adopts the next step of pretending to be a spirit in them. He will create many deceptive feelings in the believers in order to confuse their spiritual senses. If they are ignorant of the wiles of the enemy, they just may allow their spirit to be suppressed until it ceases to function. And then they heed this counterfeit feeling as though they were still following the spirit. Once their spiritual sense grows dull, Satan proceeds further in his deceit. He injects into their minds the thought that now God is leading them by their renewed mind, thus subtly covering up the fault of men in *not using* their spirit as well as covering up the work of the enemy. As soon as man's spirit ceases to operate, the Holy Spirit can no longer find any cooperative element within him; naturally then, all resources from God are cut off. And it is hence impossible for such ones to continue to experience true spiritual life.

Should Christians be insensitive to their condition, Satan assaults them even more mercilessly. He may either mislead them (at a time when they are unconscious of the presence of God) into thinking they are living by faith, or make them suffer without a cause under the delusion that they are suffering with Christ in their spirit. Wherefore Satan by means of a false spirit deceives believers into obeying his will. Such experiences occur to spiritual but undiscerning Christians.

Spiritual ones ought to possess spiritual knowledge so that all their movements can be governed by spiritual reasoning. They should not act impulsively according to fleeting emotion or flashing thought. They should never be in haste. Every action must be scrutinized with spiritual insight in order that only what is approved by the spirit's intuitive knowledge is permitted. Nothing should be done which is propelled by excited feeling or abrupt thought; everything must be carefully and quietly examined before it is executed.

To examine and test our walk is a very important element in following the spirit. Believers should not while away their spiritual life foolishly; they must examine carefully all thoughts, feelings, etc., which come to them in order to discern whether these arise from God or from themselves. The natural inclination is to take life easy, to adapt oneself to whatever happens. If so, one will often welcome what the enemy has arranged. Usually we do not investigate these matters, but Scripture commands us to "test everything" (1 Thess. 5.21). Herein lies both a characteristic and a strength of spiritual believers. They "interpret spiritual truths in spiritual language" (1 Cor. 2.13 RSV marginal). The word "interpret" here means in the original "compare" (RSV marginal), "mixing" or "putting together" (Darby note), or "determined" (Darby note). The Holy Spirit purposely gives spiritual believers such power for them to use to test anything which enters their life; otherwise, under the manifold deceits of the evil spirit, it would be most difficult to live.

THE ACCUSATION OF SATAN

Satan has another way to assault those who set their heart on following the leading of the spirit's intuition. This is by counterfeiting or fasely representing one's conscience with all sorts of accusations. To keep our conscience pure we are willing to accept its reproach and deal with whatever it condemns. The enemy utilizies this desire of keeping the conscience void of offense by accusing us of various things. In mistaking such accusations as being from our own consciences we often lose our peace, tire of trying to keep pace with the false accusations, and thus cease to advance spiritually with confidence.

Those who are spiritual ought to be aware that Satan not only indicts us before God but also to ourselves. He does this to disturb us into thinking we ought to suffer penalty because we have done wrong. He is alert to the fact that the children of God can make no progress spiritually unless they have a heart full of confidence; consequently he falsifies the accusation of conscience in order to make them believe they have sinned. Then their communion with God is broken. The problem with believers is that they do not know how to distinguish between the indictment of the evil spirit and the reproach of conscience. Frequently out of fear of offending God, they mistake the accusation of an evil spirit to be the censure of conscience. This accusation grows stronger and stronger until it becomes uncontrollable if not listened to.

Thus in addition to their willingness to yield to conscience's reproof, spiritual believers should also learn how to discern the accusation of the enemy.

What the enemy charges the saints of may sometimes be real sins, though more often than not they are merely imaginary—that is, the evil spirit makes them *feel* they have sinned. If they actually *have* sinned, they should confess it immediately before God, asking for the cleansing of the precious blood (1 John 1.9). Yet should the accusing voice still continue, it obviously must be from the evil spirit.

Here is a matter of serious consequence. Before one knows how to differentiate between the reproach of conscience and the enemy's accusation, he should ask himself whether or not he *really abhors sin. If* this particular thing is wrong, am I willing to confess my sin and eliminate it? If we truly desire to follow God's will, not having yet heeded the accusing voice, we can be quite confident in our heart for it is not in us to want to rebel against God. Then, having determined to follow God's will, we should examine ourselves as to whether or not we have actually committed that sin. We must know beyond the shadow of doubt whether or not we have done it, because the evil spirit frequently accuses us of many unrelated items. If we have done it, then before we confess to God, we first must find out through the teaching of the Bible and the leading of intuition, whether or not this thing is verily wrong. Otherwise, though we have not sinned, Satan will make us suffer for it just as though we had.

The adversary is skillful in imparting all sorts of feelings to men. He may cause them to feel happy or sad; he may induce in them a feeling of guilt or of none whatsoever. But a child of God should understand that his feeling is not necessarily accurate when he thinks he is not wrong, for often he feels right when actually he *is* wrong. Moreover, he may not be wrong even when so feeling; it may be just his feeling and not be factually grounded at all. Whatever he feels, he must *test it out for sure* so as to know where he really stands. The child of God should adopt a neutral attitude towards every accusation. He should not take any action before he is assured as to the source of it. He must not be hasty; rather, he should wait quietly for assurance as to whether it is indeed the chiding of the Holy Spirit or but the charge of the evil spirit. If it originates with the Holy Spirit, he will then deal with it honestly. The believer's present waiting is due to his uncertainty and not to rebellion. Nevertheless, he absolutely must resist making all confessions to men which are motivated by sheer force from outside, for the enemy often tries to compel him to do this.

Real conviction from the Holy Spirit leads us to holiness while the aim of Satan is solely to accuse. He indicts us to make us indict ourselves. His motive is nothing other than to make Christians suffer. Sometimes after one has accepted the enemy's imputation and confessed accordingly, Satan may next fill him with a false peace. This is no small danger for it deprives the believer of any real contrition over defeat. The reproach of conscience ceases once the sin is confessed and cleansed by the precious blood, but the accusation of the enemy continues even after what is accused has been dealt with. The former leads us to the precious blood; the latter drives us to despair, causing us to reckon ourselves irredeemable. The purpose of Satan is to engineer our fall through accusations: "Since we cannot be perfect," sighs the believer resignedly, "then what is the use?"

At times the accusation of Satan is added to the rebuke of conscience. The sin is real, but when it has been treated according to the mind of the Holy Spirit the accusation continues because the evil spirit has joined his indictment to the reproach of the conscience. It is therefore a matter of utmost concern that we preserve an uncompromising attitude towards sin: not merely yielding no ground to the enemy to indict but also learning how to differentiate between the reprimand of the Holy Spirit and the accusation of the evil spirit and learning how to distinguish what is exclusively the enemy's charge from what is his charge mixed in with the reproach of conscience. We must realize most assuredly that the Holy Spirit never reproves further if the sin is cleansed by the precious blood and forsaken.

ADDITIONAL DANGERS

Other hazards lie in the way of following the spirit besides Satan's counterfeits and his attacks. Often our soul will fabricate or sense something which urges us to take action. Christians must never forget that not all senses emerge from the spirit, for the body, the soul, and the spirit each has its own senses. It is highly important not to interpret soulical or physical senses as the intuition of the spirit. God's children should learn daily in experience what is and what is not genuine intuition. How very easy for us, once perceiving the importance of following the intuition, to overlook the fact that senses exist in other parts of the being besides in the spirit. Actually spiritual life is neither so complicated nor so easy as people usually imagine.

Here then are two causes for alarm: first, the peril of mistaking other senses to be the spirit's intuition; and second, the danger of misunderstanding the meaning of intuition. We meet these two hazards every day. Hence the teaching of the Holy Scriptures is quite essential. To confirm whether or not we are moved by, and walk in, the Holy Spirit, we must see if any given thing harmonizes with the teaching of the Bible. The Holy Spirit never moves the prophets of old to write in one way and then move us today in another way. It is categorically impossible for the Holy Spirit to have instructed people of yesteryear what they ought not to do and yet tell us in our day that we must do these very same things. What we receive in the spirit's intuition needs to be certified by the teaching of God's Word. To follow intuition alone and not in conjunction with the Scriptures will *undeniably* lead us into error. The revelation of the Holy Spirit sensed by our spirit must coincide with the revelation of the Holy Spirit in Scripture.

Since our flesh is continuously active, we must be ever vigilant against its intrusion into our keeping the teaching of the Holy Scriptures. We know the Bible discloses the mind of the Holy Spirit; but were we to observe the Bible perfectly, we still would not necessarily be following the mind of the Holy Spirit. Why? Because often we search the many teaching of the Scriptures with our natural mind and later do them with our strength. Although what is understood and is done agrees perfectly with the Scriptures, it is nevertheless done without dependence upon the Holy Spirit. The whole matter has remained within the realm of the flesh. Wherefore, not only what we know in our spirit concerning the mind of the Holy Spirit needs to be checked by the Scriptures, but also what we know from the Scriptures must be carried out through our spirit. Do we not realize that the flesh craves priority even with respect to keeping the Holy Scriptures? The spirit has intuition; but it also has power. It is consequently null and void if we understand any doctrine in our mind while at the same time it remains unexecuted by the power of the spirit.

One more matter needs to be noticed: a great danger looms before us if we live and walk by the spirit too much. Although the Word does emphasize the believer's personal spirit, the Word also informs us that the significance of one's spirit is due to the indwelling *Holy Spirit.* The reason why we must walk and live in the spirit at all is because our spirit, being the habitation of God's Spirit, is where He expresses His mind. The leading and discipline we receive therein is His leading and discipline. In stressing the significance of the Holy Spirit we are at the same time emphasizing our own spirit since the latter constitutes His base of operation. Our danger, upon apprehending the work and function of man's spirit, is to rely entirely on it, forgetting that it is merely the servant of the Holy Spirit. God's Spirit and not our spirit is the One upon Whom we wait for direct guidance into all truth. If man's spirit is divorced from the divine Spirit it becomes as useless as the other parts of man. We should never reverse the order of man's spirit and the Holy Spirit. It is because many of the Lord's people are ignorant of man's spirit and its operation that we have presented in these pages a detailed account of it. This does not mean, however, that the position of the Holy Spirit in a man is inferior to that of his own spirit. The purpose for understanding this faculty of man is to help us to obey Him more and to exalt Him more.

This should exert great influence on our guidance. The Holy Spirit is given primarily for the benefit of the whole body of Christ. He abides in each individual because He dwells in the whole body of Christ and each is a member of it. The work of the Spirit is corporate in nature (1 Cor. 12. 12-13). He guides individuals because He guides the whole body. He leads each of us for the sake of the body. The movement of one member involves the whole body. The guidance of the Holy Spirit in our individual spirits is related to the other members. Spiritual guidance *is* the guidance of the body. In order that our movements may therefore be related to the body, we need to seek sympathy and agreement from the spirit of "two or three" other members, even after we personally have received guidance in our spirit. This principle must not be neglected in spiritual work. Much of defeat, strife, hatred, division, shame, and pain has been due to the independent moves of those who mean well but who follow merely their own spirit. All who follow the spirit should accordingly test their guidance by its relationship to the spiritual body to determine whether or not it is of the Holy Spirit. In every bit of our work, conduct, faith, and teaching we should be regulated by that relationship of the "members one of another" (Rom. 12.5).

In conclusion, then, along the spiritual pathway lurk many snares. A little carelessness brings in defeat. Yet there is no short cut or bypass we can take. We are not insured because we have learned some knowledge; on the contrary, we ourselves must experience everything. Those who have preceded us can only warn us of the hazards ahead so that we may not fall prey to them. If we intend to bypass part of the pathway, we shall be disappointed, but faithful followers of the Lord can avoid many unnecessary defeats.

CHAPTER 2
THE LAWS OF THE SPIRIT

A CHILD OF GOD must learn to recognize the sense of consciousness of his inner being as the first condition for a life walked after the spirit. If he does not discern what is the sense of the spirit and additionally the sense of the soul, he invariably shall fail to do what the spirit requires of him. For instance, when we feel hungry we know we should eat; when we feel cold we know we should be clothed. Our senses express needs and requirements. We must therefore know what our physical senses mean before we can know how to satisfy them with material supplies. In the spiritual realm, too, one must come to understand the meanings of his spirit's various senses as well as their respective supply. Only after an individual comprehends his spirit with its movements can he walk by the spirit.

There are a few laws of the spirit with which every Christian ought to be acquainted. If he does not understand these laws or fails to see the significance of recognizing the sensations of the spirit, he will miss many of its movements. His failure to discern its senses undermines the proper place of the spirit in his daily walk. Hence once we have known the various functions of the inner man, such as intuition, communion and conscience, we need to identify their movements which can then enable us to walk by the spirit. Being filled with the Holy Spirit, our spirit will be operating actively. But we shall incur loss if we disregard these operations. It is thus imperative that we observe the way the spirit habitually moves. A Christian should know more about the operation of his spirit than about the activity of his mind.

(1) WEIGHTS ON THE SPIRIT

The spirit needs to be kept in a state of perfect freedom. It should always be light, as though floating in the air; only so may life grow and work be done. A Christian ought to realize what the weights laid on his spirit are. Often he feels it is under oppression, as if a thousand pound load were pressing upon his heart. He can unearth no reason for this weight, which usually steals in upon one quite suddenly. It is employed by the enemy to harass the spiritual, to deprive him of joy and lightness, as well as to disable his spirit from working together with the Holy Spirit. If he does not recognize the source of this heaviness and the meaning of the oppression in the spirit, he cannot instantly deal with it and thereby restore his spirit immediately to normalcy.

The believer may be puzzled by such a sensation, interpreting it to be something natural or something occasional. He consequently may disregard it and allow his spirit to come under suppression. How often he continues to work without paying due attention to the weight, and frequently giving the enemy ground to play his trick at will upon him. Many times when this one is supposed to be used by God, he instead is powerless to accomplish God's work because he carries this heavy weight with him. The consciousness of his spirit grows very dull beneath such oppression. That explains why Satan and his evil hosts focus their assault on placing a heavy weight upon the believer's spirit. Alas for the child of God; for he often is unaware that the source of the weight is satanic; and even if he is aware, he may not resist.

With *this* load upon his spirit the Christian is bound to suffer defeat. If he encounters it in the morning and does not deal with it at once, he experiences defeat the whole day long. A free spirit is the basis for victory. In order to fight against the enemy and to live out God's life, we must possess a spirit altogether untrammeled by weight. When it is oppressed the Christian is deprived of his power of discernment and naturally misses God's true guidance. Whenever the spirit suffers oppression the mind cannot function properly. Everything comes to a halt or else everything goes awry.

It is of utmost consequence to deal with the heavy weight or oppression of the spirit *immediately*. Never adopt an attitude of indifference, for if you do you will suffer for it. The weight will grow heavier and heavier. And should it not be dealt away with, it will become a part of your life. Whereupon you will view all spiritual affairs as bitter and acrid, retarding your spiritual advance. In case you do not treat of the weight the first time it will come upon you more easily the next. The way to handle it is to stop the work at hand at once, set your will against this weight, and exercise your spirit to oppose it. Occasionally you may have to utter words audibly against it; at other times with the power of your spirit you should resist in prayer.

It is also indispensible to deal with the cause of such heaviness because the oppressive load shall remain as long as the cause goes unresolved. In addition to resisting the enemy's work there should be the uncovering of the cause behind that work. And if successful, you will thereby regain the place you previously had yielded to the enemy. If you have the power of discernment you will come to see it was because of your failure to cooperate with God at a particular time with regard to a particular matter that the enemy gained ground to crush you with such a heavy weight. The lost ground must be regained. If we resist the enemy by discovering the cause of his working, he shall flee.

(2) BLOCKAGE OF THE SPIRIT

The spirit requires the soul and body as organs for expression. It is like a mistress who must have a steward and a servant working for her to accomplish her wish. It can also be likened to an electric current which requires wire to show forth light. Should the soul and body lose their normality under the attack of the enemy, the spirit shall be shut in and denied any means of outlet. The adversary is familiar with the requirements of the spirit; therefore he frequently acts against the believer's soul and body. When these parts cease to function properly the spirit is stripped of its means of expression and so forfeits its victorious position.

During such a period one's mind may be confused, his emotions disturbed, his will weary and impotent to actively govern the whole being, or his body overly tired and temporarily lazy. He must resist these symptoms at once or else his spirit will be blocked in and he be unfit either to engage the enemy livingly in battle or to retain his ground of victory.

Shortly after his spirit is shut in, the believer loses his "aliveness." He seems to be bashful, seeks to hide himself, and seldom undertakes anything publicly. He likes to withdraw to the back, not wanting to be seen. Perhaps he fancies he has discovered something of himself, not realizing his spirit actually is being blocked. He appears to have no interest in reading the Bible and to have no word in prayer. His past work and experience, whenever recalled, appear to be meaningless, sometimes even laughable, to him. He feels no power in preaching—as though he were merely going through the motions. Should he allow this blockage of the spirit to be prolonged, he shall be attacked even more severely by the enemy. Were not God to intervene, due to his own prayer or that of others, the believer would be suffocated spiritually. For lack of knowledge, his reaction may simply be one of surprise and he may thus assume the all-too-common attitude of giving up. Actually though, because no spiritual experience or sense occurs without a cause, we should search it out carefully and not permit any weight to persist in us.

Satan tries to imprison the spirit in a dark chamber so that the soul is without the guidance of the spirit. As soon as the blockage is lifted, however, the believer once again can breathe easily and be restored to his normal liveliness.

Whenever a child of God is in such a hemmed-in situation, it is vital that he exercise his will towards *audibly uttering* words against the foe, lifting up his voice to proclaim the victory of the cross and the defeat of the enemy. He must wholeheartedly oppose the work of the adversary in both his soul and body. Following such a proclamation he must employ his will actively to resist the blockage. Prayer is one means of opening the spirit. But given the above-described situation, one needs to pray *aloud*. The best thing for the saint to do is to claim the victorious name of the Lord Jesus over every onslaught of the enemy. In addition to prayer he should exercise his spirit to run the blockade so as to reach the outside.

(3) POISONING OF THE SPIRIT

Our spirit can be poisoned by the evil spirit. This poison is the flaming dart of the enemy, aimed directly at our spirit. Into it he shoots sorrow, grief, anguish, woe or heartbreak to cause us to have a "sorrowful spirit" (1 Sam. 1.15 ASV): and a "broken spirit who can bear?" (Prov. 18.14) It is exceedingly hazardous for anyone to accept without objection or question every sorrow which comes upon him and take for granted that these are naturally his own feelings. He has not yet examined the source nor put up any resistance. Let us remember to never accept any thought or feeling lightly. If we wish to walk after the spirit we must be watchful in all points, searching especially the source of every notion and sensation.

Sometimes Satan provokes us to harden our spirit. It can become stiff, unyielding, narrow and selfish. Such a spirit cannot work with God nor can it do His will. And so a believer will abandon his love towards men; he will shed every delicate, sympathetic, tenderhearted feeling towards others. Since he has lost the generosity of the Lord and has drawn a circle around himself, how can the Holy Spirit ever use him mightily?

Frequently the enemy entices Christians to harbor an unforgiving spirit—a very common symptom indeed among God's children. Perhaps the fall of spiritual Christians can be traced chiefly to this very cause. Such bitterness and fault-finding and enmity inflict a severe blow upon spiritual life. If believers fail to see that such an attitude is distinctly from the enemy and *not from themselves,* they shall never be emancipated from the spirit of hatred.

At still other times Satan induces the spirit of God's people to become narrow and confined. He seduces these Christians into separating themselves from others by drawing lines of demarcation. If anyone is blind to the concept of the church as a body he will be devoted to his "small circle," proving that his spirit is already shrunken. The spiritual person, however, does not consider the things of God as his own but loves the whole church in his heart. If one's spirit is open, the river of life overflows; should his spirit shrink, he hinders God's work and lessens his own usefulness. A spirit that is not large enough to embrace all the children of God has been poisoned already.

Often Satan injects pride into the believer's spirit, evoking in him an attitude of self-importance and of self-conceit. He causes him to esteem himself a very outstanding person, one who is indispensable in God's work. Such a spirit constitutes one of the major reasons for the fall of believers: "pride goes before destruction, and a haughty spirit before a fall" (Prov. 16.18).

The evil spirit infects the believer's spirit with these and other venoms. If these poisons are not opposed instantly they soon become "the works of the flesh" (Gal. 5.19). At first these are only poisons from Satan, but they can be transformed into sins of the flesh if the Christian accepts them, even unconsciously, rather than resists them.

If the venom in the spirit is not dealt with it shall immediately become the sin of the spirit, a sin severer than any other. James and John thunderously asked: "Lord, do you want us to bid fire come down from heaven and consume them? . . . And he said, you do not know what manner of spirit you are of" (Luke 9.54,55 marginal). It is most essential that we know of what kind of spirit we are. We often do not perceive that our spirit is prey to the instigation of the enemy. Everything is wrong if it is wrong. From the experience of these two disciples we observe that an erring spirit can manifest itself easily through spoken words. Even so, the words uttered may not reveal nearly as much as the tone assumed. Sometimes the words are correct but the tone is wrong. To assure victory we need to watch even the sound of our speech. Immediately the evil spirit touches our spirit, our voice loses its softness. A harsh, hard, and shrill utterance does not spring from the Holy Spirit; it simply exhibits the fact that the one who speaks has been poisoned already by Satan.

How de we usually speak? Are we able to refer to others without any tinge of condemnation? Our words may in fact be true but lurking behind those words of truth could be the spirit of criticism, condemnation, wrath, or jealousy. Whereas we should speak the truth in love. If our spirit is pure and gentle, then are we able to voice the truth. Now should the spirit of condemning be within us, we most assuredly have sinned. Sin is not only an action; it is also a condition. What is hidden behind things is what matters the most. How many times we sin while doing something for God or men, for darkly hidden away is an unfaithful, unwilling, or grudging spirit.

We must keep our spirit sweet and soft. It must be pure and clean. Do we consider an erring spirit as sin? Do we know when the enemy has attacked our spirit—when our spirit is poisoned? Suppose we do know, are we humble enough to eliminate such sin? The moment we notice our voice has turned harsh, we must stop instantly. With not the slightest hesitation we should turn to ourselves and say, "I am willing to speak with a pure spirit; I am willing to oppose the enemy." If we are reluctant to say to our brethren, "I am wrong," then our spirit remains engulfed in its sin. God's children ought to learn how to guard their spirit from being goaded by the enemy. They should know also how to preserve it in sweetness and tenderness.

In ordinary times the Lord's people should early take the shield of faith which quenches all the flaming darts of the evil one. This implies that we should swiftly exercise living faith to look for God's protection and to withstand the enemy's attack. Faith is our shield, not our extractor: faith is a weapon for quenching the flaming darts, not for pulling them out afterwards. But should anyone be hit by a flaming dart, he at once must eliminate the cause of the dart. He should maintain an attitude of resistance, immediately denying whatever comes from Satan and praying for cleansing.

(4) SINKING OF THE SPIRIT

The spirit sinking or being submerged is largely due to a turning in on oneself. It may be induced by a possessiveness over all the experiences one has had or by an intrusion of the power of darkness or by a self-centeredness in prayer and worship. When anyone's spirit is tilted inward instead of outward the power of God is at once severed and the spirit will soon be surrounded by the soul.

Sometimes this submerging of the spirit in the soul is precipitated by the deceit of the evil foe who supplies the person with physical sensations and various wonderful joyful experiences. He does not perceive that they originate with the evil spirit: he instead construes them to be from God: and thus he unknowingly comes to dwell in a sensuous world where his spirit is drowned in the soul.

Believers may be additionally deceived—and their spirit accordingly descend into the soul—when they do not understand the position of Christ. The Holy Spirit indwells the child of God to manifest the enthroned Christ to him. The books of Acts, Ephesians, and Hebrews speak very plainly on the position of Christ *in the heaven* today. The spirit of the Christian is joined to the heavenly Christ. Because of his ignorance, however, the Christian looks within to find Him. He wishes to be united with the Christ Who is in him. Hence his spirit cannot ascend above the clouds, but rather is oppressed and tumbles into the soulical realm.

All these operations tempt the individual to live in his feelings rather than in his spirit. He needs to know that before he becomes spiritual and actually walks in the spirit the enemy is not compelled at that time to resort to counterfeit; but after the person has experienced the pouring of the Holy Spirit's power into his spirit, he faces a new world never before encountered. And just here is there cause for alarm, for the enemy will work to induce him to cease abiding in the spirit. If he succeeds, the believer will incur great loss. The tactic of the adversary is to deceive him through the feelings of the soul and body into thinking these are spiritual experiences for him to enjoy.

Many who have entered into spiritual living shall meet defeats because of their ignorance of its laws. The enemy foments within them all sorts of physical sensations and supernatural experiences. Should they lean on these supernatural phenomena or on other sensational occurrences which come from the outside, their life in the spirit will be obstructed. They will dwell in their outward soul or body while their innermost spirit is denied the power to cooperate with God. Naturally soul and body once again ascend, regain their forfeited authority, and submerge the spirit completely.

While the spirit is submerged its senses are rendered inoperative. When this occurs, many spiritual Christians feel they have lost their spirit. Soul and body occupy such a large place that the entire being can live by their sensations. Man's sensory organs replace the operation of the spirit. The movements of the spirit are buried beneath the powerful sensations of the soul and body. And eventually all spiritual life and work are completely terminated. If such a condition is permitted to last for very long the believer has fallen terribly indeed. He may perhaps be possessed by the evil spirit.

Everything therefore which is capable of impairing spiritual consciousness must be denied. We must shun wild laughter, bitter crying, and every other extreme outburst of physical emotion. The body should be kept in perfect calm. We must reject inordinate supernatural or natural sensations, for these propel the mind to follow the body and not the spirit. Never allow anything to hinder us from understanding the small still throb of the spirit.

Because the soul—when the spirit begins to sink—surrounds it and reduces it to servitude, the child of God must learn how to keep his spirit continuously outgoing, never permitting it to stagnate. For unless his spirit sallies forth to attack Satan, Satan unquestionably will attack his spirit and cause it to sink. Only as our spirit is flowing out is the Holy Spirit equally able to flow out His life. The moment anyone turns in on himself and sets his spirit to sinking, the torrential flow of the divine Spirit immediately stops. He uses the believer's spirit as His channel for the flowing out of God's life.

A Christian needs to determine what has caused his spirit to slump and then must restore it to its original state. As soon as he discovers a leak in the power of his spirit, he must try to redeem the situation at once.

(5) BURDENS OF THE SPIRIT

The burdens of the spirit differ from the weights on the spirit. The latter proceed from Satan with the intent of crushing the believer and making him suffer, but the former issue from God in His desire to manifest His will to the believer so that he may cooperate with Him. Any weight on the spirit has no other objective than to oppress; it therefore usually serves no purpose and produces no fruit. A burden of the spirit, on the other hand, is given by God to His child for the purpose of calling him to work, to pray, or to preach. It is a burden with purpose, with reason, and for spiritual profit. We must learn how to distinguish the burden of the spirit from the weight on the spirit.

Satan never burdens Christians with anything; he only encircles their spirit and presses in with a heavy weight. Such a load binds one's spirit and throttles his mind from functioning. A person with a burden or concern from God merely carries it; but the one who is oppressed by Satan finds his total being bound. With the arrival of the power of darkness, a believer instantaneously forfeits his freedom. A God-given burden is quite the reverse. However weighty it may be, God's concern is never so heavy as to throttle him from praying. The *freedom* of prayer will never be lost under any burden from God: yet the enemy's weight which forces itself upon one's spirit invariably denies one his freedom to pray. The burden imparted by God is lifted once we have prayed, but the heaviness from the enemy cannot be raised unless we fight and resist in prayer. The weight on the spirit steals in unawares, whereas the concern of the spirit results from God's Spirit working in our spirit. The load upon the spirit is most miserable and oppressive, while the burden of the spirit is very joyous (naturally the flesh does not deem it so), for it summons us to walk together with God (see Matt. 11.30). It turns bitter only when opposed and its demand is not met.

All real works begin with burdens or concerns in the spirit. (Of course, when the spirit lacks any concern we need to exercise our minds.) When God desires us to labor or speak or pray, He first implants a burden in our spirit. Now if we are acquainted with the laws of the spirit we will not continue on carelessly with the work in hand and allow the burden to accrue. Nor will we neglectfully disregard the burden until it is no longer sensed. We should lay everything aside immediately to ferret out *the meaning of this burden.* Once we have discerned its import, we can act accordingly. And when the work called for is done, the burden then leaves us.

In order to receive burdens from God our spirit has to be kept continuously free and untrampled. Only an untrammeled spirit can detect the movement of the Holy Spirit. Any spirit which is already full of concerns has lost the sharpness of its intuitive sense and hence cannot be a good vessel. Due to his failure to act according to the burden which he already has received from God, the believer often finds himself painfully burdened for many days. During this period God is unable to give him any new one. Consequently, it is highly necessary to search out the meaning of a burden through prayer, with the help of the Holy Spirit and the exercise of one's mind.

Frequently the burden or concern in the spirit is for prayer (Col. 4.12). As a matter of fact we are not able to pray beyond our burden. To continue to pray without it can produce no fruit because the prayer must be emanating from our mind. But the *prayer* burden in the spirit can only be lightened *through prayer.* Whenever God concerns us with something, such as prayer, preaching the Word, and so forth, the only way to lessen that concern or burden is to do what it calls for. The prayer burden in the spirit alone enables us to pray in the Holy Spirit with sighs too deep for words. When our spirit is concerned with prayer burdens nothing can discharge that burden except prayer. It is lifted soon after the work is performed.

Because of the large accumulation of prayer burdens we often find it difficult to pray at first, but the longer we pray the more our spirit responds with amens. We should try our best to pour out all the burdens in our spirit by prayer until all of them have left us. The more life is poured out through prayer, the happier we are. A common temptation, however, is to cease praying before the burden is lifted. When we begin to feel buoyant in our spirit we assume our prayer is answered, not realizing we are just beginning to engage in spiritual work. If at that moment we turn away to attend to other matters, then spiritual work will suffer great loss.

A believer should never regard spiritual labor as altogether joyous and jubilant, as though the presence of a burden is going to deprive him of what he considers to be spiritual experience. Quite pitiful is the one who is unaware of what real spiritual exertion in the burden of the spirit is truly like. He who is willing to suffer for God and men does not live for himself; but those who daily seek sensuous pleasures and become apprehensive about bearing burdens for God and the church are living only for themselves. Now in the light of what has just been said, we must not consider ourselves as fallen or as having erred whenever God imparts a burden to us. Satan is extremely pleased if we interpret it as such for he shall thereby escape our attacks. Let us not misunderstand ourselves. And let us not listen to Satan, for if we do we shall be accused and tormented further.

Genuine spiritual work is aggressive towards Satan and travails in birth for believers. These in no wise can be termed joyous undertakings. They require a more thorough death to self. That explains why no soulish Christian is able to engage in true spiritual effort. To enjoy sensuous pleasures daily is no evidence of spirituality. On the contrary, those who go on with God and disregard their own feelings are the truly spiritual ones. When a believer in burden is contending with the enemy he often wishes to be alone, separated from all human intercourse so as to concentrate on spiritual warfare. Before the combat is over he can barely display a smiling face. A spiritual Christian should welcome any burden which the Lord brings his way.

We need to know the laws of the spirit and the way to cooperate with God as well. Otherwise, we may prolong the burden to our disadvantage or else lose the opportunity to labor together with God. Every time we receive a burden in our spirit we should find out immediately through prayer what that burden is. If it is a call to war, to war we go; if a call to preach the gospel, the gospel we preach; and if a call to pray, pray we will. Let us seek how to work together with God. Let the old burden be discharged and the new one come in.

(6) EBBING OF THE SPIRIT

God's life and power in our spirit can recede like a tide. We recognize that anyone soulish usually deems his spiritual life to be at high tide when he *feels* the presence of God; but if he feels low and dry, he is at ebb tide. These are of course but feelings; they do not represent the reality of spiritual life.

Nevertheless, spiritual life does encounter a time of decline, though it is quite unlike any feeling of the soul. After one is filled with the Holy Spirit he can proceed quite well for a period, and then *gradually,* not suddenly, his spiritual life subsides. The difference between a sensuous decline and a spiritual decline lies here: the former is usually abrupt, whereas the latter is gradual. A believer may become conscious that the life and power of God which he once received is gradually ebbing. This may cause him to lose the joy, peace and power which his spirit ought to sustain. Day by day he grows weaker. At this time he seems to lose his taste for communion with God: his Bible reading becomes meaningless: rarely, if at all, is his heart touched by any message or special verse. Moreover, his prayer turns dry and dreary as if there is neither sense nor word; and his witnessing appears to be forced and reluctant, not overflowing as before. In other words, life is no longer as vibrant, strong, buoyant or joyous as before. Everything seems to have receded.

A tide has its ebb and flow. Can God's life and power in our spirit likewise be characterized by such phenomena? By no means! God's life knows no such ebb, because it is forever flowing. It does not rise and fall as the ocean tide, but is like a river ever flowing with living water (John 7.38). God's life in us is not at all like the tide which must ebb at a certain hour, because the source of our inner life is in God with Whom there is "no variation or shadow due to change" (James 1.17). Hence the life in our spirit should flow like a river—incessantly and unto overflowing.

Wherefore if anyone becomes aware that his life is receding, he should understand that life does not subside, it simply ceases to flow. He should know as well that such ebbing is totally unnecessary. Never be so deceived by Satan as to consider it impossible for one who is still in the body to be filled permanently with the life of God. His life in us is like a river of living water. If it is not hindered it shall flow uninterruptedly. A Christian can experience a life forever flowing; an ebb tide is not only unnecessary but abnormal as well.

The question in hand is accordingly not how we may induce spiritual life to rise up after it has fallen; rather, it is how we may get it to flow. The fountain of life remains within the believer, though it is now blocked. Nothing is wrong with the inlet; it is the outlet which is obstructed. The water of life does not spring forth because the flow has no way through. Were the outlet cleared, the water of life would flow unceasingly. What a child of God therefore needs is not more life but more flow of life.

Immediately upon sensing a waning in his spiritual life, a child of God automatically should realize an obstruction must exist somewhere. Satan will accuse you of having retrogressed spiritually; other people will judge you as having lost power; and you yourself will imagine you must have committed some grave sin. These may be true, but they do not form the whole truth. Actually, such a situation is *mostly*, though not entirely, created because of our not knowing how to cooperate with God in fulfilling His conditions for the certainty of a ceaseless flow. Foolishness is a prime factor. Hence a person should immediately pray and meditate over, and test and search out the cause for, such an ebbing. He should wait upon God, asking His Spirit to reveal the reason. In the meantime, he should try to unearth where he has failed to fulfill the condition for the steady flow of life.

Not only should you confess that you have drawn back (such confession is important) but also you should actively ferret out the explanation for the falling back. While the opinions of Satan, others and yourself are undependable, they are still worth considering, since sometimes they *are* real. Upon discovering the cause, you must deal with it without delay. Life will not flow until the cause of obstruction is duly treated.

Consequently, at each ebb tide in spiritual life one must instantly begin to isolate its cause through prayer, meditation and searching. Know the law of the flow of God's life; repulse every attack of the enemy. Then life once again shall flow, stronger than before, breaking through every stronghold of the enemy.

(7) IRRESPONSIBILITY OF THE SPIRIT

Man's spirit can be compared to an electric bulb. When in contact with the Holy Spirit, it shines; but should it be disconnected, it plunges into darkness. "The spirit of man is the lamp of the Lord" (Prov. 20.27). God's aim is to fill the human spirit with light; yet the believer's spirit is sometimes darkened. Why is this? It is because it has lost contact with the Holy Spirit. To perceive whether or not one's spirit is connected with the Holy Spirit, one need only notice if it is shining.

We have said before that God's Spirit dwells in man's and that he cooperates with Him through his own spirit. If the spirit of man has been deprived of its normal condition it will seem to be disconnected from the Holy Spirit, losing all its light. It thus is very necessary for us to maintain our spirit in a healthy quiet state so as to insure its cooperation with the Holy Spirit. If it is disturbed by external forces it automatically is bereft of its power to cooperate with the Holy Spirit and is plunged into darkness.

Now these phenomena cause the spirit to fail in its responsibility of cooperating with the Holy Spirit. As long as it is irresponsible, victory remains impossible. Suppose a person, rising in the morning, feels as though he has lost his spirit. The enemy will perhaps induce him to think it is due to physical weariness lingering from yesterday's overwork. If he takes the enemy's suggestion without question and allows his spirit to become irresponsible, he shall be stripped of all his strength to repel that day's temptations as well as to accomplish that day's work. He should search right away for the real cause, for the spirit ought to be active and powerful enough to regulate the body and not be adversely affected by it. He should acknowledge that his spirit, having been assaulted by the enemy, has become irresponsible. He must seek immediate recovery or else he shall be defeated the moment he meets anyone. Never permit the early irresponsible state of the spirit to continue until midday, for this is a sure way to defeat.

Once realizing his spirit has been irresponsible, a believer should oppose without delay all the works of the enemy as well as the causes for the enemy's work. Should it be purely the attack of the adversary the spirit will regain its freedom after having resisted. But if there is justification for the attack, that is, if the person has given any ground to the enemy, then he must uncover the reason and deal with it. Usually the reason is related to the past history of the individual. He needs to pray over such various matters as his environment, family, relatives, friends, work, and so forth. When his spirit senses a release after a certain matter has been prayed over, then he has isolated the cause for the enemy's assault. Shortly after he has taken care of this matter, the believer's spirit will be freed and restored to its function.

Sometimes, however, the irresponsibility of the spirit is because the Christian has loosened the reins, allowing the spirit to stray off course. But we should note from the Word that "the spirits of prophets are subject to prophets" (1 Cor. 14.32) and "woe to the foolish prophets who follow their own spirit" (Ezek. 13.3). How extremely important for a Christian to control his spirit by exercising his will so that his spirit may not go to extremes but be kept in that state of co-operation with God. Man's spirit can go wild; hence "a haughty spirit" is remarked upon in Proverbs (16.18). The spirit of man can take action independent of God's Spirit if a believer does not exercise mastery over it and make it subject to Him. We accordingly must be watchful lest our spirit veer out of God's orbit, lose its quiet communion with God, and be disabled from laboring with Him.

Occasionally the irresponsibility of the spirit is due to its hardness. God requires a soft and tender spirit to express His mind. Should it grow harsh and unyielding, the operations of His Spirit will be hindered. Only a yielding spirit can fulfill the thought of the divine Spirit: "and every one whom his spirit made willing . . . " (Ex. 35.21 ASV). A Christian ought to be able to yield to Him on the shortest notice. His spirit should be most sensitive so that it can detect the still small voice of God and respond right away. If it is hardened the child of God not only is powerless to follow His will but is also unfit to hear the voice of the Holy Spirit in his spirit. Hence it is necessary to keep one's spirit in a tender and pliable state so as to enable that one always to follow the delicate throbbing therein. This is what the Apostle meant when he wrote: "do not quench the Spirit" (1 Thess. 5.19). A Christian should heed every word, movement, and sense in his inner man carefully. By so doing, his spiritual consciousness will be sharpened and God will be able to make His will known to him.

If a person wishes to walk by his spirit he should recognize when it is irresponsible and unable to cooperate with the Holy Spirit and also determine why. He needs to guard his spirit carefully so as to insure it against all disturbances both from the enemy and from his self life and to assure it a peaceful communion with God.

(8) CONDITIONS OF THE SPIRIT

Let us summarize. A believer should know every law of the spirit if he desires to live by it. If he is not vigilant and loses the cooperation of his spirit with God, then he unquestionably has fallen. To discern the particular condition of his inner man is one of the most central laws pertaining to the spirit. All which we have discussed in the chapter are included in this law.

A child of God ought to know what is and what is not the normal condition for his spirit. Since it should have authority over man's soul and body, occupying the highest position in him and possessing the greatest power, the Christian needs to know if such is the situation in him or not. He should also recognize whether his spirit, if it has lost its normalcy, did so through war or environment. The conditions of the spirit may be classified generally into four types:

(a) The spirit is oppressed and is therefore in decline.
(b) The spirit is under compulsion and so is forced into inordinate activity.
(c) The spirit is defiled (2 Cor. 7.1) since it has yielded ground to sin.
(d) The spirit is quiet and firm because it occupies its rightful position.

A Christian should know at least these four different conditions and also understand how to deal with each one if necessary. Often a person's spirit sinks and is "pushed aside" through his own carelessness as to the enemy's assault. During that time he seems to have forfeited his heavenly position together with its brightness and victory and subsequently feels cold and withered. Due to sadness in his spirit or to any one of a number of other reasons, his inner man is cast down and is denied the joy of floating above. When the spirit is oppressed in this fashion it drops below its normal level.

At other times it may be coerced into running wild. A person can be so stimulated by his soul that his spirit falls under compulsion and is thereby denied its tranquillity. Because of his pursuit of creaturely activities he may develop an "unruly spirit." Too much laughter as well as many other actions may produce an unmanageable spirit. Protracted war with the enemy can provoke the spirit to become overly active. The saint may find his spirit overstretched to the point where it is powerless to stop. Or the enemy may inject strange joy or other feelings into him to entice his inner man to move beyond the acceptable and right counsel of his mind or will. Whenever anyone is incompetent to guard his spirit, then is he open inevitably to defeat.

The spirit on other occasions neither sinks too low nor is elevated too high but is simply defiled. The defilement may be due to its attitude of hardness or unyieldedness; or to sins like pride, jealousy and others; or to the mixing in with the spirit of such soulical functions as natural affection, feeling, thought, and so on. The spirit needs to be purified from its every defilement (2 Cor. 7.1; 1 John 1.9).

If a Christian wishes to walk after the spirit he has to discern exactly what condition his own is in, whether it is quietly occupying its proper place, has fallen too low, is risen too high, or is simply defiled. He must learn, if required, how to uplift his oppressed spirit so that it measures up to the standard of the Holy Spirit, how to exercise his will to prevent his spirit from becoming overly active or to restore it to its normalcy if it is too active, and how to cleanse his defiled spirit that it may work together with God once again.

CHAPTER 3

THE PRINCIPLE OF MIND AIDING THE SPIRIT

IF HE IS TO WALK after the spirit the Christian must understand its every law. Without this fund of knowledge he will not be able to apprehend all the meanings of the different spiritual senses and naturally will be unable to do everything required of him. The demands of the spirit are all expressed through the motions of the spirit. To disregard spiritual movements is to ignore spiritual demands. It is this which establishes the priority of knowing the laws of the spirit in one's spiritual life.

But there is something else of no less importance for anyone wishing to walk after the spirit: the principle of the mind aiding or assisting it. This principle is to be applied constantly. Many defeats in spiritual life can be traced to ignorance of it, even though the laws of the spirit are indeed known. And why? Because these laws can only explain to us the meaning of the spirit's stirring and supply us with ways to satisfy their particular demands. Whenever the spirit senses anything, we are equipped by the knowledge of these laws to fulfill the requirement called for; if the condition is normal, we walk accordingly; and if abnormal, we can correct it. But a problem arises here; which is, that we do not always enjoy such spiritual stirrings. The spirit simply may not speak. Many have experienced an utter silence for quite a few days. It appears as though it is sleeping. Is this to say that during those days when our spirit is inactive we should do nothing? Must we quietly sit for a number of days, neither praying nor reading the Bible nor performing any work? Our spiritual common sense vigorously replies: no; by no means should we waste the time. But if we do anything during that period will it not mean that we labor in the power of the flesh and not according to the spirit?

Now this is just the moment when we should apply the principle of the mind supporting the spirit. But how? When the spirit is sleeping, our mind must come in to do the work of the spirit. And before long we shall see the latter itself joining in the work. The mind and the spirit are closely knit: they are to help each other. Many times the spirit senses something which the mind is made to understand, and then action is taken; while on other occasions the spirit is unmoved and needs to be aroused by the activity of the believer's mind. If the spirit is inactive the mind can induce it to move. And once moved, the believer should follow it. Such inducement of the spirit by the mind is what we here term as the principle or law of the mind aiding the spirit. There is a principle in spiritual life which holds that in the *beginning* we should exercise our spiritual sense to apprehend God-given knowledge, but that afterwards we must keep and use this knowledge by means of the mind. For example, you notice a great need somewhere. According to the knowledge you have received from God, you realize you should pray and petition Him for supply. But at the time you see the need your spirit does not feel at all like praying. What should you do? You should pray with your *mind* instead of waiting for the spirit to move. Every need is a call to prayer. Although at the start you pray despite silence in your spirit, as you pray on you will soon be conscious of something rising within you. It signifies your spirit has joined in at last in this work of prayer.

Occasionally our inner man is so oppressed by Satan or so disturbed by the natural life that we can hardly discern it. It has sunk so low that it seems to have lost its consciousness. We continue to feel the presence of our soul and body, but the spirit appears to be absent. If we should wait for it to stir before we pray, we shall probably never do so, nor shall it regain its freedom. What we must do is pray with what the mind remembers to be the truth we once received and in that prayer resist the power of darkness. If ever we do not sense the spirit we should pray with our mind. Such mental activity eventually will incite our spirit to move.

"Pray(ing) with the mind" (1 Cor. 14.15) can activate the spirit. Although at the outset we may appear to be praying with empty words, divested of any meaning, nevertheless as we pray along with our mind and resist with prayer our spirit soon will ascend. Whereupon the spirit and the mind will work together. And as soon as it comes in, prayer becomes meaningful and quite free. The cooperation between these two elements delineates the normal state of spiritual life.

SPIRITUAL WARFARE

Should a believer in spiritual warfare neglect the law of spirit and mind working together, he will be waiting continually for God's burden instead of warring constantly against the enemy. Because he presently has no sense of war the believer concludes he must delay until he has that sense, and that only then can he begin to pray against the enemy. He does not perceive that if he starts to pray with his mind his spirit shall immediately sense the war. Since we know how wicked the evil spirit is and how he molests the children of the Lord as well as the children of man, and since we should realize also that we must pray against him in order to send him as early as possible to the bottomless pit, how dare we tarry to pray until our spirit acknowledges the urgency? Even though we still lack the consciousness of war, we must pray anyhow. Begin to pray with the mind: curse the evil spirit with the words we have learned already: and our spirit shall soon be activated and shall add its power behind those words of curse. To illustrate. Suppose the Holy Spirit in the early morning anoints you mightily so that you can curse the enemy with your spirit, but at noon you seem to have lost this spirit. What should you do? You should do by your mind now what your spirit had done in the morning. The spiritual principle is that whatever is obtained in the spirit must be preserved and employed by the mind.

RAPTURE

This law of the mind's assistance can be applied as well to

the matter of faith concerning "the rapture." At the beginning you enjoy the "spirit of rapture," but later on you feel as though it is drained of its awareness of the nearness of the Lord's return and the reality of your rapture. In that hour you should recall the law of the mind coming to the aid of the spirit. You ought to pray with the mind even while your spiritual sense is empty. If you merely wait to have your spirit refilled with the sense of rapture, you will never possess it again; but by exercising your mind to think and to pray, you shall shortly be filled with the spiritual awareness you once had.

PREACHING

For the preaching of the truth this principle is vital. Those truths learned in the past are now stored in our brain. Communicating to others what is in our mind simply *by our mind* can produce no spiritual results whatever. No doubt at first we knew those truths in our spirit, but currently the spirit seems to have receded and all which is left are memories. How, then, can our spirit be replenished with these truths so that we may communicate them *by the spirit* to others? By exercising our mind. We should re-meditate on those truths before God and pray over them once again; that is, we should take those truths as centers and pray around them. Shortly thereafter we shall discover our spirit being permeated once more with those truths which had been there before. These initially are possessed in the spirit, later are stored in the believer's mind, and now re-enter his spirit by praying with the mind. Thus are we qualified to preach the truths we once before had known in our spirit.

INTERCESSION

We all appreciate the importance of intercession. Yet often when we have time to spend in intercession our spirit is inactive and fails to supply us with subjects for intercessory prayer. This does not mean we need not pray on that occasion or that we can utilize the time for other matters. On the contrary, it serves as a hint for us to intercede in prayer with the mind and to hope and expect the spirit will be activated into participating. You should accordingly exercise your mind to remember your friends, relatives, and fellow-workers to determine if they are in need. As you remember each one so shall you in turn intercede for them. If in interceding on their behalf your spirit remains cold and dry, then you know you are not to pray for them. But supposing at that same time you recall a special lack in your local church or a number of temptations the church is facing or certain hindrances to the Lord's work in a particular area or some distinctive truths which God's children ought to know today. In that event you should intercede for each of them as they come to your attention. If after praying awhile over these matters your spirit still fails to respond as you are yet praying with your mind, then you realize once again that these are not what the Lord desires you to pray for today. But supposing as you touch upon certain matters in your prayer you feel as though the Holy Spirit is anointing you and your spirit seems to respond: it is at this singular moment that you recognize you are at last interceding for what is on the Lord's heart. Hence the principle calls for the exercise of the mind to help the spirit locate its trend.

Frequently a slight exercise of the mind effects the spirit's response, but on other occasions—due to our narrow-mindedness or our mental dullness—we may be forced to consume considerable time before the spirit cooperates. For example, God would like to enlarge the scope of our prayer to include the nations in order to defeat all the behind-the-scene works of Satan. Or He may want us to intercede for all sinners worldwide or for the entire church. *Your* mind, however, is fixed upon the immediate. It will require some time before our mind is ready to consider these all-embracing issues and begin to pray the prayer of the Holy Spirit. Yet as soon as our spirit joins in, we can and must discharge all the burdens which it has concerning this particular matter. We ought to pray carefully and thoroughly over each and every facet of this matter till our spirit is lightened of its burden. Only thereafter can we turn to intercede for other concerns.

This is indeed an important principle in our spiritual life. Whenever God gives us new prayers they usually are received in our spirit, but afterwards we cannot expect *God* to refill our spirit with those prayers. Instead, *we* should exercise our mind to pray continuously over them until our spirit once more regains its burdens.

KNOWING GOD'S WILL

God's guidance does not always come to us directly; it is sometimes indirect. In direct guidance the Spirit of God moves in our spirit and so enables us to know His will. If our mind is attentive to the movement in the spirit we shall easily understand the will of God. But in the various affairs of life God does not necessarily tell us many things directly. There may be many needs of which we as men are aware. What should we do about these conscious needs? We may be invited to work somewhere or something else may suddenly happen. Such matters as these obviously are not sponsored directly by our spirit, for they come to us from other people. Our mind sees the urgency of solving these problems, yet our spirit is unresponsive. How may we experience the guidance of God in such a situation? Well, when we encounter something of this kind, we must with our mind ask God to lead us in the spirit. By so doing we are experiencing the indirect guidance of God. This is the moment the mind must assist the spirit. When one notices his spirit is inactive he should exercise his mind. It is not necessary for it to assist if the spirit is exuding its thought incessantly: only as the spirit remains silent must the mind fill the gap for it.

In such circumstances the believer should exercise his mind by pondering this unsolved matter before God. Although such prayer and consideration emerge from his mind, before long his spirit will collaborate in the prayer and consideration. His spirit which he did not sense before he now begins to sense, and soon the Holy Spirit will be found leading him in his spirit. We should never sit back because of a lack of early movement therein. Rather should we use the mind to "scoop up" our spirit and activate it to help us know whether or not this matter is of God.

THE PRINCIPLE GOVERNING THE ACTIVITY OF THE SPIRIT

In our spiritual experience the operation of the mind is indispensable. Unlike the ocean tide, the spirit is not filled by spontaneous comings and goings. For it to be filled we must comply with the conditions for its filling. This is where the mind assumes its responsibility: to set in motion what the spirit will soon carry forward by itself. If we endlessly wait for the permeation of the spirit we shall be disappointed. On the other hand we should not too highly esteem the work of the mind. By this time we ought to know that unless our action comes from the spirit it serves no useful purpose. We must not walk after the mind. Why then do we engage the mind? We exercise it not for its sake but for the sake of inducing the *spirit* to work. Hence we continue to esteem the spirit as most important. Now if after our mind has been functioning for some time the spirit still fails to respond, as though there is no anointing, we must cease exercising it. Should we detect in spiritual warfare a prolonged emptiness deep within and our spirit continues to sense nothing, we ought to halt the working of the mind. We should not, however, stop its working because of the unwillingness of the flesh. Occasionally we feel tired and yet we know we must proceed. At other times we know we must cease. There is no fixed law over spiritual matters.

The mind supporting the spirit can be likened to operating a hand water pump. In some pumps it is essential to pour into it a cup of water just to provide suction for the machine while pumping. The relation of our mind to the spirit is similar to that between the cup of water and the water pump. If you do not use this cup of water as a starter you shall be powerless to pump up water from the well. Even so, our spirit will not rise up unless we exercise the mind first. Not to start praying with the mind for the sake of the spirit is like a man who neglects to pour in that cup of water first and concludes after pumping twice that there is not any water in the well.

How varied are the works of the spirit. Oftentimes it is like a lion full of strength; whereas at other times it is like a babe possessing no will of its own. When it is weak and helpless the mind must act as its nurse. The mind is never a subsitute for the spirit; the mind merely helps us to activate it. Should the spirit cease to assert its ruling position, the believed must use the power of his mind in prayer to provoke its reassertion. If the spirit has sunk through oppression he should employ his mind to survey the situation and to pray earnestly until it rises up and regains its freedom. A *spiritual* mind can maintain the spirit in a steady position. It can restrain the spirit from being overly active; it can also uplift the spirit from its fallen state.

Let us elaborate a bit further. As has been said, the spirit can be replenished only with the ministration of the spiritual mind. The principle is that all matters in which the spirit formerly took a hand should now be done by the mind. If the Holy Spirit grants anointing later on, He is attesting to you that you are doing this particular thing in the spirit. In the beginning there was nothing of a spiritual sensing about it but currently the sense in the inner man assures you that this is what it intended in the first place. The spirit was impotent to do it then because it was too weak; now, however, through the help of the mind, it can express what it could not express at the first. We can secure whatever we need in the spirit if we ponder and pray with the mind. This will cause us to be filled again in our spirit.

Another point needs to be observed. In spiritual conflict spirit struggles against spirit. But all the powers of man's entire being should join his spirit in wrestling against the enemy. Of these the mind is the most important. The spirit and the mind join forces in battle. Should the former become oppressed and begin to lose its power to resist, the latter must carry the fight forward on its behalf. As the mind contends and resists in prayer the spirit is thereby replenished and once more rises to the occasion.

THE CONDITION OF THE MIND

Inferior though it be to the spirit, the mind nonetheless can assist it. Besides bolstering a weak spirit, it should be able to read and search out the spirit's thought as well. How necessary, therefore, that the mind be kept in its normal state. Just as the movements of the spirit have their laws, so the activity of the mind is governed by its particular laws. The mind that can work freely is one which is light and lively. If it be expanded too far, like overstretching a bow, it shall sacrifice its effectiveness to work. The enemy well knows how we need our mind to attend the spirit so that we may walk by the spirit. Thus he frequently induces us to overuse it that it may be rendered unfit to function normally and hence be powerless to reinforce the spirit in time of weakness.

Our mind is much more than an organ of assistance to the spirit; it also is the place where we obtain light. The Spirit of God dispenses light to the mind through the spirit. If the mind is overexerted it relinquishes the power of receiving His light. The enemy understands that if our mind is darkened our whole being enters into darkness; he consequently strives with all his effort to provoke us to think so very much that we are unable to work quietly. To walk after the spirit a believer must inhibit his mind from revolving endlessly. If it turns too long around one topic, worries or grieves too much over matters, and ponders too intensively to know God's will, it may become unbearable and hamper its normal operation. The mind needs to be kept in a steady and secure state.

Since the mind occupies such a signal position, the Christian, when working together with others, must be careful not to break into his brother's thought. Such action creates much suffering for that one's mind. When his thoughts are being guided and led on by the Spirit, the believer is terribly apprehensive of interference. Any such act will terminate his thought and set his mind to stretch beyond its proper measure, rendering it unfit to cooperate with the Holy Spirit. Accordingly, not only must we keep our own mind free but we additionally must respect our brother's mind. We first must find out the trend of our brother's thought before we can respond to him; otherwise, we shall cause that brother to suffer unduly.

CHAPTER 4
THE NORMALCY OF THE SPIRIT

AN ERRING SPIRIT is often responsible for much of our incorrect conduct. If anyone desires to walk in a spiritual way he must keep himself continually in a proper state. Just as the mind may become loose and haughty or retreat and grow shy, so may his spirit. Should it not be maintained in the Holy Spirit, then it shall be defeated and his outward conduct shall equally suffer defeat. We ought to understand that numerous outer failures stem from the failure of the inner spirit. Were one's inner man strong and powerful it could control the soul and body and, under any circumstances, inhibit their license; but if it be weak, the soul and body shall oppress the spirit and cause that one to fall.

God is interested in our spirit. It is there that the new life dwells, there that His Spirit works, there that we fellowship with Him, there that we know His will, there that we receive the revelation of the Holy Spirit, there that we are trained, there that we mature, there that we resist the attacks of the enemy, there that we receive authority to overcome the devil and his army, and there that we secure the power for service. It is by the resurrection life in the spirit that our body eventually shall be changed into a resurrection one. As the condition of our spirit is so is the condition of our spiritual life. How essential for us to preserve our spirit in its normal state. What the Lord is especially concerned with in the Christian is not his outer man, the soul, but his inner man, the spirit. No matter how highly developed out outer man may be, if this inner component of ours is abnormal, our whole walk shall go askew.

The Bible is not silent about the normalcy of a believer's spirit. Many matured ones have experienced what the Bible exhorts; they recognize that to retain their triumphant position and to cooperate with God they must preserve their spirit in the proper conditions laid down in the Word. We shall shortly see how it is to be controlled by the renewed will of the believer. This is a principle of great consequence, for by the will one is able to set his spirit in its proper place.

A CONTRITE SPIRIT

"*Jehovah is nigh unto them that are of a broken heart, and saveth such as are of a contrite spirit*" (Ps. 34.18 ASV).
"*For thus says the high and lofty One who inhabits eternity, whose name is Holy: I dwell in the high and holy place, and also with him who is of a contrite and humble spirit*" (Is. 57.15).

God's people often erroneously think that they need a contrite spirit only at the time they repent and believe in the Lord or whenever they subsequently fall into sin. We should know, however, that God wishes us to keep our spirit in a state of contrition at all times. Although we do not daily sin we are nonetheless required by Him to be of humble spirit constantly, because our flesh still exists and may be stirred up at any moment. Such contrition precludes our losing watchfulness. We ought never sin; yet we always should have sorrow for sin. The presence of God is felt in such a spirit.

God takes no pleasure in our repenting over and over again as though this were sufficient; rather does He wish us to live in perpetual contrition. Only a spirit of this kind can equip us to detect and mourn immediately all disharmony with the Holy Spirit present in our conduct and deeds. It also helps us to acknowledge our faults when told of them. This penitent spirit is very necessary, for despite the fact a person has been joined to the Lord to be one spirit, he is not forever afterwards infallible. The spirit can err (Is. 29.24); even if it has not erred, the mind can be so confused as to paralyze it from executing the thought of the spirit. A contrite inner life helps one to confess instantly and to not hide those little points others have noticed in him as being unlike the Lord. God saves those who possess a contrite spirit; others He cannot save for it requires contrition to know His mind. People who cover their faults and excuse themselves do not have a repentant spirit; hence God cannot save them to the uttermost. How we need a spirit susceptible to the correction both of the Holy Spirit and of man, a spirit willing to concede to having lived below par. And then we shall daily experience the salvation of the Lord.

A BROKEN SPIRIT

"The sacrifice acceptable to God is a broken spirit" (Ps. 51.17).

A broken spirit is one which trembles before God. Some Christians do not sense any uneasiness in their inner man after they have sinned. A healthy spirit will be broken before God—as was David's—upon once having sinned. It is not difficult to restore to God those who have a broken spirit.

AN AFFLICTED SPIRIT

"But to this man will I look: to the afflicted and contrite in spirit, and who trembleth at my word" (Is. 66.2 Darby).

The spirit with which God is delighted is an afflicted one, because it reverences Him and trembles at His Word. Our spirit must be kept in continual reverential fear of the Lord. All self-reliance and self-conceit must be shattered; the Word of God must be accepted as the sole guide. The believer must possess within him a holy fear: he must have absolutely no confidence in himself: he must be as one whose spirit is so stricken that he dare not raise his head but humbly follows the command of God. A hard and haughty spirit always impedes the way of obedience. But when the cross is working deeply a believer comes to know himself. He realizes how undependable are his ideas, feelings and desires. Hence he dare not trust himself but trembles in all matters, acknowledging that except he be sustained by the power of God he shall unquestionably fail. We must never be independent of God. The moment our spirit ceases to tremble before Him at that precise moment it declares its independence from Him. Except we sense our helplessness we shall never trust in God. A spirit which trembles before Him shields one from defeat and helps him to truly apprehend God.

A LOWLY SPIRIT

"It is better to be of a lowly spirit with the poor than to divide the spoil with the proud" (Prov. 16.19) *"He who is lowly in spirit will obtain honor"* (Prov. 29.23). *"And also with him who is of a contrite and humble spirit, to revive the spirit of the humble"* (Is. 57.15).

Lowliness is not a looking down on one's self; rather is it a not looking at one's self at all. As soon as a believer's spirit becomes haughty he is liable to fall. Humility is not only Godward but is manward as well. A lowly spirit is demonstrated when one associates with the poor. It is this spirit alone which does not despise any who are created by God. God's presence and glory is manifested in the life of the spiritually humble.

A lowly person is a teachable person, easily entreated and open to explanation. Many of our spirits are too arrogant: they can teach others but can never themselves be taught. Many possess a stubborn spirit: they stick to their opinions even if they realize they are wrong. Many are too hard in spirit to listen to an explanation for a misunderstanding. Only the humble have the capacity to bear and forbear. God needs a lowly man to express His virtue. How can a proud man hear the voice of the Holy Spirit and then cooperate with God? No trace of pride should be found in our spirit: tenderness, delicacy, flexibility—these shall be the norm. A tiny bit of harshness in the inner man may hinder fellowship with the Lord, for this certainly is most unlike Him. To walk with the Lord the spirit must be lowly, forever waiting on Him and offering no resistance to Him.

POOR IN SPIRIT

"Blessed are the poor in spirit" (Matt. 5.3).

The poor in spirit views himself as possessing nothing. A believer's peril lies in his having too many things in his spirit. Only the poor in spirit can be humble. How often the experience, growth and progress of a Christian become such precious matters to him that he loses his lowliness. The most treacherous of all dangers for a saint is to meditate on what he appropriates and to pay attention to what he has experienced. Sometimes he engages in this unconsciously. What, then, is the meaning of being poor? Poor bespeaks having nothing. If one endlessly reflects upon the deep experience which he has passed through, it soon shall be debased to a commodity of his spirit and hence become a snare. An emptied spirit enables a person to lose himself in God whereas a wealthy spirit renders him self-centered. Full salvation delivers a believer *out* of himself and into God. Should a Christian retain something for himself his spirit immediately shall turn inward, unable to break out and be merged in God.

A GENTLE SPIRIT

"In a spirit of gentleness" (Gal. 6.1).

Gentleness is a most necessary feature of the inner man. It is the opposite of harshness. God requires us to cultivate a gentle spirit. Amid the most prosperous work anyone with a gentle spirit can instantly stop on short notice from God, just as Philip did when sent from Samaria to the desert. A gentle spirit turns easily in God's hand however He wills. It knows not how to resist God nor how to follow its own will. God needs such a yielding spirit to accomplish His purpose.

A gentle spirit is no less important in human relationships. It is the spirit of a lamb which characterizes the spirit of the cross. "When he was reviled, he did not revile in return;

when he suffered, he did not threaten" (1 Peter 2.23). This is a description of a gentle spirit. Such gentleness is willing to suffer loss; though it has the power of revenge and the protection of the law, it nevertheless has no wish to avenge itself with the arm of flesh. It is a spirit which in suffering harms no one. The one who can boast such a spirit as this lives righteously himself but never demands righteousness from others. He is full of love and mercy; wherefore he can melt the heart of those around him.

A FERVENT SPIRIT

"In diligence not slothful; fervent in spirit; serving the Lord" (Rom. 12.11 ASV).

For a time the flesh may be fervent when it is emotionally excited, but this fervency does not endure. Even when the flesh seems most diligent it actually may be quite lazy, since it is diligent solely in those things with which it agrees; hence the flesh is impelled by emotion. It cannot serve God in matters which do not appeal to it nor when emotion is cold and low. It is impossible for the flesh to labor with the Lord in cloud as well as in sunshine, step by step, slowly but steadily. "Fervent in spirit" is a permanent feature; he therefore who possesses this spirit is qualified to serve the Lord endlessly. We should avoid all fervency of the flesh but allow the Holy Spirit to so fill our inner man that He may keep it perpetually fervent. Then our spirit will not turn cold when our emotion becomes chilled, nor will the work of the Lord collapse into a seemingly immovable state.

What the Apostle stresses here amounts to an order. This order must be taken up by our renewed will. We should exercise it to choose to be fervent. We should say to ourselves, "I want my spirit to be fervent and not to be cold." We should not be overwhelmed by our icy and indifferent feeling; instead we should permit our fervent spirit to control everything, even where our emotion is extremely unconcerned. The sign of a fervent spirit is serving the Lord *always*.

A COOL SPIRIT

"He who has a cool spirit is a man of understanding" (Prov. 17.27).

Our spirit needs to be fervent yet also to be cool. Fervency is related to "diligence in serving the Lord" whereas coolness is related to knowledge.

If our spirit lacks coolness we often take inordinate action. The enemy purposes to drive us off track in order that our spirit may be deprived of its contact with the Holy Spirit. Frequently we observe saints who, in the hour of a feverish spirit, change their principled life into a sensational one. The spirit is closely knit with the mind. The moment the spirit loses its composure the mind is excited; when the mind becomes heated the conduct of the believer grows abnormal and goes out of control. Consequently it is always profitable to keep the inner man calm and collected. By disregarding the ardor of the emotion, the increase of desire, or the confusion of thought and by measuring every problem with a cool spirit instead, we shall maintain our feet on the pathway of the Lord. Any action taken when our spirit is excited is likely to be against the will of God.

The knowledge of God, self, Satan and all things brings calmness to our spirit; it effects a kind of spirit which soulish believers never experience. The Holy Spirit must fill our inner man while the outer man must be consigned entirely to death; then the spirit will enjoy an unspeakable calm. Neither the soul nor the body nor changing environment takes away that calm. It is like the ocean: although the waves rage on the surface, the bottom of the sea remains composed and undisturbed. Before a Christian experiences the dividing of soul and spirit he will be disturbed and shaken immediately by the slightest perturbation. This is due to lack of spiritual knowledge. Hence to keep the inner and outer man divided is the way to keep the spirit cool. A person with an imperturbable spirit experiences a kind of "untouchableness." However chaotic may be the outside situation he does not lose the calm and peace inside. Though a mountain should fall at his face he remains as composed as ever. Such composure is not achieved through self-improvement but is secured through the revelation of the Spirit Who discloses the reality of all things and through the control the believer exerts over his soul so that it no longer may influence his spirit.

The key, therefore, is the rule of the will. Our spirit must accept this rule. Fervency is what our will desires, but so is coolness. We should never permit our spirit to be in such a condition as to extend beyond the control of the will. We must will both to have a fervent spirit towards the Lord's work and to maintain a cool spirit in executing that work.

A JOYFUL SPIRIT

"*My spirit rejoices in God my Savior*" (Luke 1.47).

Towards himself a Christian should have a broken spirit (Ps. 51.17), but towards God it should be one of rejoicing always in Him. He rejoices not for its own sake nor because of any joyful experience, work, blessing or circumstance, but exclusively because God is his center. Indeed, no saint can genuinely rejoice out of any cause other than God Himself.

If our spirit is oppressed by worry, weight and sorrow it will commence to be irresponsible, next sink down, then lose its proper place, and finally become powerless to follow the leading of the Holy Spirit. When pressed down by a heavy load the spirit loses its lightness, freedom and brightness. It quickly topples from its ascendant position. And should the time of sorrow be prolonged, damage to spiritual life is incalculable. Nothing can save the situation except to rejoice in the Lord—rejoice in what God is and how He is our Savior. The note of hallelujah must never be in short supply in the spirit of the believer.

A SPIRIT OF POWER

"*For God did not give us a spirit of timidity but a spirit of power and love and self-control*" (2 Tim. 1.7).

Timidity is not humility. While humility is self-forgetfulness completely—a forgetting both its weakness and strength—timidity recalls all the weakness and hence is self-remembering. God does not delight in our cowardice and withdrawal. He wants us, on the one hand, to tremble before Him because of our emptiness, yet on the other hand, to proceed courageously in His might. He requires us to bear Him witness fearlessly, to suffer pain and shame for Him valiantly, to accept loss of all things with courage, and to rely on the Lord's love, wisdom, power and faithfulness with confidence. Whenever we discover ourselves shrinking from witnessing for the Lord or withdrawing in other ways where boldness is demanded, we should realize that our spirit has abandoned its normal state. We ought to preserve it in a condition of "dauntlessness."

We need to have a spirit of power, of love, and of self-control. It should be strong, but not to the point of becoming unloving. It is also mandatory that it be quiet and controlled so that it may not be excited easily. We must have a spirit of power towards the enemy, a spirit of love towards men, and a spirit of self-control towards ourselves.

A QUIET SPIRIT

"Let it be the hidden person of the heart with the imperishable jewel of a gentle and quiet spirit, which in God's sight is very precious" (1 Peter 3.4).

Granted that this is a word directed towards the sisters, it nonetheless is spiritually applicable to the brothers as well.

"To aspire to live quietly" (1 Thess. 4.11). This is the duty of every Christian. Modern Christians talk far too much. Sometimes their unuttered words surpass in number those that are spoken. Confused thought and endless speech set our spirits to wandering away from the control of our wills. A "wild spirit" often leads people to walk according to the flesh. How hard for believers to restrain themselves from sinning when their spirits become unruly. An errant spirit invariably ends up with an error in conduct.

Before one can display a quiet mouth he first must possess a quiet spirit, for out of the abundance of the spirit does the the mouth speak. We ought to carefully keep our spirit in stillness; even in time of intense confusion our inner being should nevertheless be able to sustain an independent quietude. A placid spirit is essential to anyone walking after the spirit: without it he shall quickly fall into sin. If our spirit is hushed we can hear the voice of the Holy Spirit there, obey the will of God, and understand what we cannot understand when confused. Such a quiet inner life constitutes the Christian's adornment which betokens something manifested outwardly.

A NEWNESS OF SPIRIT

"*We should serve in newness of spirit*" (Rom. 7.6 Darby).

This too is a serious facet of spiritual life and work. An old spirit cannot inspire people: the best it can do is pass on some thought to others: even so, it is weak and therefore powerless to stimulate earnest consideration. An aged spirit can only produce aged thought. Never can dynamic life flow out from an old spirit. Whatever issues from a decrepit spirit (words, teaching, manner, thought, life) are but old, stale and traditional. Perhaps many doctrines do in fact reach another believer's mind, but they gain no footing in his spirit; as a consequence, it is impossible to touch the spirits of others because there is no spirit behind one's teaching. It is conceivable that the one who harbors an old spirit has once experienced some of the truths, but they have now become mere remembrances of the past, purely pleasant memories. These truths have been transferred from the spirit to the mind. Or perhaps they have just been new ideas freshly conceived in his mind, and due to lack of confirmation in life they simply do not impart the touch of a fresh spirit to the audience.

Time and again we meet various Christians who habitually convey something new from the Lord. While we are with them we feel they have *just* left the Lord's presence, as though they would bring us right back to the Lord. This is what newness means; anything else is oldness. Such ones appear to enjoy renewed strength all the time, soaring like eagles and running like youths. Instead of imparting dried, corrupted, and worm-eaten manna of the mind to people, these give fish and bread freshly cooking on the fire of the spirit. Deep and wonderful thoughts never move people as a fresh spirit can.

We must maintain a fresh spirit continually. How can we face people if our inner man does not give the impression of having been newly with the Lord and newly blessed of the Lord? Anything—life, thought, experience—which has reduced itself to a remembrance of the past is old and aged. Moment by moment we must receive everything anew from the Lord. To imitate the experiences of another without ourselves having it in life is forbidden; but to copy from the relics of our own past experience is likewise ineffective. Thus we can grasp the import of what Christ enunciated as recorded in John: "'I live because of the Father" (6.57). Our inner man shall remain unceasingly fresh if we momentarily draw upon the life of the Father to be our life. A stale spirit generates no fruit in work, inspires no walk after the spirit, and achieves no victory in warfare. An old spirit cannot face others because it has not faced God. To enjoy a spirit that is always fresh and new, one's inner being must be in constant touch with God.

A HOLY SPIRIT

"To be holy in body and spirit" (1 Cor. 7.34). *"Let us cleanse ourselves from every defilement of body and spirit"* (2 Cor. 7.1).

For anyone to walk in a spiritual manner it will be necessary for him to keep his spirit holy at all times. An unholy spirit leads people into error. Inordinate thought towards men or things, assessing the evil of others, a lack of love, loquacity, sharp criticism, self-righteousness, refusing entreaty, jealousy, self-pride, and so forth—all these can defile the spirit. An unholy spirit cannot be fresh and new.

In our pursuit of spiritual life we must not overlook any sin, because sin inflicts more harm upon us than does anything else. Even though we already have learned how to be delivered from sin and how to walk by the spirit, we nevertheless must guard against unknowingly returning to the old sinful ways. For such a return renders a walk after the spirit utterly impossible. The child of God therefore needs to maintain an attitude of death towards sin lest it overcome him and poison his spirit. Without holiness no one can see the Lord (Heb. 12.14).

A STRONG SPIRIT

"Become strong in spirit" (Luke 1.80).

Our spirit is capable of growth and should increase gradually in strength. This is indispensable to spiritual life. How often we sense our spirit is not strong enough to control our soul and body, especially the moment the soul is stimulated or the body is weak. Sometimes in helping others we notice how heavily weighed down they are in their spirit, yet ours lacks the power to release them. Or when battling with the enemy we discover our spiritual strength is inadequate to wrestle long enough with the enemy until we win. Numberless are those occasions when we feel the spirit losing its grip; we have to force ourselves to proceed in life and in work. How we long for a more robust inner man!

As the spirit waxes stronger the power of intuition and discernment increases. We are fit to resist everything not of the spirit. Some who wish to walk after the spirit cannot because their inner man lacks the strength to control the soul and the body. We cannot expect the Holy Spirit to do anything for us; our regenerated spirit must instead cooperate with Him. We should learn how to *exercise* our spirit and use it to the limit of our understanding. Through exercise it will become progressively sturdier till it possesses the strength to eliminate all obstructions to the Holy Spirit; such hindrances as a stubborn will, a confused mind, or an undisciplined emotion.

"A man's spirit will endure sickness; but a broken spirit who can bear?" (Prov. 18.14) Clearly the spirit can be broken or wounded. A wounded spirit must be a very weak one. Were our spirit sturdy we would be able to endure the stimulation of the soul and *not shake*. Moses' spirit is usually portrayed as being a very strong one; yet because he failed to keep it continually firm, he found that the Israelites "made his spirit bitter" (Ps. 106.33) and consequently he sinned. If our inner being remains vigorous we can triumph in Christ however much our body may suffer or our soul be afflicted.

The Holy Spirit alone can grant us the strength required by the inner man. The might of our spirit accordingly derives from the power of God's Spirit. Ours itself, though, needs additionally to be trained. After one has learned how to walk by his spirit, he will then know how to live by its life in place of soul life, how to use its power instead of his natural power in performing God's work, and how to apply its strength rather than his soulical strength in warring against the enemy. Naturally, such experiences are progressive and must be entered into progressively. Yet the principle is clear: as a believer moves according to the spirit he will gain increased power of the Holy Spirit and his inner man will grow stronger. A Christian ought to maintain his spirit in strength at all times lest at the critical moment he is powerless to meet the need.

ONE SPIRIT

"Ye stand fast in one spirit" (Phil. 1.27 ASV).

We have observed previously how the life of a spiritual man flows with that of other Christians. Oneness of the spirit is a matter of great moment. If by His Spirit God dwells in the believer's spirit and He fully unites with him, how can his spirit not be one with other believers? A spiritual man is not only one with Christ in God but also one with God indwelling each of His children. Should a Christian permit thought or feeling to control his spirit, it will not be one with that of other saints. Only when mind and emotion are subject to the spirit's rule can he disregard or restrain differences in thought and feeling and so be one in the spirit with all children of God. It is necessary for him to guard unceasingly the oneness of spirit with *all* believers. We are not united with a small group—those who share the same interpretation and outlook as we—but with the body of Christ. Our spirit should harbor neither harshness nor bitterness nor bondage but be completely open and entirely free, thus creating no wall in our contact with all other brethren.

A SPIRIT FULL OF GRACE

"The grace of our Lord Jesus Christ be with your spirit" (Gal. 6.18). *"The grace of the Lord Jesus Christ be with your spirit"* (Philemon 25).

The grace of the Lord Jesus Christ is exceedingly precious to our spirit. There we find the Lord's grace to help us in time of need. This is a word of benediction: but this also represents the peak a believer's spirit can ever reach. We should always season our spirit with the grace of our lovely Lord.

A SPIRIT OF RAPTURE

One other facet of the normal spirit needs to be discussed besides those features mentioned already. This one we would term the spirit of rapture. Christians ought to have a spirit which is perpetually in an out-of-this-world and ascending-into-heaven state. Such a spirit as this is deeper than one of ascension, for those who possess the former not only live on earth as though in heaven but also are truly led of the Lord to wait for His return and their own rapture. When a believer's spirit is united to the Lord's and they become one spirit, he commences to live in the world as a sojourner, experiencing the life of a heavenly citizen. Following that, the Holy Spirit will call him to take one further step and will give him the spirit of rapture. Formerly his impetus was "Go forward!"—now it becomes "Ascend up!" Everything about him rises heavenward. The spirit of rapture is that spirit which has tasted the powers of the age to come (Heb. 6.5).

Not all who accept the truth of the Second Coming possess this spirit of rapture. Men may believe in the Lord's return, preach His Second Coming, and pray for His return and yet not have this spirit. Even mature ones do not necessarily possess it. The spirit of rapture is the gift of God. It is sometimes dispensed by God as He pleases and sometimes granted by Him in response to prayers of faith. When possessed of this spirit the believer's inner being seems always to be in a state of rapture. He believes not only in the return of the Lord but also in his being transported. Rapture is more than an article of faith; it is to him a fact. Just as Simeon, through the revelation of the Holy Spirit, trusted that he would not taste death before he had seen the Lord's Christ (Luke 2. 26), so believers should have the assurance in their spirit that they will be transported to the Lord before they die. Such faith is the faith of an Enoch. Now we are not being stubbornly superstitious here; but if we live in the time of rapture, how can we be lacking in such faith? Such belief will help us to understand more of what God is doing in this age as well as obtain heavenly power for our work.

In other words, if the spirit of a Christian is in a state of rapture he will be more heavenly and will not think his way to heaven must necessarily traverse the valley of death.

How frequently God's child, when engaged in spiritual labor, entertains many expectations and plans. He is full of the Holy Spirit, wisdom and power; he believes God will greatly use him; and he looks forward with anticipation that before long his labor shall produce much fruit. However, in the very midst of prosperity the hand of the Lord suddenly sweeps down upon him, suggesting to him that he must conclude all his undertaking and be ready to take another course. This comes as a genuine surprise to man. He naturally asks why it must be so. Is not my power for working? Is not the profound knowledge I have for helping people? Need everything be closed in and cold? Nonetheless, under guidance of this kind the believer learns that the purpose of God for him is an alteration in his course. Previously everything was going forward; henceforth it is to ascend. It does not signify there is no more work; what it does mean is that that work can be concluded at any time.

God continually has employed such circumstances as persecution, opposition, plunder, etc., to cause saints to comprehend that He wishes them to have the spirit of rapture rather than to make progress in the work on earth. The Lord desires to change the course of His children, many of whom do not realize there is this far better spirit of rapture.

This spirit has its definite effect on life. Before one secures it his experience is bound to be changing constantly; after he receives the witness and assurance of rapture in his spirit, however, his life and labor will be sustained on a level worthy of this kind of spirit, thus preparing him for the Lord's return. Such preparation includes more than outward correction: it is making the spirit, the soul, and the body of the believer wholly ready to meet the Lord.

Hence we should pray and petition the Holy Spirit to show us how to obtain this spirit of rapture and how to retain it. We should believe and then be willing to eliminate all obstacles to the realization of such a spirit. And once we have appropriated it we should habitually check our life and work against it. In case we lose this spirit we should determine at once how it was lost and how it can be restored. Such a spirit once obtained can be easily forfeited. This may be due chiefly to our ignorance (at this stage of life) of how to preserve such a heavenly position through special prayer and effort. We must therefore ask the Holy Spirit to teach us the way to retain this spirit. Such prayer usually leads us to seek "the things that are above" (Col. 3.2), and this is one of the requisites for preservation.

Since he now stands at the door of heaven and can be transported at any moment, the Christian should choose to wear the heavenly white garment and perform heavenly work. Such a hope separates him from earthly matters while joining him to the heavenly.

The fact that God wishes a believer to look for rapture does not suggest that he should be concerned only with his rapture and forget the remainder of the work God has appointed him. What God actually designs to convey to him is that he should not permit God-given labor to hinder his rapture. In both his walk and work, heavenly attraction should always be greater than earthly gravitation. The child of God should learn to live for the Lord's service, but even moreso for the Lord's receiving him. May our spirit be uplifted daily, looking for the return of the Lord. May the things of this world so lose their power over us that we do not in the slightest wish to be "worldly"; nay, we even delight in not remaining "in the world." May our spirit daily ascend, asking to be with the Lord earlier. May we so seek the things above that not even the best work on earth can distract our hearts. May we henceforth pray in spirit and with understanding, "Come, Lord Jesus!" (Rev. 22.20)

PART SEVEN

THE ANALYSIS OF THE SOUL—EMOTION

CHAPTER 1

THE BELIEVER AND EMOTION

ALTHOUGH A CHRISTIAN may have experienced deliverance from sin, he shall continue to be soulish—that is, powerless to overcome his natural life—if he fails to experience additionally the deep work of the cross wrought by the Holy Spirit. A limited description of the life and work of soulish Christians has been given earlier. Careful study of the soulish reveals that the conduct and action of such ones stem principally from their emotion. While the soul possesses three primary functions most soulish or carnal Christians belong to the emotional category. Their whole life appears to revolve largely around the impulses of emotion. In human affairs it seems to occupy a greater area than mind and will: it apparently plays a bigger role in daily life than do the other parts of the soul. Hence nearly all the practices of the soulish originate with emotion.

THE FUNCTION OF EMOTION

Our emotion emits joy, happiness, cheerfulness, excitement, elation, stimulation, despondency, sorrow, grief, melancholy, misery, moaning, dejection, confusion, anxiety, zeal, coldness, affection, aspiration, covetousness, compassion, kindness, preference, interest, expectation, pride, fear, remorse, hate, *et al.* The mind is the organ of our thinking and reasoning and the will, of our choices and decisions. Aside from our thought and intent and their related works, all other operations issue from emotion. Our thousand and one diverse feelings manifest its function. Feeling comprises such a vast area of our existence that most carnal Christians belong to the emotional type.

Man's sensational life is most comprehensive, hence highly complicated; to help believers understand it, we can gather all its various expressions into the three groups of (1) affection, (2) desire, and (3) feeling. These groups cover the three aspects of the function of emotion. Should a saint overcome all three, he is well on the way to entering upon a pure spiritual path.

To be sure, man's emotion is nothing but the manifold feelings he naturally has. He may be loving or hateful, joyful or sorrowful, excited or dejected, interested or uninterested, yet all are but the ways he feels. Should we take the trouble to observe ourselves we will easily perceive how changeful are our feelings. Few matters in the world are as changeable as emotion. We can be one way one minute and feel quite opposite the next. Emotion changes as feeling changes, and how rapidly the latter can change. He therefore who lives by emotion lives without principle.

The emotion of man often displays a reactionary motion: a time of activity in one direction will sometimes produce an opposite reaction. For example, unspeakable sorrow usually follows upon hilarious joy, great depression after high excitement, deep withdrawal after burning fervor. Even in the matter of love, it may commence as such but due to some emotional alteration it may end up with a hatred whose intensity far exceeds the earlier love.

A BELIEVER'S EMOTIONAL LIFE

The more one probes the workings of an emotional life the more he will be convinced of its vacillation and undependability. No one should wonder that a child of God who walks by emotion rather than by spirit usually comports himself in a wavelike fashion. He bemoans his existence because it is so unstable. Sometimes he appears to live in the third heaven transcending everything, while at other times he plunges to the low level of an ordinary man. His experience is replete with ups and downs. It does not require an enormous circumstance to change him, for he is unable to withstand even the tiniest mishap.

Such phenomena exist because a person is controlled by feeling and not by spirit. Since the dominant impulse in his walk continues to be emotion, it not having yet been delivered to the cross, his spirit will receive no strengthening of the Holy Spirit. Wherefore this one's spirit is weak, helpless to subdue emotion and through it to govern the whole man. If, however, by the power of the Holy Spirit he has his emotional life crucified and accepts the Holy Spirit as the Lord over all things, he most assuredly can avoid this kind of alternating existence.

Emotion may be denominated the most formidable enemy to the life of a spiritual Christian. We know a child of God ought to walk by the spirit. To walk this way he needs to observe every direction given by his inner man. We know also, however, that these senses of the spirit are delicate as well as keen. Unless the child of God waits quietly and attentively to receive and discern the revelation in his intuition, he never can secure the guidance of his spirit. Consequently, the *total silence* of emotion is an indispensable condition to walking by the spirit. How often its small and delicate motion is disturbed and overpowered by the roaring of one's emotion. On no account can we attribute any fault to the smallness of the spirit's voice, for we have been endowed with the spiritual capacity to be able to hear it. No, it is entirely the mixing in of other voices that causes the

Christian to miss the spirit's voice. But for that person who will maintain his emotion in silence, the voice of intuition can be detected easily.

The upsurge and decline of feeling may not only disqualify a believer from walking in the spirit but may also directly cause him to walk in the flesh. If he cannot follow the spirit he will naturally follow the flesh. Because he is unfit to obtain the guidance of his spirit, he invariably turns to his emotional impulse. Be it therefore recognized that when the spirit ceases to lead, emotion will do so. During such a period the believer will interpret emotional impulses to be motions of inspiration. An emotional Christian can be compared to a pond of sand and mud: as long as no one disturbs the water the pond looks clear and clean; but let it be agitated a moment and its true muddy character appears.

INSPIRATION AND EMOTION

Many saints cannot distinguish inspiration from emotion. Actually these two can be defined readily. Emotion always enters from man's *outside,* whereas inspiration originates with the Holy Spirit in man's spirit. When a believer surveys the beauty of nature, he naturally senses a kind of feeling welling up within him. As he admires the fascinating landscape he is moved with pleasure. This is emotion. Or when he meets his loved one there surges through him an unspeakable feeling as though some sort of power is attracting him. This too is emotion. Both the beautiful scenery and the beloved one are outside the man—hence the stirrings aroused by these external elements belong to emotion. Inspiration, on the other hand, is quite the reverse. It is exclusively effected by the Holy Spirit *within* man. God's Spirit alone inspires; since He dwells in the human spirit, inspiration must come from within. Inspiration may be imparted in the coldest and most tranquil environment; it does not require the encouragement of scenic wonder or of dear ones. Emotion is just the opposite: it withers the instant outside help is removed. And so an emotional person thrives wholly in accordance with the particular environment of the given moment: with stimulation he can press on, without it he folds up. But inspiration needs no such outside aid; on the contrary, it becomes confused should emotion be unduly influenced by external environment.

The Lord's people should be cautious, however, lest they view coldness and absence of constraint to be barometers of spirituality. Such an assumption is far from the truth. Know we not that the mark of emotion is dejection as well as excitation? Know we not that emotion cools as well as stirs? When emotion arouses a man he is elated, but when it mollifies him he feels depressed. Driven by high emotion, the Christian commits many errors. Upon awakening to this fact, however, he tends to suppress his feelings altogether. And so now he conceives himself as spiritual. Yet what he does not realize is that this is but a reactionary impulse of that self-same *emotion* of his which has calmed him down; that following a time of excitement, there is bound to emerge an emotional *re*-action. Such coldness and dullness precipitates the believer to lose interest in God's work: it deprives him as well his brotherly affection towards God's children. Because of the reluctance of the outer man to work, the believer's inner man is imprisoned and the life of the spirit is powerless to flow out. Now during this episode the saint may deem himself to be walking after the spirit, for, he reasons within himself, am I not today an extremely cold person and no longer burning wildly as before? Little does this Christian comprehend that he continues to walk after emotion anyway, only this time after the other extreme of emotion!

Few are the cases, however, of Christians turning cold. Most of them continue to be propelled forward by their high emotion. In the moment of excitement they do many things beyond proper bounds, actions which during subsequent periods of calmness they themselves would deride and consider nonsense. Deeds done under excitement often induce pangs of regret and remorse in retrospect. How distressing that Christians lack the spiritual strength to consign their inordinate feeling to death and to deny its control.

Two reasons can be offered why many walk according to their emotion. First, since they do not understand what walking according to the spirit is nor have ever sought to so walk, they will naturally walk according to the movement of emotion. Because they have never learned how to deny the agitation of their emotion, they are simply swept along by it and do those deeds which they ought not do. Their spiritual sense verily raises its objection, but these individuals so lack spiritual power that they completely disregard its objection and heed their feeling instead. The latter beats stronger and stronger in them until they are completely carried away. They do what they should not; and after having done it they repent for having so done. Second, even those who have experienced the dividing of spirit and soul and who recognize the stirrings of emotion as being soulish and instantly resist can nonetheless walk after emotion. This is due to the success of "spiritual" counterfeit. Before anyone becomes spiritual he is overwhelmed by his powerful emotional feelings; but after he becomes spiritual his emotion often pretends to be his spiritual sense. Outwardly these two are difficult to differentiate, because they appear to be nearly identical. For lack of knowledge, the saints can be deceived. And as a consequence they exhibit many carnal actions.

We should remember that in walking after the spirit all our actions must be governed by *principles*, since the spirit has its own laws and principles. To walk by the spirit is to walk according to its laws. With spiritual principles everything becomes sharply defined. There is a precise standard of right and wrong. If it is "yes" it is "yes" whether the day is clear or cloudy; if it is "no" then it is "no" whether exciting or depressive. The Christian's walk should follow a distinct standard. But if his emotion is not handed over to death, he cannot abide a permanent standard. He will live by the whim of his vacillating feelings and not according to a definite principle. A principled life differs enormously from an emotional life. Anyone who acts from emotion cares neither for principle nor for reason but only for his feeling. Should he be happy or thrilled he may be tempted to undertake what he ordinarily knows is unreasonable. But when he feels cold, melancholy or despondent he will not so much as fulfill his duty, for his feeling fails to go along. If God's children would pay a little attention to their emotion, they would note how changeable it actually can be and how dangerous it therefore is to walk by it. So often their attitude is: if the Word of God (spiritual principle) agrees with their feeling, they observe it; if the Word does not, they simply reject it. What an enemy emotion can be to spiritual life! All who desire to be spiritual must conduct themselves daily according to principle.

One quality which characterizes a spiritual person is the great calm he maintains under every circumstance. Whatever may happen around him or however much he may be provoked, he accepts it all calmly and exhibits an unmovable nature. He is one who is able to regulate his every feeling, because his emotion has been yielded to the cross and his will and spirit are permeated with the power of the Holy Spirit. No extreme provocation has the strength to unsettle him. But if one has not accepted the dealing of the cross upon his emotion, then he will be easily influenced, stimulated, disturbed, and even governed by the external world. He will undergo constant change, for emotion shifts often. The slightest threat from outside or the smallest increase in work shall upset him and render him helpless. Whoever genuinely desires to be perfect must let the cross cut deeper into his emotion.

If the Christian would simply bear in mind that God does not lead anyone who is in turmoil, he might be spared many errors. Never decide on anything or start to do anything while emotion is agitating like a roaring sea; it is in times of great emotional upheaval that mistakes are readily made. Our mind too becomes undependable in such periods because it is easily affected by feeling. And with a powerless mind, how can we ever distinguish right from wrong? Again, during that time even our conscience is rendered unreliable. As emotion pulsates, the mind becomes deceived and conscience is denied its standard of judgment. Whatever is decided and performed in such circumstances is bound to be improper and will be something to be regretted afterwards. A believer should exercise his will to resist and to terminate such fomented feeling; solely when his emotion is no longer boiling but returns to perfect calm can he decide what he should do.

Similarly, one should refrain from doing anything which might stir up his emotion unnecessarily. Sometimes it is peaceful and quiet, but subsequently we do something willfully our own which immediately activates the emotion unduly. Such cases are frequent, with great damage inflicted upon our spiritual life. We must deny all that disturbs the peace of our soul. Not only should we not do anything during emotional crisis; we also should not do anything which tends to induce such a crisis. Does this therefore imply the opposite: that we can do nothing wrong if what we do is decided or performed in a time of emotional quietude? Not necessarily at all, for instead of being led by the spirit we may unfortunately be led by our "cold emotion." If such be the case, the work we do shall soon activate our "warm" emotion. Those who have had experiences along this line may recall how in writing a letter or meeting a person their emotion became greatly agitated, proving that what they were undertaking was out of God's will.

EMOTION AND WORK

Heretofore we have stressed the truth that the spirit alone can do spiritual work, so that any work not achieved by it counts for nothing. This truth is so vital that we feel led to restate it in additional detail.

Today men give much attention to psychology. Even many who serve the Lord feel they *must* diligently study psychology. These believe if only their words, teachings, presentations, manners and interpretations can be made psychologically appealing to people, that many could be won to Christ. Psychology naturally refers in large part to the workings of man's emotion. Occasionally it does seem to be helpful, but a child of God who relies on emotion serves no productive purpose for the Lord.

We recognize already that regeneration of the spirit is the paramount need of man. Any work which cannot quicken man's dead spirit or impart to man God's uncreated life or give him the Holy Spirit to indwell his regenerated spirit proves thoroughly futile. Neither our psychology nor that of the unbelievers can impart life to them. Unless the Holy Spirit Himself performs the work, all is vain.

A Christian should understand that his emotion is wholly natural; it is not the source of God's life. If he in fact acknowledges that no life of God resides in his emotion, he will never attempt to secure the salvation of people by means of his power of emotion through tears, mournful face, cries, or other emotional devices. No efforts of his emotion can affect in the slightest the darkened human spirit. Except the Holy Spirit gives life, man can have no life. If we do not rely on the Spirit and use emotion instead, our work will yield no real fruit.

Those who labor for the Lord need to see distinctly that nothing in man can generate God's life. We may exhaust every psychological method to excite man's emotion, to arouse his interest in religion, to make him feel sorry and shameful for his past history, to create in him a fear of the coming penalty, to foster admiration of Christ, to induce him to seek communication with Christians, or to be merciful to the poor: we may even cause him to feel happy in doing these things: *but* we cannot regenerate him. Since interest, sorrow, shame, fear, admiration, aspiration, pity and joy are merely various impulses of emotion, man can experience all these and his spirit still be dead for he has not yet apprehended God intuitively. From the human viewpoint, might not one be tempted to assert that if a man possesses all these qualities must he not be a first-class Christian? Yet these are but the manifestations of emotion; these do not prove regeneration. The first and foremost sign of new birth in anyone is that he knows God intuitively, for his spirit has been quickened. Let us not be misled or be content in our work if people should change their attitude towards us, become friendly with us, and manifest the above-mentioned expressions. This is *not* regeneration!

If everyone who serves the Lord would take to heart today that our aim is to help people to receive the life of Christ, then none would ever employ an emotional approach to obtain men's approval of the teaching of Christ and their preference for Christianity. Only if we completely acknowledge that what man requires today is God's life—the quickening of the spirit—will we then perceive how vain is any work performed by ourselves. No matter how extensive a man may undergo a change, this alteration effected by emotion occurs exclusively within the pale of his very "self": never does he step outside that boundary and exchange his life for the life of God. May we truly appreciate the reality of the fact that "spiritual aims require spiritual means." Our spiritual aim must be to secure man's regeneration, and to effect that transformation we must use spiritual means. Emotion is altogether useless here.

The Apostle Paul tells us that any woman who prays or prophesies must have her head veiled (see 1 Cor. 11). Many and diverse interpretations surround this matter. We have no intention to join the dispute by deciding on an interpretation. Of one thing we can be sure, however; which is, that the Apostle intends to restrain the operation of emotion. He signifies that everything which can foment emotion must be veiled. It is especially easy for women in preaching to agitate people's emotion. Physically merely the head is covered; but spiritually everything pertaining to feeling must be delivered to death. Although the Bible does not call for the brothers to veil their heads physically, spiritually speaking they should be as veiled as the sisters.

Paul would have no necessity to give such an order of prohibition if emotion were not so greatly being displayed in the Lord's work. Today the power of attraction has developed into nearly the biggest problem in so-called spiritual service. Those who are naturally attractive are more successful; whereas others less attractive experience less success. The Apostle nevertheless insists that everything belonging to the soul, naturally attractive or not, must be covered. Let all the servants of the Lord learn this lesson from the sisters. Our natural appeal does not help us in spiritual work and neither will our lack of natural appeal hinder it. We shall abandon our heart of dependence on the Lord if we stress our power to attract others; likewise, if we pay attention to any lack of power to attract we also shall not walk after the spirit. Far better is it not to think of this matter at all.

What are the servants of the Lord seeking today? Countless ones aspire to spiritual power. But this power is obtained solely by paying a price. Should a Christian die to his emotion he will possess spiritual might. It is because he leans too much on his emotion and is bound too strongly to his desire, affection and feeling that the Christian forfeits real power. Only a deeper operation of the cross can fill us with spiritual dynamite; other than that there is no way to it. When the cross works upon our desire enabling us to live completely for God, spiritual power will naturally be evidenced in us.

A believer's emotion, if not overcome, will additionally hamper him in spiritual work. As long as its influence obtains, his spirit is impotent to control it and consequently unqualified to fulfill the highest will of God. Take physical weariness as an example. We should be able to distinguish (1) the need for rest due to bodily fatigue, (2) the need for rest due to emotional weariness, and (3) the need for rest due to both. God does not intend us to overwork. He wishes us to rest when genuinely tired. Yet we should understand whether we have need to rest due to bodily fatigue or emotional weariness or both. Frequently what we say is rest is merely *laziness*. Our body requires respite and so does our mind and spirit. But a person should never rest because of a laziness which arises from the evil nature in his emotion. How often laziness and emotional distaste for work join to employ physical fatigue as a cover-up. Since man's emotion is highly self-favoring, believers should guard against laziness intruding into what should be exclusively a good and proper kind of rest.

THE PROPER USE OF EMOTION

If God's children permit the cross to operate deeply upon their emotion they shall find afterwards that it no longer obstructs, but rather cooperates with, their spirit. The cross has dealt with the natural life in the emotion, has renewed it, and has made it a channel for the spirit. A spiritual man we have said before is not a spirit, but neither is he a person devoid of emotion; on the contrary, the spiritual man will use his feeling to express the divine life in him. Before it is touched by God emotion follows its own whim. And hence it habitually fails to be an instrument of the spirit. But once it is purified it can serve as the means of the spirit's expression. The inner man needs emotion to express its life: it needs emotion to declare its love and its sympathy towards man's suffering: and it also needs emotion to make man sense the movement of its intuition. Spiritual sensing is usually made known through the feeling of a quiet and pliable emotion. If emotion is pliably subject to the spirit the latter, through the emotion, will love or hate exactly as God wishes.

Some Christians, upon discerning the truth of not living by feeling, mistake spiritual life as one without it. They accordingly try to destroy it and to render themselves as insensate as wood and stone. Because of their ignorance of the meaning of the death of the cross, they do not understand what is meant by handing over one's emotion to death and living by the spirit. We do not say that, in order to be spiritual, a Christian must become exceedingly hard and void of affection like inanimate objects—as though the term spiritual man means for him to be emptied of feeling. Quite the contrary. The most tender, merciful, loving, and sympathetic of persons is a spiritual man. To be entirely spiritual by delivering his emotion to the cross does not denote that henceforth he is stripped of his feeling. We have observed numerous spiritual saints and have noticed that their love is greater than that of others, which demonstrates that a spiritual man is not without emotion and additionally that it differs from that of the ordinary man.

In committing our soul to the cross we must remember that what is lost is the soul *life*, not its *function*. Were its function nailed to the cross we then could no longer think, choose, or feel. We must therefore remember this basic fact: to lose soul life means to doggedly, resolutely, and continuously deny the natural power and to walk exclusively by the power of God; it means to live no longer after self and its desires but to submit unexceptionally to the will of God. Moreover, the cross and resurrection are two inseparable facts: "for if we have become united with him in the likeness of his death, we shall be also in the likeness of his resurrection" (Rom. 6.5 ASV). The death of the cross does not connote annihilation; hence the emotion, mind and will of the soul are not extinguished upon passing through the cross. They only relinquish their natural life in the death of the Lord and are raised again in His resurrection life. Such death and resurrection cause the various operating organs of the soul to lose their life, to be renewed, and to be used by the Lord. Consequently a spiritual man is not emotionally deprived; rather, his emotion is the most perfect and the most noble, as though newly created out of God's hand. In short, if anyone has trouble here, the trouble lies with his theory and not with his experience, for the latter will bear out the truth.

Emotion must go through the cross (Matt. 10.38-39) in order to destroy its fiery nature, with its confusion, and to subject it totally to the spirit. The cross aims to accord the spirit authority to rule over every activity of emotion.

CHAPTER 2
AFFECTION

GOD'S DEMAND

YIELDING ONE'S AFFECTION TO THE LORD may be viewed by the Christian to be a most difficult task, yet the Lord is concerned with one's affection more than with any other matter. He demands him to present his affection wholly to Him and let Him lord over it. The Lord asks for first place in our affection. We often hear people talk about consecration, but this act is simply the first step in one's spiritual walk. Consecration is not the destination of spirituality, it is but its beginning. It leads a Christian to a sanctified position. In a word, without consecration there can be no spiritual life. Even so, nothing is more paramount in one's consecration than is his affection. Whether or not this has been yielded determines the truth or falsity of consecration. Its acid test is affection. Relatively easy is it for us to hand over our time, money, power, and countless other items; but to offer our affection is exceedingly difficult. This is not to imply we do not love Christ; perhaps we love our Lord very much. Nevertheless, if we grant first place in our affection to another and relegate Christ to second place, or if we love someone else while loving the Lord, or if we ourselves direct our affection, then what we have offered is not considered consecration for we have not yielded our affection. Every spiritual believer appreciates the necessity for affection to be offered first. For without that, nothing really is offered.

God the Father demands absolute love from His children. He is unwilling to share our heart with anyone or anything else: even if He should receive the bigger share, He is still not pleased. God demands all our love. Naturally this strikes a fatal blow to one's soul life. The Lord bids us part with what we ourselves cling to, for it divides our heart. He asks us to love Him totally and to utterly follow Him in love: "You shall love the Lord your God with all your heart, and with all your soul, and with all your mind" (Matt. 22.37). "All" denotes every ounce of it for the Lord. He enjoins us to reserve not one tiny particle of affection which we ourselves can direct. He calls for all. He is a jealous God (Ex. 20.5), therefore He does not allow anybody to steal the love of His children.

Yet how many dearly beloved ones have their claim on the believer's affections besides God! Perhaps an Isaac, a Jonathan, or a Rachel. Wherefore God insists we lay our beloved ones on the altar. He cannot tolerate any competition. Our all must be on the altar. This is the Christian's way to spiritual power. And shortly after the sacrifice is laid on the altar—nay, after the *last* sacrifice is duly placed thereon—fire will come down from heaven. Without the altar, there can be no heavenly fire. How, then, will one ever have the power of the Holy Spirit if he does not take up his cross and offer everyone whom he loves to the Lord? This is not an empty altar, for fire consumes the sacrifice on it. What can the fire consume if there is no sacrifice? Brethren, neither our mental understanding of the cross nor our endless talk about it will give us the power of the Holy Spirit; only our laying everything on the altar will. If we continue to harbor some secret rope uncut, if our heart secretly retains some oxen and sheep and an Agag, we will still not experience the manifestation of the Holy Spirit's power in our lives.

How much the work of God has suffered because of our failure to let the Lord be the Lord of our affections. Many parents cling to their children for themselves and permit the kingdom of God to incur loss. Countless husbands or wives are unwilling to make sacrifice and thus the harvest is left ungathered. Numerous Christians are so attached to their friends that they sit back and let their brethren fight at the front alone. It is deplorable how many think they can love their dear ones and the Lord simultaneously, not comprehending that by loving these, they cannot love the Lord. We persist in living in the soul if we cannot say with Asaph: "Whom have I in heaven but thee? And there is nothing upon earth that I desire besides thee" (Ps. 73.25).

We cannot but stress the significance of our loving the Lord with our whole heart. Nothing satisfies His heart as does our love. The Lord looks not for our laboring for Him but for our loving Him. The church at Ephesus, according to Revelation 2, works and toils for the Lord, yet He is displeased with them because they have abandoned their first love. If our service is rendered for love's sake the Lord will certainly be pleased; but what value is it to Him if we undertake endeavors for Him without truly possessing a heart for Him? We should be aware how possible it is to labor for the Lord and yet not love the Lord. Let us ask God to cast light on the reason for our activity. Is love for the Lord strong within us? What is the use of calling out "Lord, Lord" and working diligently for Him while simultaneously the heart has no love for Him? May we have a perfect heart towards our dearly beloved Lord!

God's children have never fully understood how their loved ones could hinder their spiritual growth. As we begin to have other loves besides a love for God, however, we do discover that He gradually loses significance for us. And even should our loved ones love God, we probably will love Him for the sake of our dear ones rather than because of God Himself. Hence our relationship with God descends from the spiritual to the carnal level. We never ought to love God for the sake of another person or thing; we must love Him for His sake alone. Should a believer love the Lord for his dear one's sake, his devotion towards Him is governed by the one whom he loves. God has thus been done a favor in that the loved one has been responsible for turning the believer's love towards God. And consequently God becomes indebted to that loved one for the devotion He receives from the believer. Today the loved one propels the believer to love God; tomorrow the same one may cause him to abandon his love to God.

Moreover, when we are inclined towards someone we can hardly preserve our heart in quietness; usually we will be stirred by our emotion to seek feverishly to please the other one. Most likely the desire to draw near to God will be less than the desire to draw near to the loved one. In such a case the Christian will doubtlessly exhibit diminished interest in spiritual affairs. Outwardly nothing seems changed: inwardly though his heart is entangled with his dear one. Spiritual interest, if not totally lost, is surely greatly decreased. Furthermore, the Christian's aspiration for the vainglory of this world is excited beyond restraint. In order to obtain the attention of his loved one he will seek to impress that one with the things, fashion, beauty, glory, and other aspects of the world. God and His demands go by the board. Be it therefore known that man can love but one person and serve but one master at a time: if he loves man, he cannot love God. We must sever all secret relationships with man.

Actually, only God can satisfy a Christian's heart; man cannot. The failure of many is to seek from man what can be found only in God. All human affection is empty; the love of God alone is able to fully satisfy one's desire. The moment a Christian seeks a love outside God his spiritual life immediately falls. We can only live by the love of God.

What then? Does this indicate we need not love man? The Bible repeatedly charges us to love the brethren and even to love our enemies. Accordingly we know it is not God's will we should not love man, but He does desire to *manage* our affection towards all men. God does not want us to love others for our sake but to love for His sake and in Him. Our natural likes and dislikes do not have any part here; natural affection must lose its power. God wants us, for love's sake, to accept His control. When He wishes us to love someone, we instantly are able to; should He also desire us to terminate our relationship with someone, we can do that too.

This is the pathway of the cross. Only as we allow it to cut deeply so that we have our soul life delivered to death can we be rid of self in our affections. If we genuinely have undergone death we will not be *attached* to anyone but will be guided solely by the command of God. Our soul life, as it experiences death, loses its power and becomes as much as dead in the matter of affection. God will then direct us how in Him to renew our love for men. God wants us to create in Him a new relationship with those we formerly loved. Every natural relationship has been terminated. New relationships are established through death and resurrection.

How contrary such a course seems to Christians, and yet how blessed it is to those who so experience it! In order to substantiate, for the believer's own profit, his consecration to God, God often "strips" him of that which he holds dear. God endeavors either to secure our love towards Him or to strip us of our love. When He employs the second way He will either cause our loved ones to change their hearts towards us or make it impossible for us to love them by setting up environmental obstacles such as their moving or passing away. If our heart is sincere in consecration, God will deprive us of everything so that He shall be the only One left. To possess spiritual life in reality we must be willing to forsake all we love. Whatever conflicts with our love to God, God demands us to forsake. Spiritual life forbids the dividing of our affection. Any error in our affection—be it an error of intention or purpose or excessiveness—is judged by God to be as wrong as an error in our hatred. Love and hate, when from ourselves, are equally defiled in the sight of God.

Once the believer has passed through a purifying process he will observe how unalloyed his affection towards men *now* is: no longer is self mixed in with his love: all is for God and all is in God. In his former affection he loved others but loved himself more, because he esteemed his own self more important than they. But now he is able to share the sorrow and joy of others, to bear their burdens, and to serve them with affection. No longer does he love what his own self loves, but loves those whom God loves; no more does he count himself above others, but regards them as his own self. He is today in God and loves himself as well as others for God's sake: he can therefore love others as his very self.

Let us understand that the lordship of God over our affection is an indispensable requirement to spiritual growth. How undisciplined and wild is our affection! If it is not subject to God's will it shall endanger our spiritual walk at all times. A mistaken thought may be corrected easily, but an errant affection is nearly unmanageable. We should love the Lord with all our heart, permitting Him to direct our love.

LOVING THE LORD SOULISHLY

Right here we should sound a note of warning. Never think we ourselves can love the Lord. Whatever comes from us is rejected by Him; even loving Him is unacceptable. On the one hand, the believer's lack of deep affection towards the Lord grieves Him greatly; on the other hand, one's loving Him with *soul power* is not welcomed by God either. Our affection, even when used to love the Lord, must be entirely under the spirit's management. Too many love the Lord with a worldly love and too few, with God's pure love.

Nowadays the Lord's people primarily employ their soulical power to absorb the things of God. They speak about their Father God, call the Lord their most beloved Lord, and contemplate His suffering. By so doing their hearts are filled with joy and they feel they are now loving the Lord. They conclude this feeling is from God. Sometimes while meditating on the Lord's cross they cannot withhold their tears because they seem to experience such an unspeakable burning affection for the Lord Jesus. These things nonetheless pass through their lives like ships sailing through the sea: no lasting trace is left behind. Such is the love of countless Christians. But what is this kind of love after all? Such love as this is the sort which only serves to make one's self happy. This is not loving God, it is loving pleasure. The visualization of the Lord's suffering seems to have touched his heart, but its inner truth has not affected his life.

How powerless is the suffering of the Lord in a believer's heart when merely mentally or emotionally conceived! In contemplating His suffering one becomes inflated and proud, viewing himself as loving the Lord far more than do others. He talks as though he is a heavenly man; actually, he has not moved one breath away from his pitiful self. He gives the impression of loving the Lord so much, and for this reason others admire him. Even so, his love is nothing but self-love. He thinks and talks and desires after the Lord only because in so doing he can feel happy. His motive is for deriving pleasure and not for the sake of the Lord. Such meditation secures to himself a comfortable and pleasant stirring, and so he continues to meditate. All is soulish and earthly, neither of God nor of the spirit.

What, therefore, is the distinction between spiritual love and soulish love towards God? These two are not readily distinguishable outwardly, but inwardly every Christian can detect the true source of his love. As the soul is our very self so all which belongs to it cannot draw away from self. A soulish affection is one in which self is working. To love God for the sake of personal pleasure is carnal love. If a love is spiritual it has no self mixed in with loving God. It means to love God for His Own sake. Any affection which is totally or partially for one's own pleasure or for reasons other than for God Himself emanates from the soul.

Another way we can distinguish the source of love is through its results. If one's love is soulical it does not empower him to be delivered permanently from the world. The believer must continue to worry and struggle to break away from the world's attraction. Not so with spiritual love. Here the things of the world just naturally fade away before it. The one who participates in that kind of love despises the world, considering its things abhorrent and abominable. Henceforth he appears to be unable to see the world because the glory of God has blinded his physical eyes. Furthermore, a person who experiences such love as this becomes humble as though he has dried up before men.

The nature of God's love is unchangeable. Ours alternates all too readily. If it is our habit to love God with our own affection we shall turn cold towards Him whenever we are unhappy. We shall lose our own love should we have to go through a long period of trial. Our affection towards God will recede when we cannot obtain the pleasure we expect, because we love Him with our own love and for our own sake. If it were God's love it would remain in the condition of loving Him through every circumstance. "For love is strong as death, jealousy is cruel as the grave . . . Many waters cannot quench love, neither can floods drown it" (S. of S. 8.6,7). The believer who genuinely loves God will persist in loving Him regardless what he encounters or how he feels. A soulical affection ceases when the movement of emotion ceases; but a spiritual affection is strong, ever unrelenting, for it never relinquishes.

The Lord frequently leads the saint through painful experiences in order that he may not love the Lord for his own sake. When one loves with his own affection and for his own sake he can only love when he senses the affection of the Lord. However, one who loves with God's love and for His sake will be made by God to believe in His love rather than to feel it. At the beginning of a Christian life the Lord uses many ways to attract the believer to, and to assure him of, His love. Later, He desires to guide him further on by withdrawing the feeling of love while leading him on into *believing* His heart of love. Please note that that first step of being attracted by the feeling of the Lord's love is *necessary* for the believer's subsequent deeper walk with the Lord, because unless he has been drawn by the Lord's love he shall be powerless to forsake all and follow Him. During the initial stage on a Christian's spiritual path the feeling of the love of the Lord is vital and helpful, something to be sought diligently. After an appropriate time, though, he ought not *cling* to such feeling, for to do so will bring damage to his spiritual life. Various spiritual experiences are apportioned to different steps in one's spiritual walk. To encounter a certain experience in its corresponding stage of life is both proper and profitable; but to hanker again for those early experiences at a later stage in our walk constitutes retreat or retardation. After the Lord has made a person feel His love, He wishes Him to *believe* in His love. Hence when one has experienced for a time the love of the Lord in his emotion, God will remove that feeling (although not immediately) in order to create in him the essential belief that the love of the Lord never changes. Consequently, let that one not be surprised should he, following a period of feeling the Lord's love, lose that feeling. The time has now arrived for him to believe in the Lord's love.

GUARD AGAINST ONE THING

We have learned that in walking after the spirit we need to keep our emotion calm and quiet; otherwise we cannot hear the voice of intuition. Unless our affection is thoroughly quiet under the will of God our heart will be intermittently disturbed and the guidance of the spirit will hence be interrupted. A believer should always notice in his spirit what person or thing easily activates his affection. Should Satan be impotent to overcome a believer in any other respect, he will tempt him through this particular point involving his affection. Innumerable Christians have failed on just this issue. Great caution must accordingly be exercised.

Nothing activates our affection more than friends, and among friends the opposite sex stirs us the most. Due to differences in natural endowment, the opposite sexes attract each other. Here is not only a physical complement but a psychological one as well. Yet such attraction belongs to the soul: it is natural: it ought to be denied. It is an established fact that the opposite sex can easily stimulate affection. The stimulation by the same sex is much less prevalent than that by the opposite sex. For some psychological reason there is overwhelmingly more attraction to the opposite sex. This is the common and natural tendency. A slight stimulation occasioned by the opposite sex generally stirs up deep affection.

Obviously we are now speaking of the natural tendency of man. For this very reason a Christian who wishes to walk by the spirit must take note of it. In our association with people, especially in the matters of love, if we treat the same sex in one way and the opposite sex in another we know we are already under the operation of the soul. If we treat them differently for no reason other than that one is of the opposite sex, then our affection remains natural. To be sure, such stimulation by the opposite sex can be mixed in with proper motive. A Christian must nonetheless recognize that should there be such mixed motives in friendship his social intercourse is not purely spiritual.

A worker in his work and while at work needs to watch lest the thought of the opposite sex makes its intrusion. He must resist all desire to be glorified among the opposite sex. All words uttered and mannerisms affected due to the influence of the opposite sex diminish spiritual power. Everything must be done quietly with a pure motive. Remember that it is not sin alone which defiles; whatever issues from the soul can defile as well.

Does all this signify, then, that a believer should not have friends of the opposite sex? The Bible does not so teach. Our Lord when on earth had friendly fellowship with Martha, Mary, and other women. So the question fundamentally must be: is our affection wholly under God's control? Or is the working of the flesh somehow mixed in with it? It is perfectly proper for brothers and sisters to fellowship; only there should not be mixed in with it the working of the soul.

To sum up, a Christian's affection must be entirely offered to God. Whenever we feel it too difficult to hand someone over to God, we know our soul life has ruled in that area. Where our affection is unable to yield fully to God's will, much unspiritual mixture must be there. All soulish affections lead us to sin and draw us to the world. An affection which is not inspired by the Lord will soon be transformed into lust. Samson is not alone in the history of man in failing in this regard. Delilah is still cutting the hair of man today!

We stated earlier that affection is the hardest element for a believer to offer: *ergo,* its consecration becomes the sign of true spirituality: *ergo,* this is the greatest test. He who has not died to worldly affection has not died to anything. Death to natural affection proves one's death to the world. To covet and to lust after man's affection demonstrates that the Christian has not yet died to self life. His death to soul life is substantiated by his forsaking every affection other than that for God. How transcendent is a spiritual man! He walks far above human natural affection.

CHAPTER 3
DESIRE

DESIRE OCCUPIES the largest part of our emotional life: it joins forces with our will to rebel against God's will. Our innumerable desires create such confused feelings in us that we cannot quietly follow the spirit. They arouse our feelings and make for many turbulent experiences. Before one is set free from the power of sin his desire unites with sin in making him love sin and in depriving the new man of his freedom. After he is liberated from sin's outward manifestations the same desire drives him to seek for *himself* many things outside God. And while a person is still in the emotional state he is controlled mainly by his desire. Not until the cross has performed its deeper work and one's desire has been judged in the light of the cross can he wholly live in the spirit and for God.

When a Christian remains carnal he is ruled vigorously by his desire. All natural or soulish desires and ambitions are linked with *self* life. They are for self, by self, or after self. While carnal, one's will is not yielded fully to the Lord, and so he holds many ideas of his own. His desire then works together with his ideas to make him delight in what he wills to have and to expect to have his own ideas realized. All self-delight, self-glory, self-exaltation, self-love, self-pity and self-importance issue from man's desire and render self the center of everything. Can we conjure up anything man himself desires which is not linked to something of self? If we examine ourselves in the light of the Lord we shall see that all our aspirations, no matter how noble, cannot escape the bounds of self. All are for it! If they are not self-pleasing, then they are self-glorifying. How can a Christian live in the spirit if he is engulfed in such a condition?

A BELIEVER'S NATURAL DESIRES

Pride springs from desire. Man aspires to obtain a place for himself that he may feel honored before men. All secret boastings about one's position, family, health, temperament, ability, good looks, and power flow from man's natural desire. To dwell on how differently one lives, dresses and eats and to feel self-content in these differences is also the work of emotion. Even to esteem the gift one receives from God as superior to that of others is inspired by natural desire as well.

How extensively an emotional believer comes to display himself! He loves both to see and to be seen. He cannot abide the restraints of God. He will try every means to push himself to the front. He is unable to be hidden according to the will of God and to deny himself when he is hidden. He wishes others to notice him. When he is not duly respected his desire of self-love suffers a deep wound. But if he is admired by people his heart is overjoyed. He loves to hear praising voices and considers them just and true. He also attempts to elevate himself in his work, whether in preaching or in writing, for his secret self motive goads him on. In a word, this one has not yet died to his desire of vainglory. He is still seeking what *he* desires and what can inflate *him*.

Such natural inclination makes a believer ambitious. Ambition arises through the unleashing of our natural inclination and desire. All ambitions to spread one's fame, become a man above others, and attract the world's admiration proceed from the emotional life. Often in spiritual work the aspirations for success, fruit, power and usefulness are but pretenses for glorifying oneself. The quest for growth, depth, and nobler experience is frequently a search for self-pleasure and the admiration of others. If we trace the course of our life and work back to their source, we may be surprised to discover that our desires are the springs behind many of our undertakings. How we live and work for ourselves!

However good, praiseworthy and effective one's walk and labor may appear to be, if they are motivated by his ambition they are nevertheless judged by God to be wood, hay and stubble. Such conduct and exertion possess no spiritual worth. God deems a believer's craving for spiritual fame just as corrupt as his desiring sin. If one walks according to his natural propensity he will esteem himself well in everything he does; but God is most displeased with this "self."

This natural desire is equally active in other aspects of one's walk. His soulish life hankers after worldly conversation and intercourse. It urges him to see what he should not see and read what he should not read. He may not do these things habitually, yet because of a strong urge within him he sometimes does what he knows he should not. Soulish desire can also be detected in a person's attitude. His soulishness can be spotted even in his mannerisms; for instance, in the way he walks. Unquestionably it is discerned most easily in his words and deeds. Now these are admittedly little things, but all who faithfully walk after the spirit realize how impossible it is for them to so walk should they be propelled in these matters by their soulish desire. A Christian needs to remember that in spiritual affairs nothing is too small to hinder his progress.

The more a person is spiritual the more real he becomes, for he has been united with God and is at rest. But when one is goaded by his natural life he becomes very pretentious. He carries a reckless spirit and likes to do daring things in order to satisfy himself and impress others. How he pretends to be mature and wise when actually he is immature in many of his undertakings. He may regret his pretension afterwards but for the moment he feels great. Anyone who pursues such desires cannot avoid going off on a tangent.

Pleasure-loving also is a prominent manifestation of an emotional believer. Our emotion cannot abide living wholly for God; it will most certainly rebel against such a commitment. When a person accepts the demand of the cross in consigning his soulish emotion to death that he may live utterly for the Lord, he will discover experientially how his emotion pleads and maneuvers for a little ground of activity. For this very reason numerous Christians are powerless to walk totally after the Lord. How many Christians, for example, are able to engage in prayer warfare for a *whole day* without reserving some period for recreation, for refreshing their emotion? It is difficult for us to live in the spirit for an entire day. We always set aside for ourselves some time to converse with people in order to relieve our emotion. Only when we are shut in by God—seeing neither man nor sky, living in the spirit and serving Him before the throne—do we begin to appreciate how much emotion demands of us, how imperfectly we have died to it, and how much we yet live by it.

Desire for haste is another symptom of the emotional Christian. One who moves by his natural feeling does not know how to wait on God nor is he acquainted with the leading of the Holy Spirit. Emotion is usually hasty. A Christian emotionally excited acts hastily. It is extremely hard for him to wait on the Lord, to know the will of God, and to walk step by step in that will. Indeed, the Lord's people are incapable of following the spirit unless their emotion is truly yielded to the cross. Let us remember that out of a hundred impulsive actions scarcely one is in the will of God.

Judging by the time we need to pray, to prepare, to wait, and to be filled again with the power of the Holy Spirit, can we really be faultless if we move impulsively? Because He knows the impetuosity of our flesh God frequently uses our fellow-workers, brethren, family, circumstances, and other material factors to wear us out. He wants our hastiness to die so that He can work for us. God never performs anything hurriedly; consequently He will not entrust His power to the impatient. He who wishes to act impulsively must depend upon his own strength. Haste clearly is the work of the flesh. Since God does not desire anyone to walk after the flesh, the Christian must commit his precipitate emotions to death. Each time emotion demands hurry we should tell ourselves: "Emotion is now urging towards hastiness; oh Lord, may Thy cross operate here." He who walks by the spirit must not be hasty.

God takes no pleasure in what we ourselves do, but He is delighted with our waiting on Him, waiting for His orders. Our actions must be ordered by God. Only what is commissioned in the spirit is His undertaking. How impossible this is for the Christian who follows his own inclination. Even when he wants to do God's will he is extremely impatient. He does not comprehend that God has not only a will but also a time. Frequently He reveals His mind but bids us linger for His time to come. The flesh cannot tolerate such waiting. As God's child advances spiritually he shall discover that the Lord's time is as important as the Lord's will. Do not rashly beget an Ishmael lest he become the greatest enemy to Isaac. Those who cannot submit themselves to God's time are unable to obey God's will.

Due to his self-desiring, an emotional believer cannot wait on God. Whatever he undertakes he does in himself, for he cannot trust God nor allow God to work for him. He does not know how to commit a matter completely into God's hand and refrain from employing his own strength. Trust is beyond him because this requires self-denial. Until his desire is restrained, his self will be very active. How he is eager to help God! For God seems to work too slowly, so help Him along he must! Such is the operation of the soul, motivated by natural desire. Often God renders the believer's work ineffectual and thereby seeks to induce him to deny himself.

Self-justification is a common symptom among emotional Christians. The Lord's people often encounter misunderstandings. Sometimes He enjoins them to explain their situations; but unless one is so instructed by the Lord, his explanations are but the agitations of his soul life. More often than not the Lord wishes His people to commit all matters into His hand and not defend themselves. How we like to speak on our own behalf! How awful for us to be misunderstood! It diminishes one's glory and deflates one's self-esteem.

The self in man cannot remain silent when an unjustified fault is leveled at him. He cannot accept what is given him by God nor can he stay for God to justify him. He believes God's justification will come too late; he demands the Lord to justify him at once so that everybody may behold his righteousness in no uncertain terms. All this is but the ferment of soulish desire. Were the believer willing to humble himself beneath the mighty hand of God at the instance of misunderstanding, he would discover that God wishes to use this occasion to equip him to deny his self more deeply; that is, to deny once again his soulish desire. This constitutes the Christian's practical cross. Each time he accepts a cross he experiences once more its crucifixion. Should he follow his natural concern and rush to defend himself, he shall find the power of self more formidable to subdue on the next occasion.

Before's one natural desire is dealt with he inevitably will pour out his heart to someone in the hour of suffering, discomfort, or despondency. His emotion has been aroused within and he longs to confide his trouble to someone so as to release the miserable pressure upon his breast and thus relieve his burden. Man's soulish inclination is to inform people about his distress as though their very knowledge of it will lessen it. By such action the individual is attempting to derive sympathy and comfort from other people. He yearns intently for this condolence and commiseration for these afford him a certain pleasurable feeling. He does not know how to be satisfied with God knowing his problems: he cannot commit his burdens to the Lord alone, quietly letting Him lead him to deeper death through these circumstances. He seeks man's comfort rather than God Himself. His self life is greedy for what man can give him but despises the ordering of God. Believers should perceive that their soul life will never be lost through *man's sympathy and comfort*—these but nourish that life. The spirit life commences with God and finds in Him its all sufficiency. The power to welcome and endure solitude is the spirit's power. When we locate human ways by which to soften our burdens we are adhering to the soul. God desires us to maintain silence, letting those crosses He has arranged for us work out His purpose. Each time we open not our mouth in suffering, we witness the cross working. To be dumb is the cross! He who loosens not his tongue truly tastes its bitterness! Nevertheless his spiritual life is nourished by the cross!

GOD'S AIM

God aims to have His people dwell exclusively in the spirit, willing to offer their soul life completely to death. To attain this objective He will have to touch severely their natural desire. God wants to destroy their natural inclinations. How often He does not allow His child either to do or to possess things which in themselves are not bad (they may in fact be quite legitimate and good), simply because, as the result of emotional impulses, he wants them for himself. If a Christian walks according to his personal aspirations he cannot avoid being rebellious towards God. Our Lord's aim is to destroy absolutely the believer's craving for anything *besides Himself*. The Lord is not concerned with the nature of a thing; He only asks what directs him to this thing—his own desire or the will of God? The best work or walk, if it arises out of one's desire and not from intuitive revelation, has positively no spiritual value before God. Many works which God had intended to lead His child into He must temporarily suspend because that one is motivated by his own wish. God will begin to lead His child again to these works once he has completely yielded to Him. God longs for His will (made known in our intuition) to be the guiding principle of our life and labor. He does not want us to heed our own propensity even when it seems to agree with His purpose. What we ought to heed is God's will; what we must deny is our own desire. Here is the wisdom of God. Why does He forbid us to follow our inclination even when it coincides with His will? Because it is still *our own desire*. For if we are allowed to obey our good aspirations, does there not remain a place for our "self"?

Despite the fact our desires occasionally agree with His will, God is not delighted with them because they are nonetheless of ourselves. He charges us to break completely with our longings for anything *other than Himself*. This "anything" may include some very excellent desires but He will give no ground to any of them that are independent. We must rely on Him in all matters. What does not emerge from dependence on Him He rejects. Step by step He leads us to deny our soul life.

If anyone wishes to maintain a true spiritual course he must cooperate with God in putting to death his own desire. All interests, inclinations and preferences must be denied. We should gladly accept man's contradicting, despising, discounting, misunderstanding, and harsh criticising and permit these matters which are so antagonistic to natural desire to deal with our soul life. We should learn how to receive suffering, pain, or a lowly place as apportioned us by God. However much our self life feels pained or our natural feeling is hurt, we must bear them patiently. If we bear the cross in practical matters we shall shortly see our self life crucified on the cross we bear. For to carry the cross is to be crucified thereon. Every time we silently accept what goes against our natural disposition we receive another nail which pins our soul life more firmly to the cross. All vainglory has to die. Our longing to be seen, respected, worshiped, exalted and proclaimed needs to be crucified. Any heart for self-display must equally be crucified. Every pretension to spirituality in order to be praised must be cut down; so must all self-importance and self-exaltation. Our desire, whatever its expression, must be denied. Anything which is initiated by ourselves is defiled in the sight of God.

The practical cross which God dispenses runs counter to our desires. The cross aims at crucifying them. Nothing in our total make-up suffers more wounding under the lash of the cross than does our emotion. It cuts deeply into everything pertaining to ourselves. How then can our emotion be happy when our desire is dying? The redemption of God requires a thorough setting aside of the old creation. God's will and our soul's delight are incompatible. For anyone to pursue the Lord he must oppose his own desire.

Since this is God's purpose He therefore arranges to have His children experience many fiery trials so that all these offscourings of desire may be consumed in the fire of suffering. A Christian may aspire to high position, but the Lord brings him low: he may cherish many hopes, yet the Lord allows him no success in anything: he may entertain many delights, but the Lord gradually takes away each of them till none remains: he yearns for glory, yet the Lord inflicts upon him humiliation. Nothing in the ordering of the Lord seems to coincide with the Christian's thought; everything strikes him down as would a beating rod. Though he struggles with all his might he soon deduces that he is heading straight for death. He does not discern at first that it is the Lord Who leads him to this demise. Everything seems to speak of helplessness, seems to remove any hope of life, seems to demand that he should die. During this period when he cannot escape death, he begins to realize he owes this end to God, and so he yields and accepts it with composure. This death, however, bespeaks the cessation of his soul life that he may live utterly in God. To achieve this death in the Christian's life God has worked long and hard. How foolish then for him to resist such an expiration for so long. For is it not true that after he has passed through this death all turns out well and God's aim in him is also fulfilled? Thereafter he can advance rapidly in spiritual growth.

Once he loses his heart for "self" the believer can be wholly God's. He is ready to be molded into any form God wishes. His desire no longer strives against God; nay, he relishes nothing but God. His life has now become quite simple: he has no expectations, no requests, no ambitions other than to be willingly obedient to the Lord's will. A life of obedience to His intent is the simplest kind on earth, because he who so lives seeks nothing but to quietly follow God.

After a person has forsaken his natural longings he obtains a genuinely restful life. Formerly he had many desires.

To satisfy them he planned, plotted and contrived, exhausting every ounce of his wisdom and power. His heart was in constant turmoil. While contriving, he agitated to attain what he desired. When defeated, he agonized because of failure to achieve. How the restful life eludes him! Furthermore, the person who has not yet abandoned what is his and surrendered to what is God's cannot help but be affected by his surroundings. People's capricious attitudes, changing environments, loneliness, and many other elements in the external world work to induce melancholia. This is quite a common trait among emotional saints. But natural desire can also arouse wrath in such a one. When externals go against his wish or do not turn out exactly as he prefers, when matters appear to be unjust and unreasonable to him, he becomes disturbed, anxious, and angry. These different emotional expressions are provoked by external causes. How easily one's emotion can be stirred, perturbed, and wounded. One's natural desire thus seeks out man's love, respect, sympathy and intimacy; but if he fails to realize his desire he murmurs against heaven and cries out against men. Is there anyone exempt from such sorrow and grief? Living in this bitter world as we all do, can anyone realistically expect to have his desire fully realized? If this is impossible, then how can an emotional believer ever secure rest in life? He cannot. But that child of God who purely follows the spirit and seeks not his own pleasure is satisfied with what God gives to him: and his restlessness immediately ceases.

The Lord Jesus speaks to His disciples saying: "Take my yoke upon you, and learn from me; for I am gentle and lowly in heart, and you will find rest for your souls" (Matt. 11.29). The soul here alludes especially to the emotional part of our being. The Lord knows that His Own people must pass through many trials, that the heavenly Father is going to arrange for them to be lonely and misunderstood. As no one understands Him except the Father, so no one will understand His disciples (v.27). Jesus knows that the heavenly Father must permit many unpleasant occurrences to befall the believers in order that they may be weaned from the world. He also appreciates what the feelings in their souls will be like as they are put through the fire. For this reason He tells them in advance to learn from Him so that they may find rest for their emotion. Jesus is gentle: He is able to receive any treatment from men: He joyfully accepts the opposition of sinners. Jesus is likewise lowly: He heartily humbles Himself: He has no ambition of His Own. The ambitious are hurt, angry, and restless when they cannot obtain their wishes. But Christ at all times lives gently and humbly on earth; there is consequently no occasion for His emotion to boil and erupt. He teaches we should learn from Him, that we should be gentle and lowly as He is. He says for us to bear His yoke as a restraint upon ourselves. He bears a yoke too, even the yoke of God. He is satisfied with His Father's will alone; as long as the Father knows and understands Him, why should He be concerned about the opposition of others? He is willing to accept the restrictions given him by God. He explains that we must bear His yoke, accept His restraint, do His will, and seek no freedom for the flesh. If this is done, then nothing can disturb or provoke our emotion. This is the cross. If anyone is willing to receive the cross of Christ and submit completely to the Lord, he shall find rest for his emotion.

This is none other than a *satisfied life.* The Christian cherishes nothing but God; henceforth he is satisfied with His will. God himself has filled his desire. He regards everything God has arranged or given, asked or charged him with, as good. If he can but follow the will of God his heart is satisfied. He seeks his own pleasure no longer, and not because of force but because God's will has satisfied him. Since he is now filled, he has no more requests to make. A life such as this can be summed up in one word: satisfied. The characteristic of spiritual life is satisfaction—not in the sense of self-centeredness, self-sufficiency, or self-filling but in that of the person having found all his needs fully met in God. To him God's will is the very best; he is satisfied. What else need he ask for? Only emotional Christians find fault with God's arrangement and aspire to have more by conceiving numberless expectations in their hearts. But one who has allowed the Holy Spirit to operate deeply in him by the cross no longer yearns for anything according to himself. His desire is fulfilled already in God.

At this point the believer's desire is totally renewed (this does not mean that thereafter there can be no failure); it is united with God's desire. Not only is he, negatively, resisting the Lord no longer; but positively, he is delighting in His delight. He is not suppressing his desires; he is simply delighted with what God requires of him. If *God* desires him to suffer, he asks Him to make him suffer. He finds sweetness in such suffering. If *God* desires him to be afflicted, he willingly seeks such affliction. He loves affliction more than healing. If *God* desires to bring him low, he gladly cooperates with Him in bringing himself down. He delights now only in what God delights in. He covets nothing outside Him. He expects no uplifting if God does not so desire. He does not resist God but rather welcomes whatever He bestows, whether sweet or bitter.

The cross produces fruits. Each crucifixion brings to us the fruit of God's life. All who are willing to accept the practical cross which God gives shall find themselves living a pure spiritual life. Daily there is for us the practical cross God desires us to bear. Every cross has its peculiar mission to accomplish a particular work in our life. May no cross ever be wasted upon us!!

CHAPTER 4

A LIFE OF FEELING

A BELIEVER'S EXPERIENCE

WHEN CHRISTIANS BECOME affectionately attached to the Lord they are usually experiencing a life of feeling. Such an experience for them is most precious. They enter this phase of their Christian walk generally following their emancipation from sin and before their entrance upon a true spiritual life. Because they lack spiritual knowledge, these Christians often assume this kind of emotional experience to be most spiritual and most heavenly since it is encountered primarily after release from sin and affords them great pleasure. The delight it bestows is so satisfactory that they find it difficult to cut loose and forsake it.

During this period the believer senses the nearness of the Lord, so near that the hands can almost touch Him. He is alive to the delicate sweetness of the Lord's love as well as gripped by his own intense love towards the Lord. A fire seems to be burning in his heart; it leave him with an unspeakable joy which makes him feel he is already in heaven. Something is heaving in his bosom, yielding indescribable pleasure, as though he were in possession of a priceless treasure. This sensation continues with him as he walks and works. Whenever the believer passes through this type of experience he wonders where his abode is, for he seems to have shed his earthly tent and now soars away with the angels.

For the moment Bible reading becomes a real delight. The more he reads the more joyous he feels. Prayer is also very easy. How wonderful to pour out his heart to God. The more he communes the brighter the heavenly light shines. He is able to make many decisions before the Lord which indicates how much he loves Him. Great is his longing to be quiet and alone with God; if only he could close his door forever and commune with the Lord his joy would be full, for no tongue can speak nor pen can write of the joy that lies therein. Formerly he was gregarious, as though crowds and individuals could satisfy his needs; but today he cherishes solitude because what he could derive from the crowds can never be compared to the joy he now receives when alone with his Lord. He favors seclusion more than companionship for fear that among men he may lose his joy.

Moreover, service assumes considerable spontaneity. Hitherto he appeared to have nothing to say, but now with the fire of love aglow in his heart he experiences multiplied pleasure in telling others of the Lord. The more he speaks the more anxious he is to speak. To suffer for the Lord becomes sweet to him. Since he senses Him so near and dear, he gladly embraces the thought of martyrdom. All burdens turn light and all hardships grow easy.

With such a consciousness of the closeness of the Lord, the Christian's outward conduct also undergoes change. In days gone by he was fond of talking, yet currently he is able to remain silent. In his heart he may even criticize others who talk incessantly. Previously he was rather frivolous, today he is quite serious. Very sensitive is he to any ungodliness appearing in other brethren, for which he judges them sternly. In a word, the Christian at this stage is increasingly careful about his outward deportment as well as possessed with more insight into the shortcomings of others.

Such a person always secretly pities those who are lacking in his experience. He estimates his joy to be most excellent; how pitiable his brethren know nothing of it. While he watches other brothers and sisters serving the Lord coldly and quietly, he considers their lives tasteless. Must not his be the highest life since he is so flushed with the joy of God? It seems to him that he himself is floating on the cloud above the mountains while ordinary saints are plodding along down in the valley.

Does this kind of experience last long however? Can one possess such exultation daily and be happy for life? Most of us cannot maintain such an experience for very long. And so what grieves the believer most is that upon enjoying such an experience—generally speaking, for about a month or two—his most beloved joy suddenly vanishes. He rises as usual in the morning to read his Bible yet where is the former sweetness? He prays as before but finds himself exhausted after a few words. He feels as if he has lost something. Not long ago he was judging others for being far behind him in the spiritual race, but now he considers himself to be one of *them*. His heart has turned cold; the earlier sense of a fire burning within has been smothered. No longer is he conscious of the presence and proximity of the Lord; instead the Lord appears to be quite remote from him. He now begins to wonder where the Lord has gone. To suffer becomes a real suffering now because he cannot sense any more the former joy he had in suffering. Moreover, he has lost interest in preaching: he no longer feels like continuing on after saying but a few words. In sum, during such an episode everything seems to be dark, dry, cold and dead. It appears to the believer as though he has been abandoned by the Lord in a tomb; nothing can comfort his heart. His former expectation of lasting bliss has faded completely away.

At this moment the child of God will naturally surmise that he must have sinned and that the Lord has consequently forsaken him (for if he had not sinned, he reasons, the Lord would not have withdrawn His presence, would He?). Accordingly, he probably sets about scrutinizing his recent conduct, trying to ascertain how he has sinned against the Lord. He hopes that upon confession the Lord will return and replenish him with that previous feeling of intimacy and high spirits. As he examines himself, however, he cannot detect any special sin; he seems to be just the same as before. And so the believer once more resumes his inward inquiry: if today's condition provokes the Lord to depart from me, he asks himself, why did He not forsake me before? And if I have not sinned, then I say again why has the Lord left me? The believer is completely mystified. He can only conclude that he *must* have sinned against the Lord somewhere and hence this forsaken condition. And Satan accuses him too, reinforcing the false notion that he has actually sinned. Wherefore he cries in prayer to the Lord for forgiveness, hoping to regain what he has lost.

The believer's prayer is nonetheless ineffectual. Not only is he unable to have the lost experience instantly restored; he also day by day grows colder and drier in his feelings. He loses interest in everything. Previously he could pray for hours: today even a few minutes becomes forced. He has no inclination to pray at all. The reading of the Bible, which in the past greatly interested him, currently looms before him as a massive rock from which he can derive no nourishment. He experiences no pleasure when fellowshiping with others or undertaking any task; he engages in these affairs merely because a Christian is expected to do them. All is dull and forced.

Confronted by such a sensation some Christians, not all, shrink back. Many matters which they know belong to God's will are left undone because they have fallen into despondency. Many duties go unfulfilled. Their former conduct which they had corrected during the period of ecstasy returns to them. What they pitied others for in earlier days has presently become their own experience. They adopt talkative, frivolous, jesting and fun-loving manners. Although they had undergone a change, that change did not last.

When a child of God is stripped of his joyous feeling, he concludes that all is gone. Since he no longer senses the Lord's presence, surely the Lord cannot possibly be with him. If he does not feel the warm affection of the Lord, he most certainly must have displeased Him. As this experience lengthens, the believer seems to lose even the sense of God. He will therefore seek earnestly to recover what he has lost, so long as he does not faint in his heart. For does he not love the Lord and has he not longed to be near Him? How can he abide the absence of the sensing of God's love?

He goes forth to find God. He struggles to free himself from this desolate state, but without success. Even when he can force himself into manifesting some good conduct, his heart secretly condemns him as being hypocritical. It is not easy for him to succeed in anything for his failures are many. This naturally intensifies his suffering. If anyone should praise him at this moment he is keenly embarrassed, because no one can appreciate how miserable he is inside. On the other hand if anyone should blame him, he senses the rightness of it because he understands his own weakness. He deeply admires those who are advancing in the Lord and who are having sweet communion with Him. He looks upon all others around him as better than he since they each possess some measure of good while he has not a shred.

Will this barren condition continue forever? Or will he regain his former experience? What usually happens is as follows. After awhile, perhaps within a few weeks, the coveted feeling suddenly returns to him. This may occur at the hour of listening to a sermon, or following earnest prayer in his early morning devotion or during his midnight meditation. The time varies but the joy does return. During this break in the believer's condition, all which had been forfeited is restored. The presence of the Lord is as precious as before; the glow of love fires up again in his bosom; prayer and Bible reading become sweet as in days gone by; and the Lord is so lovely and so approachable that He can almost be touched. To draw nigh to Him is not a burden but the pleasure of his heart. Everything is transformed: no more darkness, suffering and staleness: all is now light, joy and refreshment. Since he considers his unfaithfulness the reason for the Lord's departure, he thereafter uses all diligence to preserve what is regained, lest he be deprived of this life of feeling all over again. His outward conduct is more careful than ever; he serves the Lord daily with all his strength, hoping to sustain his joy and never again fail as before.

Yet strange as it may seem, despite all his faithfulness, the

Lord shortly afterwards leaves the saint once more. His transport of delight has altogether taken flight. He again slumps into anguish, blackness, and barrenness.

If we examine the biography of many Christians we discover that this type of experience is shared by many after they have been delivered from sin and encounter God as a Person. Initially the Lord causes them to sense His love, His presence, His joy. But soon such feeling disappears. It subsequently comes back, rendering them extremely happy; not long afterwards, though, it vanishes a second time. At least several times the Christian undergoes these come and go occurrences. Such phenomena will not happen while he is still fleshly, before he learns to love the Lord; only after he has made some progress spiritually and begun to love the Lord will he meet with this kind of situation.

THE MEANING OF THIS EXPERIENCE

According to the believer's interpretation, he is at his spiritual peak when in possession of the wonderful feeling: he is at his lowest when deprived of it. He often characterizes his walk as full of ups and downs. By this he means that while he is feeling joyful, loving the Lord and sensing His presence he is at his spiritual best; but if his inward sensation is marked by dryness and pain he must be at his spiritual worst. In other words, he is spiritual so long as the warm fire of love is burning in his heart but soulish if his heart turns icy cold. Such is the common notion among Christians. Is is accurate? It is totally inaccurate. Unless we understand how it is wrong we shall suffer defeat to the very end.

A Christian should recognize that "feeling" is exclusively a part of the soul. When he lives by sensation, no matter what the kind, he is being soulish. During the period that he feels joyful, is loving the Lord and senses His presence, he is walking by feeling; likewise, during the period that he feels just the opposite he is *still* walking by feeling. Just as he is soulish whose life and labor are dictated by a refreshing, bright and joyous sensation, so is he equally soulish whose walk and work are determined by a dry, gloomy and painful one. A real spiritual life is never dominated by, nor lived in, feeling. Rather does it regulate feeling. Nowadays Christians mistake a life of feeling for spiritual experience. This is because many have never entered into genuine spirituality and hence interpret happy sensation to be spiritual experience. They do not know that such feeling is still soulical. Only what occurs in the intuition is spiritual experience—the rest is merely soulical activity.

It is here that Christians make one of the grossest mistakes. Under the stimulation of emotion a child of God may feel he has ascended to heaven. And naturally he assumes he has an ascended life. But he does not realize this is solely how he *feels.* He thinks he possesses the Lord whenever he is conscious of His presence, yet he believes he has lost the Lord whenever he cannot sense Him; once more he knows not that this is but the way he feels. He thinks he is truly loving the Lord as he senses a warmth in his heart; but should there be no burning sensation then he concludes that he has veritably lost his love for Him; yet again he is ignorant of the truth that such are only his *feelings.* We know that fact may not agree with feeling for the latter is exceedingly untrustworthy. Indeed, whether one senses much or senses nothing, the fact remains he is *unchanged.* He may feel he is progressing and yet may make no progress at all; he may likewise feel he is regressing and yet may not regress in the slightest. These are simply his feelings. When full of lively stirrings he reckons he is advancing spiritually; this, however, is just a time of emotional excitement which soon will subside to its former state. The working of emotion seems to assist soulical people to advance but the working of the Spirit causes spiritual men to advance. The progress of the former is false; only what is attained in the power of the Holy Spirit is true.

THE AIMS OF GOD

Why then does God impart and later withdraw these feelings? Because He has a number of aims He wishes to fulfill.

First. God grants joy to believers to draw them closer to Him. He uses His gifts to attract men to Himself. He expects His children to believe in His love in every circumstance after He has once shown how gracious and loving He is towards them. Unfortunately Christians love God only when they sense His love and forget Him the moment they do not.

Second. God deals with our lives in this fashion in order to help us understand ourselves. We realize the hardest lesson to learn is that of knowing oneself—to appreciate how corrupt, empty, sinful, and void of good one is. This lesson has to be absorbed *throughout life.* The deeper one learns it the more one perceives the depth of uncleanness of his life and nature in the eyes of the Lord. Yet this is instruction which we do not relish learning nor is our natural life able to learn it. Hence the Lord employs many ways to teach and to lead us into this knowledge of self. Among His numerous ways the most important is this giving of joyous feeling and later taking it away. Through such treatment one begins to comprehend his corruptness. In the state of aridity he may come to see how in the former days of joy he misused God's gift in uplifting himself and despising others, and how he many times acted through the ferment of emotion rather than with the spirit. Such realization evokes humility. Had he understood that this experience is arranged by God to assist him to know himself, he would not have sought blissful sensation so intently as though it were the summit. God desires us to recognize that we may act just as often in dishonoring God's name when in ecstasy as when in anguish. We progress no more during the bright than during the dull period. Our life is equally corrupt in either condition.

Third. God aims to help His children overcome their environment. A Christian should not allow his surroundings to change his life. He whose path is altered by the influence of environment is not deeply experienced in the Lord. We have learned already that what can be affected by environment is emotion. It is when our emotion is influenced by environment that our lives undergo change. How imperative therefore for us to conquer emotion if we wish to overcome environment. To conquer his surroundings the Christian must prevail over all his various sensations. If he cannot surmount his ever vacillating feeling how can he overcome his environment? It is our feeling which is alive to any shift in environment and which varies accordingly. If we do not override our sensation our lives shall oscillate with our changing sensation. Thus do we need to overcome feeling before we can overcome environment.

This explains why the Lord leads one through different feelings in order that he may learn how to quell these feelings and thereby triumph over his surroundings. If he can subdue his strong and contrasting sensations he surely will be able to cope with the changing atmosphere. Thus will he achieve a steadfast and established walk, no longer drifting with the tide. God desires His child to remain the same with or without high feeling. He wants His child to commune with Him and serve Him faithfully whether he is happy or is sad. God's child must not reshape his life according to how he feels. If he is serving the Lord faithfully and making intercession for others, then he should do so in gladness or in sorrow. He should not serve only when he feels refreshed and cease serving when he is parched. If we cannot subdue our many varied sensations then we can in no wise conquer our diverse surroundings. He who fails to surmount his environment is one who has failed to subjugate his feeling.

Fourth. God has another objective in view. He purposes to train our will. A genuine spiritual life is not one of feeling; rather, it is a life of will. The volition of a spiritual man has been renewed already by the Holy Spirit: it now awaits the spirit's revelation before it issues a command to the whole being. Unfortunately the will of quite a few saints is often so weak that either it cannot carry through the commands given it or, under the influence of emotion, it rejects God's will. To train and strengthen the will consequently becomes a very essential step.

A Christian who is excited can easily advance because he has the support of his high emotion. But if he grows despondent he finds the going rough because he then has solely his will on which to rely. God intends to make the volition strong but not to excite the emotion. From time to time He permits His child to experience a kind of weary, barren and insipid feeling so as to compel him to exercise his *will* through the strength of the spirit to do precisely the same thing as he would in a time of emotional stimulation. When stimulated, emotion undertakes the work; but now God aims for the believer's *will* to work in lieu of emotion. The will gradually can be strengthened through exercise only during periods of receiving no aid from feeling. How many mistake sensation for the measure of spiritual life. They erroneously construe the hour of strong feeling to be their spiritual apogee and the hour bereft of such feeling as their spiritual perigee. They are unaware of the fact that one's true life is lived *by his spirit through the will.* The position to which his volition attains in the hour of barren sensation represents the reality of the Christian's attainment. The way he dwells amid drought is his *authentic* life.

Fifth. Via such leading God longs to guide the Christian onto a higher level of existence. If we carefully examine the Chrisitian's walk we shall realize that the Lord at each instance He has desired to lead His own to a higher spiritual plateau first gave that one a taste of such a life in his feeling. We may say that on every occasion that one experiences a life of feeling, he has reached one more station on his spiritual journey. God grants him a foretaste of what He desires him to have: first He arranges for the Christian to sense it and next He withdraws the sensation so that by his spirit through his will he may keep what he has felt. If his spirit can press on with the assistance of his will, the Christian, by disregarding his emotion, can then see that he has made real progress in his walk. This is confirmed by our common experience. While we are pursuing an up-and-down type of existence we usually assume we have not made any advance. We conclude that during these months or years we have simply gone forward and then backward or simply backwards and then forwards. If, however, we were to compare our current spiritual state with that which obtained at the *commencement* of such alternating phenomena, we would discover we have actually *made some progress*. We advance unknowingly.

A great number err because they have not appropriated this teaching. Upon fully consecrating themselves to the Lord for entering upon a new experience such as sanctification or victory over sin, they truly and distinctly step into a new kind of life. They believe they have made progress, for they are brimming with joy, light and lightness. They account themselves already in possession of that perfect course which they admired and sought. But after awhile their new and happy circumstance suddenly evaporates: gone are the joy and thrill. Most of them faint in their hearts. They judge themselves unqualified now for perfect sanctification and unfit to have the more abundant life which others possess. Their judgment is based on the fact that they have lost what they had long admired and had possessed for but a brief moment. What they do not realize is that they have been experiencing one of God's vital spiritual laws, which is: *that what has been possessed in the emotion must be preserved in the will: that only what is retained in the will truly becomes a part of one's life*. God has only withdrawn the feeling; He wants us to exercise our volition to do what we had formerly been stimulated to do by our feeling. And before long we shall discover that what had been forfeited in our feeling has unconsciously become a part of our life. This is a spiritual law. We would do well to remember it so as never to faint.

The whole problem is therefore the will. Is our organ of volition still yielded to the Lord? Is it free to follow the spirit's leading as before? If so, then however much feeling has changed, *it* is of no *concern*. What we must be concerned with always is this: is our will obeying the spirit? Let us not indulge our feelings. Rather let us wisely heed the example of what occurs surrounding the experience of new birth: on that occasion the believer is usually full of joyous sensation; yet soon this sensation disappears; has he consequently perished all over again? Of course not! He has already possessed life in his spirit. How he subsequently feels makes not a particle of difference.

THE DANGER OF THIS LIFE

There is positively no danger if, while having such an experience, we comprehend its meaning and press forward in accordance with God's will. But it can be highly hazardous to spiritual life if we do not apprehend God's will and fail to resist our living by feeling; that is, when we encounter a buoyant feeling we advance unhesitatingly, but in the absence of such sensation we refuse to move at all. Those who make feeling their principle of life expose themselves to many dangers.

Anyone who walks by blissful emotions is usually weak in his will. It is unable to follow the direction of the spirit. The development of spiritual sensing is hampered by substituting his feeling for the spirit's intuition. He walks by his emotion. His intuition on the one side is suppressed by emotion and on the other is left unused; it is barely growing. Now intuition is active solely when emotion is quiet; only then can it communicate its thought to man. It waxes strong if it is often exercised. But the will of that person who leans on feeling is deprived of its sovereign power: his intuition is stifled and cannot transmit a distinct voice. Since the will thereby slips into a withered condition, the believer requires even more *help from feeling* to provoke the will to work. The will turns by feeling. If the latter is high the will is active; but should it be taken away the will suspends action. It is powerless to do anything by itself; it relies on the activation of emotion to propel it. Meanwhile the believer's spiritual life naturally sinks lower and lower until it seems that whenever emotion is absent no spiritual life is indicated at all. The operation of emotion has become an opiate to such ones! How tragic that some remain unconscious of this fact and seek emotion as the zenith of spiritual life.

The cause behind this error lies in the deception which feeling imparts. At the moment of great ecstasy the child of God not only senses love from the Lord but feels an intense love of his own towards the Lord as well. Must we deny our feeling of loving the Lord? Can such a warm sensation of affection towards Him hurt us? This very interrogation discloses the folly of these saints.

Let the question be asked instead: Is a person actually loving the Lord when he is full of exultation? Or is it that he loves the *exultant feeling?* Granted, this joy is given us by God; but is it not God Who also takes it away? If we genuinely loved Him we should fervently love Him in whatever circumstances He may put us. If our love is present merely when we feel, then perhaps what we love is not God but our feeling.

Moreover, a person may misinterpret such a feeling to be God Himself, not aware that a vast distinction exists between God and the joy of God. Not until the time of barren feeling shall the Holy Spirit show this one that what he so earnestly sought was not God but His joy. He does not really love God; what he loves is the feeling which makes him joyous. The sensation does in truth give him the sense of God's love and presence, yet he does not love Him for His sake alone but rather does he love because he feels refreshed, bright and buoyant. Thus he craves such feeling again whenever it recedes. What brings him pleasure is the joy of God and not God Himself. Were he actually loving God he would love Him even if he must suffer through "many waters" and "floods" (S. of S. 8.7).

This of course is a most difficult lesson to learn. We must indeed have joy, and the Lord delights to give us that joy. If we enjoy His felicity *according to His will,* such enjoyment is profitable rather than harmful. (This means we do not seek this joy ourselves, though we are thankful should God desire to grant it; yet we are equally thankful if He wishes us to be barren: we shall not try to force the matter). Nonetheless, should we deem it so pleasurable that we afterwards seek it daily, then we already have forsaken God in favor of the joy which He dispenses. The happy feeling God gives can never be separated from God the Giver. Should we try to enjoy the delightful sensation He gives, yet without Him, our spiritual life is in peril. That is to say, we are not able to progress spiritually if we find satisfaction in the joy God gives rather than in God as our joy. How often we love Him not because of Himself but because of ourselves. We love, for in loving God we experience a kind of joy in our hearts. This sharply reveals that we do not actually love Him; what we love is only joy, even if that is the joy of God.

This indicates that we esteem God's *gift* higher than God the *Giver!* It also proves we continue to walk by our soul life and do not appreciate what a true spiritual life is. We deify joyous feeling and incorrectly regard it as pleasurable. To cure His children of this mistake God withdraws the joyous feeling as He wills and topples them into suffering that they may know that pleasure is in Himself, not in His joy. If they verily make *God* their joy they will uplift Him and love Him even in the hour of suffering; if not, they will sink into darkness. God, in so undertaking, aims not to destroy our spiritual life but purposes to destroy all idols we worship other than Himself. He wants to eliminate every obstacle to our spiritual walk. He wants us to live in Him, not in our feelings.

Another danger may arise for those who live by sensation rather than by the spirit through the will: they may be deceived by Satan. This is one matter about which we ought to inform ourselves. Satan is skillful in counterfeiting the feelings which come from God. If with diverse kinds of sensations he attempts to confuse Christians who aspire to walk wholly after the spirit, how much more will he play his tricks on those who desire to follow their feeling. In their pursuit of emotion they fall directly into the hand of Satan, for he delights to supply them with all kinds of feeling which they assume to be from God.

The evil spirit is able to excite or to depress people. Once a person is misled into accepting Satan-dispensed feeling, he has yielded ground to Satan in his soul. He shall continue to be further deceived until Satan has gained control over nearly all his feeling. Sometimes Satan will even induce him to experience supernatural sensations of shaking, electrifying, freezing, overflowing, floating in the air, fire burning from head to foot and consuming all his uncleanness, etc. When anyone has been beguiled to this extent his whole being comes to thrive on feelings, his will is totally paralyzed, and his intuition is entirely surrounded. He exists altogether in the outer man; his inner man is completely bound. At this stage he follows Satan's will in almost everything, for the enemy merely needs to supply him with some particular feeling to goad him to do what he wants him to do. The tragedy is that the believer is not aware he is being tricked by Satan; he instead pictures himself as being more spiritual than others since he enjoys such supernatural experiences.

Supernatural phenomena such as those described damage the spiritual life of many a Christian most severely today. Countless numbers of Gods children have fallen into this pit. They consider these supernatural occurrences—which give them a physical feeling of the power of the spirit and render them happy or sad, hot or cold, laughing or crying and which supply them with visions, dreams, voices, fires and even inexpressible wonderful sensations—as most definitely bestowed by the Holy Spirit, and thus represent the highest attainment of a Christian. They are unable to recognize that these are but the works of the evil spirit. They would never dream that the evil spirit as well as the Holy Spirit could perform such work. Totally ignorant are they of the fact that the Holy Spirit operates in the spirit of men. Whatever induces feeling to the *body* proceeds nine out of ten times from the evil spirit. Why have so many fallen into this snare? Simply because they do not live in the spirit but love to live in their feeling! They accordingly provide the wicked power opportunity to play his tricks. Christians must learn to deny their sensational life or else they shall give ground to the enemy to deceive them.

Let us seriously warn every one of God's children to take note of their *bodily* feeling. We should never allow any spirit to create any feeling in our body against our will. We should resist each of these outward bodily feelings. We should not believe in any of these physical sensations. Rather than follow them we should forbid them, for they constitute the enemy's initial deception. We ought solely to follow intuition in the *depths* of our beings.

A careful observation of a Chritian's life of feeling can uncover an underlying principle in such a life—which is none other than "for the sake of self." Why is joyous sensation so sought after? For the sake of self. Why is barrenness so abhorred? Again for self's sake. Why seek bodily feelings? For self. Why crave supernatural experiences. Also for self. Oh, may the Holy Spirit open our eyes to behold how full of self is a so-called "spiritual" life of feeling! May the Lord show us that when we are filled with joyous emotions our life is still centered on self. It is the love of self-pleasure! The reality or falsity of spiritual life can be gauged by the way we treat self.

CHAPTER 5
THE LIFE OF FAITH

THE BIBLE DISCLOSES for us the normal path of a Christian's walk in such passages as "the righteous shall live by faith"; "the life I now live in the flesh I live by faith in the Son of God"; and "we walk by faith, not by sight" (Rom. 1.17 ASV; Gal. 2.20; 2 Cor. 5.7). By faith are we to live. But while this principle may be quickly grasped in the mind it is not so readily experienced in life.

The life of faith is not only totally different from, but also diametrically opposite to, a life of feeling. He who lives by sensation can follow God's will or seek the things above purely at the time of excitement; should his blissful feeling cease, every activity terminates. Not so with one who walks by faith. Faith is anchored in the One Whom he believes rather than in the one who exercises the believing, that is, himself. Faith looks not at what happens to him but at Him Whom he believes. Though he may completely change, yet the One in Whom he trusts never does—and so he can proceed without letting up. Faith establishes its relationship with God. It regards not its feeling because it is concerned with God. Faith follows the One believed while feeling turns on how one feels. What faith thus beholds is God whereas what feeling beholds is one's self. God does not change: He is the same God in either the cloudy day or the sunny day. Hence he who lives by faith is as unchanging as is God; he expresses the same kind of life through darkness or through light. But one who dwells by feeling must pursue an up-and-down existence because his feeling is ever changing.

What God expects of His children is that they will not make enjoyment the purpose of their lives. God wants them to walk by believing Him. As they run the spiritual race they are to carry on whether they feel comfortable or whether they feel painful. They never alter their attitude towards God according to their sensations. However dry, tasteless or dark it may be, they continue to advance—trusting God and advancing as long as they know this is God's will. Frequently their feeling appears to rebel against this continuation: they grow exceedingly sorrowful, melancholic, despondent, as though their emotions were pleading with them to halt every spiritual activity. They nonetheless go on as usual, entirely ignoring their adverse feeling; for they realize work must be done. This is the pathway of faith, one which pays no heed to one's emotion but exclusively to the purpose of God. If something is believed to be God's mind, then no matter how uninterested one's feeling is he must proceed to execute it. One who walks by sensation undertakes merely what he feels interested in; the one however who walks by faith obeys the complete will of God and cares not at all about his own interest or indifference.

The life of feeling draws people away from abiding in God to finding satisfaction in joy, while the life of faith draws believers into being satisfied with God by faith. They having possessed God, their joyful feelings do not add to their joy nor do their painful sensations render them woeful. A life of emotion induces the saint to exist for himself but a life of faith enables him to exist for God and cedes no ground to his self life. When self is entertained and pleased it is not a life of faith but simply a life of feeling. Exquisite feeling does indeed please the self. If one walks according to sensation it indicates he has not yet committed his natural life to the cross. He still reserves some place for self—wishing to make it happy—while simultaneously continuing to tread the spiritual path.

The Christian experience, from start to finish, is a journey of faith. Through it we come into possession of a new life and through it we walk by this new life. Faith is the life principle of a Christian. This is of course acknowledged by all saints; but strangely enough many seem to overlook this in their experience. They forget that to live and to move by emotion or happy sensations is to do so by sight and not by faith What is the life of faith? It is one lived contrary to a life of feeling because it disregards feeling altogether. If Christians desire to live by this principle they should not alter their demeanor or bitterly cry as though bereft of their spiritual life whenever they feel cold, dry, empty, or pained. We live by faith and not by joy.

THE DEEPER WORK OF THE CROSS

When we forsake physical happiness and mundane pleasures we are apt to conclude that the cross has finished its perfect work in us. We do not perceive that in God's work of annulling the old creation in us there remains a deeper cross awaiting us. God wishes us to die to His joy and live to His will. Even if we feel joyous because of God and His nearness (in contrast to being joyous because of fleshly and earthly things), God's aim nevertheless is not for us to enjoy His joy but to obey His will. The cross must continue to operate till His will *alone* is left. If we rejoice in the bliss God dispenses but renounce the suffering He also dispenses, then we have yet to experience the deeper circumcision by the cross.

Great is the contrast between the will of God and the joy of God. The first is ever present, for we can behold God's mind in His providential arrangement; but the second is *not* always present, since it is experienced only in certain circumstances and at certain times. When a Christian seeks the joy of God he takes simply that part of His purpose which makes him happy; he does not desire the entire will of God. He chooses to obey God's aim when God makes him happy; but if He should cause him to suffer he at once revolts against His will. But the person who receives His will as his life will obey regardless how God makes him feel. He can discern divine arrangement in both joy and suffering.

During the initial stage of a Christian's experience God allows him to delight in His joy; after he has advanced somewhat in his spiritual walk God withdraws His joy, since this is profitable for the Christian. God appreciates the fact that should the believer seek and enjoy this kind of bliss too long he shall not be able to live by every word which proceeds from His mouth; instead he shall live wholly by that word which makes him glad. Thus he abides in the comfort of God but not in the God Who gives comfort. For this reason God must remove these pleasurable sensations so that His child may live exclusively by Him.

We know that the Lord at the commencement of our spiritual walk normally comforts us during those times we suffer on His behalf. He causes the believer to sense His presence, see His smiling face, feel His love, and experience His care in order to prevent him from fainting. When the believer apprehends the mind of the Lord and follows it He usually gives him great pleasure. Although he has paid some price for following the Lord yet the joy he obtains far surpasses what he has lost and hence he delights to obey His will. But the Lord perceives a danger here: upon having experienced comfort in suffering and happiness in heeding His mind, the child of God naturally looks for such comfort and joy the next time he suffers or obeys the Lord's will or else expects to be helped immediately by His comfort and joy. Hence he suffers or does the Lord's will not purely for His sake but for the sake of being rewarded with consolation and happiness as well. Without these crutches he is powerless to continue. The will of the Lord becomes inferior to the joy which He bestows at the moment of obedience.

God realizes His child is most eager to suffer if he is comforted, and is delighted to follow His will if he is accorded joy. But God now wishes to learn what motivates him: whether he suffers exclusively for the Lord's sake or for the sake of being consoled: whether he heeds God's mind because it should be heeded or because he derives some joy by so heeding. For this reason, after a Christian has made some progress spiritually God commences to withdraw the consolation and delight which He gave him in the hour of suffering and obedience. Now the Christian must suffer without any ministration of comfort from God: he suffers externally while feeling bitter inwardly. He is to do the will of God without the least thing to stimulate his interest; indeed everything is dry and uninteresting. By this process God will learn precisely why the believer suffers on His behalf and obeys His will. God is asking him: are you disposed to endure without being compensated by My comfort? Are you ready to endure just for Me? Are you amenable to perform labor which does not interest you a bit? Can you do it just because it is *My* purpose? Will you be able to undertake for Me when you feel depressed, insipid and parched? Can you do it simply because it is *My* work? Are you able to accept joyfully physical suffering without any compensation of refreshment? Can you accept it because it is given by *Me?*

This is a practical cross by which the Lord reveals to us whether we are living for Him by faith or living for ourselves by feeling. Frequently have we heard people say, "I live for Christ." What does this really convey? Many saints assume that if they labor for the Lord or love the Lord they are living for Christ. This is far from being exactly so. To live for the Lord means to live for His will, for His interest, and for His kingdom. As such, there is nothing for self—not the slightest provision for self-comfort, self-joy, or self-glory. To follow the mind of God because of comfort or joy is strictly forbidden. To recoil from, to cease or delay in, obedience because of feeling depressed, vapid or despondent is positively impermissible. We ought to know that physical suffering alone may not be regarded as enduring for the Lord, for often our bodies will be bearing pain while our hearts are full of joy. If we actually suffer for Him, then not only do our bodies suffer but our hearts feel pained as well. Though there is not the least joyfulness, we yet press on. Let us understand that to live for the Lord is to reserve nothing for self but to deliver it willingly to death. He who is able to accept everything gladly from the Lord—including darkness, dryness, flatness—and completely disregard self is he who lives for Him.

Should we walk by emotion we can perform God's desire only as we have a happy feeling. But should we live by faith we can obey the Lord in all regards. How often we do realize a certain matter is in fact God's will yet we have not the least interest in it. And so we feel parched when we try to perform it. We have no registration that the Lord is pleased nor do we experience His blessing or strengthening. Rather do we feel as if we are passing through the valley of the shadow of death, for the enemy is contesting our way. And alas, without mentioning the innumerable believers who today do not even follow God's will, there are those few following it who more or less only follow that part which interests them. They obey the mind of God solely when it suits their emotion and desire! Unless we advance by faith we shall flee to Tarshish (see Jonah 1.3, 4.2).

We should inquire once again as to what the life of faith is. It is one lived by believing God *under any circumstance*: "If he slay me," says Job, "yet would I trust in Him" (13.15 Darby). That is faith. Because I once believed, loved and trusted God I shall believe, love and trust Him wherever He may put me and however my heart and body may suffer. Nowadays the people of God expect to feel peaceful even in the time of physical pain. Who is there who dares to renounce this consolation of heart for the sake of believing God? Who is there who can accept God's will joyfully and continuously commit himself to Him even though he *feels* that God hates him and desires to slay him? That is the highest life. Of course God would never treat us like that. Nevertheless in the walk of the most advanced Christians they seem to experience something of this apparent desertion by God. Would we be able to remain unmoved in our faith in God if we felt thus? Observe what John Bunyan, author of *Pilgrim's Progress*, proclaimed when men sought to hang him: "If God does not intervene I shall leap into eternity with blind faith come heaven, come hell!" There was a hero of faith! In the hour of despair can we too say, "O God, though You desert me yet will I believe You"? Emotion begins to doubt when it senses blackness, whereas faith holds on to God even in the face of death.

How few have arrived at such a level! How our flesh resists such a walk with God alone! The natural disinclination for cross-bearing has impeded many in their spiritual progress. They tend to reserve a little pleasure for their own enjoyment. To lose everything in the Lord, even self-pleasure, is too thoroughgoing a death, too heavy a cross! They can be fully consecrated to the Lord, they can be suffering untold pain for Him, they can even pay a price for following the will of God, but they cannot forsake that obviously trifling feeling of self-pleasure. Many cherish this momentary comfort; their spiritual life rests on this tiny twinge of feeling. Were they to exercise the courage to sacrifice themselves to God's fiery furnace, showing no pity or love for self, they would make great strides on their spiritual pathway. But too many of God's people remain subservient to their natural life, trusting what is seen and felt for safety and security: they have neither the courage nor the faith to exploit the unseen, the unfelt, the untrodden. They have already drawn a circle around themselves; their joy or sorrow hinges upon a little gain here or a little loss there; they accept nothing loftier. Thus are they circumscribed by their own petty self.

Were the Christian to recognize that God wishes him to live by faith, he would not murmur against God so frequently nor would he conceive these thoughts of discontent. How swiftly would his natural life be cut away by the cross if he could accept the God-given parched feeling and could esteem everything given him by God as excellent. Were it not for his ignorance or unwillingness, such experiences would deal with his soul life most practically, enabling him to live truly in the spirit. How sad that many succeed at nothing greater in their lives than the pursuit of a little feeling of joy. The faithful, however, are brought by God into genuine spiritual life. How godly is their walk! When they examine retrospectively what they have experienced they readily acknowledge that the ordering of the Lord is perfect: for only because of those experiences did they renounce their soul life. Today's crying need is for believers to hand themselves over completely to God and ignore their feeling.

This should not at all be misconstrued to signify, however, that henceforth we shall become joyless persons. "Joy in the Holy Spirit" is the greatest blessing in the kingdom of God (Rom. 14.17). The fruit of the Holy Spirit, moreover, is joy (Gal. 5.22). If this is so, then how can we reconcile this apparent inconsistency? Simply come to see that though we do lose joy in our feeling, nevertheless the joy we gain issues from a pure faith and cannot be destroyed. Joy of this caliber runs far deeper than emotion. In becoming spiritual we abandon the old desire for self-pleasure and hence additionally the former search for bliss; but the peace and joy of the spirit which arises from faith remains forever.

AFTER THE SPIRIT

To walk after the spirit a Christian must deny every scintilla of his life of feeling. He must move by faith and eliminate the crutches of wonderful sensation to which the flesh naturally clings. When he is following the spirit he neither fears if he receives no help from feeling nor if feeling opposes him. But when his faith is weak and he follows not the spirit, he then will heed the support of the visible, the sensible and the touchable. Emotion replaces intuition in guidance whenever spiritual life grows weak. He who abides in feeling will come to see that, having long sought pleasurable sensations, he shall soon seek as well the help of the world, because feeling rests nowhere save in the world. An emotional Christian often employs his own way and seeks man's help. To follow the leading of the spirit requires faith, for it usually is contrary to feeling. Without faith no one can actually march forward. A soulish person ceases to serve God the moment he becomes depressed; on the other hand one who lives by faith does not delay in serving the Lord until he becomes joyful: he simply goes forward while beseeching God to increase the strength of his spirit that he may overcome any depressed feeling which may descend.

THE LIFE OF THE WILL

The life of faith can be called the life of the will since faith is impervious to how one feels but chooses through volition to obey God's mind. Though the Christian may not *feel* like obeying God, even so he *wills* to obey Him. We find two opposite kinds of Christians: one depends on emotion, the other relies on the *renewed* will. A Christian who trusts in feeling can obey God solely while he is deriving stimulus from his feeling, that is, excitable feeling. The one however who depends on volition determines that he shall serve God amid whatever circumstance or feeling. His will reflects his real opinion whereas his feeling is only activated by outside stimulus. From God's viewpoint not much value accrues in doing His will out of a pleasurable sensation: to do so is merely to be persuaded by the joy of God and not by a wholehearted aspiration to do His will. Except he neither feels a bit of joy nor is stimulated by some wonderful feeling and yet decides to do God's will can the Christian's obedience be counted truly valuable, because it flows from his honest heart and expresses his respect for God and disregard of self. The distinction between the spiritual and the soulish Christian lies precisely there: the soulish primarily considers himself and therefore only obeys God when he feels his desire is satisfied; the spiritual has a will fully cooperating with God and hence accepts His arrangement without wavering even though he has no outside help or stimulus.

Of what have we to boast if we obey God merely while we experience joy in our body? Or how can we brag if we enjoy the cheer of the Lord while suffering? Precious is it in God's sight if we determine to obey His mind and suffer for Him even when the comfort, love, help, presence and joy of the Lord are absent.

A great number of believers are unconscious of the fact that to walk by the spirit is to walk by the will which is joined to God. (A will which is not so joined is untrustworthy and inconsistent; it requires a will that is entirely yielded to God's to always choose what the spirit desires). In the early stage of their Christian experience they heard how other saints enjoyed unutterable bliss during obedience or suffering. They ardently admired such a life, so they too offered themselves exclusively to the Lord with the hope of possessing this "higher" life. In truth, following their consecration they did experience time and again the Lord's intimacy and love, which prompted them to conclude that their hope had been realized. But far too soon did these wonderful experiences become past history.

Because they are unaware that the expression of true spiritual life issues not from feeling but from the will many suffer endless pains, for these believe they have lost their spiritual life when no happy sensation is felt. Such ones, at a time of low feeling, need to ascertain whether their original heart of consecration has been changed or whether they still harbor the desire to do God's will. Are they yet disposed to suffer for Him? Is there any change in their readiness to do anything or go anywhere for God? If these have not been altered, then their spiritual life has not receded. But if these have changed, their life in the spirit has indeed receded.

Just as one's retrogression is not due to any loss of joy but to the weakening of his will in obedience to God, so his progress is not because he possesses many delightful feelings now which he previously did not, but because of a deeper union of his will with God. It is this which renders him more inclined to follow God's will, more amenable to His desires. The touchstone of genuine spiritual life is how much one's volition is united with God's; good or bad sensation, happy or sad feeling does not in the slightest serve as an indicator. If one is willing, however dry he may feel, to be faithful to God even to death, his spiritual course becomes the noblest. Spirituality is measured by our volition because it unfolds our undisguised condition. When our choices and decisions are yielded to God we may safely say we have yielded to God and no longer act as our own sovereign. Self stands in opposition to spiritual life. With self broken down that life grows up: should self remain strong that life will suffer. We accordingly can judge one's spirituality by looking into his will. Feeling, on the contrary, is distinctly different. For even if we possess the most glorious sensations, we are nonetheless full of self, being self-gratified and self-pleased.

Let not those who sincerely strive after spiritual growth be deceived into thinking that feeling is their life principle, because this shall entice them to be mindful always of tingling sensation. Just be certain that the will is utterly offered to God. Joy or no joy is not to be the consideration. God wants us to live by faith. Should He wish us to live by faith and be satisfied solely with His will bereft of consolation or ecstatic delight for long duration, would we be inclined to so live? We should delight in our having obeyed the mind of God, not in being accorded some joy. God's will alone should be sufficient to make us joyful.

THE DUTY OF MAN

While a Christian is governed by feeling he invariably will neglect his duty towards others. This is because he makes himself the center and is consequently unfit to care for the needs of others. For a Christian to fulfill his duty it requires faith and will. Responsibility ignores feeling. Our duty towards men is defined and our responsibility in the mundane affairs of life is certain. These cannot be altered according to one's changing emotion. Duty must be performed according to principle.

During the period that a Christian knows the truth merely in his feeling he certainly cannot fulfill his duty. He is so taken up with the joy from fellowshiping with the Lord that that is all he pursues. His greatest temptation is to want to do nothing but be alone with the Lord and bask in this joy. He does not like the work in which he formerly was engaged because it holds out no other prospect than many trials and troubles. When face to face with the Lord he senses intense holiness and victory, but when he emerges to perform his daily tasks he finds himself as defeated and defiled as before. What he wants is to escape his duties: he hopes that by lingering lengthily before the Lord he can remain holy and victorious the longer. He views these matters of duty as earthy and unworthy of occupying the attention of so pure and triumphant a person as he. Since he cares so much about finding time and place to commune with the Lord and hates so deeply those works which are his duties, he naturally neglects the need and welfare of those around him. Parents and servants who think like this do not, respectively, take good care of their children nor serve their masters faithfully because they judge these duties as worldly, therefore of negligible worth. They believe they must seek something more spiritual. The reason for this unbalanced approach is the believer's failure to walk by faith; he continues to look for self-support. He has not yet been united fully with God. Hence he needs *special* time and *special* place to commune with God. He has not learned to discern the Lord in all matters and to cooperate accordingly with Him. He does not know how to be united with the Lord in the daily details of living. His experience of God is but in his feeling; and so he loves to erect a tent on the mountain and dwell there permanently with the Lord but hates to descend to the plain to cast the demon away.

The loftiest Christian experience is never contradictory to the duties of one's pathway. In reading the letters to the Romans, Colossians and Ephesians we can plainly see how perfectly a Christian must perform his duty as a man. His highest life does not necessitate special hour and situation in order to be manifested; it can be thoroughly expressed at any time or place. To the Lord there is no dichotomy between household work and preaching or praying. The life of Christ can be exhibited through all sorts of activity.

As a consequence to living an emotional life we become dissatisfied with our present position and are loathe to perform the duties connected with that position. We revolt because in those duties we do not find the pleasure we seek. But our life is not for pleasure; why do we therefore look for it again? The path of feeling bids us neglect our duty; the path of faith calls us not to forsake our duty to friends or foes. If we are united with God in every detail of living, we shall know what are our tasks and how we should properly fulfill them.

IN THE WORK OF GOD

To deny the life of emotion and live by faith completely is one of the basic requirements for serving God. An emotional believer is useless in God's hand. He who walks by feeling knows how to enjoy pleasure but not how to work for God. He has not yet attained the status of a worker, since he lives for himself and not for God. Living for the Lord is the prerequisite to working for Him.

A Christian must realize the way of faith before he can be a useful instrument to God and actually perform His work. Otherwise his aim in life is pleasure. He works for the sake of feeling and for that reason he will stop working. His heart is brimming with self-love. If he is placed by the Lord in a field of labor filled with physical and emotional suffering he begins to pity himself and finally gives up. But even as the work of the Lord Jesus was that of the cross, exactly so is the work of a Christian to be. What pleasure is there in such work? Except Christians utterly commit their emotion and their heart of self-love to death, God can hardly find any real workers.

Today the Lord needs men to be His followers who shall trail Him to the end. Too many saints labor for the Lord when the task is prosperous, is suited to their interest, or does not imperil their feeling; but how quickly they retreat should the cross come upon them and require them to die and give them no help except to lay hold of God by faith. We know that if a work is veritably accomplished by God there cannot but be results. Yet supposing one has been commissioned by the Lord and has labored for eight or ten years without achieving any results. Can he continue to labor faithfully simply because God has commanded it? How many saints are there who serve purely because it is God's command? Or how many work just to produce fruits? Since God's work is eternal in nature, He demands men with faith to labor for Him. It is difficult for human beings who live in time to perceive and to understand the work of God, for it is replete with eternal character. How, then, can those who live by feeling ever join in in God's work since nothing in it can please their feeling? Unless the death of the cross cuts penetratingly into the soul of a believer so that he reserves nothing for self, he cannot follow the Lord in work except to a limited extent. Beyond that he is unable to go. God asks for men who are totally broken and who will follow Him even to death to work for Him.

IN BATTLING THE ENEMY

Those who live by feeling are even more worthless in spiritual warfare, because to battle the enemy in prayer is truly a self-denying work. What incalculable suffering is involved! Nothing for satisfying one's self can be found here; it is pouring out one's all for the body of Christ and the kingdom of God. How unbearable must be this resisting and wrestling in the spirit! What pleasure is there for the spirit to be laden with indescribable burden for the sake of God? Is it interesting to attack the evil spirit with every ounce of strength one can summon? This is a prayer warfare. But for whom is the believer praying? Not for himself surely, but for the work of God. Such prayer is for warfare which is thoroughly lacking in interest one usually encounters during ordinary prayer. Is there anything in this that can make him feel comfortable when he must travail in his soul and pray to destroy and to build? No element in spiritual warfare can gladden the flesh—unless of course one is contending merely in his imagination.

An emotional Christian is easily defeated in conflict with Satan. While he is praying to assault the enemy the latter by his evil spirit will attack his emotion. He will set the Christian to feeling that such contesting is painful and such prayer is lifeless. So as he becomes sorrowful, insipid, dark and dry, he immediately stops fighting. An emotional Christian is powerless to war against Satan, for as soon as his feeling comes under attack by Satan he quits the field of battle. If one's emotion has not experienced death, he may provide opportunity to Satan to strike at any hour. Each time he rises to oppose the enemy he is defeated by a satanic touch upon his feeling. Can anyone expect victory over Satan unless he has first overcome his life of sensation?

Spiritual warfare accordingly demands an attitude of total death to feeling and an absolute trust in God. Only a person with this attitude can bear up alone and not seek companions or man's approval in fighting the enemy. Only this caliber of Christian can proceed under all sorts of anguished feelings. He cares not at all for his life nor about death but only cares for the leading of God. He indulges no personal interest, desire or longing. He has offered himself to death already and then lives exclusively for God. He neither blames nor misunderstands Him because he considers all His ways to be loving. This is the class of person who is able to fill the breach. Though he may appear to be deserted by God and forgotten by men, yet he mans his battle station. He is a prayer warrior. He overcomes Satan.

REST

After a believer has thus been dealt with, he can commence the walk of faith which is true spiritual life. And the one who arrives at this position enters upon a life of rest. The fire of the cross has consumed his every greedy pursuit. He at last has learned his lesson: he recognizes that God's will alone is precious. All else, though naturally desirable, is incompatible with the highest life of God. Now he rejoices in relinquishing everything. Whatever the Lord deems necessary to withdraw, he gladly allows His hand to do it. The sighing, mourning and grieving which arose out of his former anticipation, seeking and struggling have today entirely disappeared. He realizes that the loftiest life is one lived for God and one obedient to His will. Though he has lost everything yet is he satisfied with the fulfillment of God's purpose. Though he is left with nothing to enjoy, yet is he humble under the ordering of God. So long as the Lord is pleased he cares not the least what happens to him. He now has perfect rest; nothing external can any longer stimulate him.

Presently the child of God abides by a will which is united with the Lord. His volition, today filled with spiritual strength, is competent to control his emotion. His walk is steady, firm, restful. His former situation of ups and downs has vanished. Even so, we must not now rush to the conclusion that henceforth he shall never again be ruled by emotion, for before we enter heaven itself such sinless perfection is not possible. Nonetheless, in comparing his present state with his former condition, this one can indeed be described as experiencing rest, being established, and continuing firm. He suffers no further from that incessant confusion he encountered heretofore, though occasionally he may still be disturbed by the operation of his emotion. That is why watchful prayer continues to be indispensable. Let us therefore hasten to add: do not misunderstand what has been said to mean that from here on there shall be no possibility of feeling either joy or sorrow. As long as our organ for emotion is not annihilated (it never will be), our feeling shall continue to exist. We still can sense pain, blackness, aridity and sorrow. Yet those sufferings can penetrate our outer man only, leaving our inner man untouched. Due to the clear division between spirit and soul, outwardly our soul may be disturbed and consequently suffer but inwardly our spirit remains calm and composed as though nothing had happened.

Upon arriving at this restful position the believer shall find that all he heretofore had lost for the Lord's sake has today been restored. He has gained God, and therefore everything belonging to God belongs to him as well. What the Lord had withdrawn before he now can properly enjoy in Him. The reason why God at the beginning had led him through many sorrows was because his soul life lay behind everything, seeking and asking too much for *himself*, desiring even things which were outside God's will. Such independent action had to be circumscribed by God. Now that he has lost himself—that is, his natural life—the Christian is in a position to enjoy the bliss of God within its legitimate boundary. Not till today was he qualified to be rightly related to His joy. Hereafter he can thankfully accept whatever is given him, because the eagerness to secure something for self has already been put to nought; he does not petition inordinately for that which was not bestowed upon him.

Such a child of God has advanced onto a pure ground. Where there is mixture there is impurity. The Bible views impurity as something defiled. Before one reaches this ground of no mixture he cannot express a pure walk. He lives for God yet also lives for self: he loves the Lord but loves himself as well: his intention is unto God, yet simultaneously he aims at self-glory, self-pleasure, self-comfort. Such a life is a defiled one. He walks by faith but also walks by feeling, he follows the spirit but also follows the soul. While he does not in fact reserve the larger portion for himself, nonetheless this smaller portion held back is sufficient to render his life impure. Only what is pure is clean; anything mixed with foreign matter becomes defiled.

When a believer has experienced the practical treatment of the cross he finally arrives at a pure life. All is for God and in God, and God is in all as well. Nothing is unto self. Even the tiniest desire for pleasing one's self is crucified. Self-love has been consigned to death. The present aim of existence becomes single: to do the will of God: so long as He is pleased, nothing else really counts: to obey Him becomes the sole objective of life. It does not matter how he feels; what matters is obeying God. This is a pure walk. Although God affords him peace, comfort and bliss, he does not enjoy them for the sake of gratifying his desire. He from now on views everything with God's eye. His soulish life has been terminated and the Lord has granted him a pure, restful, true and believing spiritual life. While it is God Who does destroy him, it equally is God Who builds him up. That which is soulish has been destroyed but that which is spiritual has been established.